The Double Act

The Double Act

A History of British Comedy Duos

Andrew Roberts

The
History
Press

First published 2018

The History Press
The Mill, Brimscombe Port
Stroud, Gloucestershire, GL5 2QG
www.thehistorypress.co.uk

British Library Cataloguing in Publication Data.
A catalogue record for this book is available from the British Library.

ISBN 978 0 7509 8432 4

Typesetting and origination by The History Press
Printed and bound in Great Britain by TJ International Ltd

Contents

Introduction

The first double act that I saw starred a short pompous man who wore the sort of round glasses associated with shopkeepers in the later Ealing comedies. 'Hello boys and girls,' he exclaimed, full of enthusiasm, only for his panegyric about a recent trip to the zoo to be ruined by a rude interruption from a younger man with the ready smile of a door-to-door salesman. The would-be lecturer was decidedly put out by the intervention of this individual, but it did not prevent him from being in the other's company on a weekly basis. The second featured a charming yet very formidable middle-aged lady who swore whenever she heard mention of a colour while her twin brother blew raspberries at the name of a food.

The acts in question were, of course, Don Maclean and Peter Glaze on *Crackerjack*, and Hattie Jacques and Eric Sykes on *Sykes*,[1] each displaying one fundamental essence of comic duo; one could not be envisaged without the presence of the other. Another is the difference in status, nature or appearance, a comic trope that literally harks back millennia.

---

1   'The Hypnotist' (1978).

In Aristophanes' *The Frogs* Dionysus is superior in status; Xanthius is his slave but yet the latter enters the play riding a donkey while his master is having to walk while (unconvincingly) disguised as Heracles – 'How's that for arrogance and being spoiled rotten?' complains the god.

To prevent this book from approaching the length of *War and Peace*, the starting point is the late nineteenth century, when the comedy double act was being forged from the influences of music hall and even minstrel shows. The cross-talk and the use of song pervaded well into the twentieth century with the participants often trapped by economic circumstance (Bud Flanagan and Chesney Allen) or institutionalisation (those comic duos who used an armed forces scenario). One very common theme is that the straight man represents the forces of English life who bully the shorter, more vulnerable-looking comic for their own good, be he an army NCO, a government official or the forces of business, be they large or small. The act might appear in the guise of a sketch, which itself was the foundation of the situation comedy, while in 'legitimate theatre', two best friends would be discovering that a farce is what occurs to you on the worst day of your lives. In a farcical comedy, the laughter so often derives from the audience's relief that the pragmatists' trials are not theirs.

The narrative ends in the late 1980s, the last days of *Terry and June* and when the older Variety tradition, whether screened on television or in a seaside resort that was last repainted when Shane Fenton & The Fentones were in the Hit Parade, was starting to look tired. By that stage the divide between 'alternative' and 'traditional' was starting to dissolve, but as comedy is apparently about *breaking rules*,[2] we will encounter Lee and Herring, Armstrong and Miller and *The Mighty Boosh*. This cut-off point is also born of subjectivity. What amuses is inevitably a personal matter and while the thought of engaging in any nostalgia for Baddiel and Skinner with *Fantasy Football League* and any form of 1990s

---

2   Why is this statement so often prefixed to naked abuse towards the disabled, the poor or the generally vulnerable?

'New Lad nostalgia'[3] is appealing to some, others would derive greater entertainment from a 1965 Public Information Film about tyre repair.

On a somewhat more regretful note, the issues of space mean that Hinge and Bracket, Les Dawson and Roy Barraclough, Les Dennis and Dustin Gee, Hope and Keen and so many more acts will have to await a further tome. The focus is on pairings that may be reasonably said to be comedic in form and content – although I have included one unintentionally funny action-adventure duo – and this sadly means excluding Stan and Hilda Ogden and Jack and Vera Duckworth. It also means there was no space for Fanny and Johnny Craddock who were a double act of public notoriety if not public renown. Another challenge is possibly that of what may best be described as 'comedy orthodoxy'; if you want to start a fevered online debate, merely post an opinion and the ensuing rants will frequently last for months. The remake of *The Wicker Man* (Neil LaBute, 2006) would have enjoyed far more success had it eschewed irate bees attacking Nicolas Cage and set the narrative in a Comedy Club somewhere near Portsmouth.

What this book will explore are the influences on the British comedy double act. Such acts hail from diverse backgrounds but their common denominators are the manner in which they simultaneously perform to each other and the audience without any extraneous effort. On occasions their legacies are of shadow and ephemera, which might be playbills for variety shows with advertisements for the Azena Danse Salon – 'Sheffield's most Luxurious Ballroom with the Seaside Atmosphere' – or an edition of the *TV Times* which features Reg Varney's favoured recipe for sponge cake or comedy acts proclaiming that they may be booked via a FLAXman or PRImrose Hill telephone number. A comedy duo could seek to extend the medium of radio, especially when engaged on a quest of the ultimate answer, while television situation comedy represented a bridge between the Variety sketch and drama. In the

---

3   *The Word*, the Ford Mondeo, 'Three Lions' … it was a drab era.

post-war years it both established a new interpretation of the double act and brought the names of the writers to the fore. The impact of the Cambridge Footlights, the Edinburgh Fringe and 'alternative comedy'[4] will be discussed, as will the impact of cinema. Films so often have the power to 'function as stories, dreams and shows, and how they become as potent in our imagination as the rooms in which we spent our childhoods' (Thomson, 2014: 8). To many Britons, this can apply to a pair of out-of-work actors who went on holiday by mistake as it does to a tall bald headmaster who is attempting to mask his growing hysteria as his authority is challenged by a short and unspeakably determined headmistress of another establishment. The latter picture was, of course, *The Happiest Days of Your Life* (Frank Launder, 1950), and even if Alastair Sim and Margaret Rutherford were never again teamed on screen, the memories abide of a film comedy that was quite perfect. Patrick Macnee and Diana Rigg worked together for only two years; they will forever be Steed and Mrs Peel.

This book does not claim to be the definitive guide; it is rather a starting point written by one who owes a debt to the comedians. It is also a tribute to the works of entertainment historians who inspire as much as they inform and divert: John Fisher, Benny Green, Roy Hudd, Andy Medhurst, Eric Midwinter and Roger Wilmut. My sincere thanks go to Patrick Barlow, Kenneth Cope, Barry Cryer, Dick Fiddy, Chris Gidney, Syd Little, Don Maclean, Gary Morecambe and Brian Murphy for their time and patience in enduing my questions.

And it is the public that is the final arbiter, who perceives the chemistry between the two parties or note its absence. They often ignore the importance of the straight man, but while Tony Hancock and Sidney James were never a formal double act, to their audience they were indivisible. It is the audience who can discern the difference between watching a unified theatrical creation – a double act with a single vision – and those born of professional expediency. Perhaps the mark of a truly great comedy duo is the sadness when it dissolves; you feel as though

---

4   A phrase that now appears almost quaint.

you have lost an aspect of everyday existence. Or, as Eric Morecambe told Ernie Wise: 'Don't be long, when you're not here I get a draught all down one side.'

Bibliography

Thomson, David (2014). *Moments That Made the Movies*. London: Thames & Hudson.

1

From the Music Hall to the Idiot's Lantern

Historians of live entertainment will forever debate when music hall began to be succeeded by 'Variety'. The terms seem to have surfaced in the 1880s as the means of listing a diverse bill of entertainments to the audience, while John Fisher argues that 'music hall flourished from about 1850 and had run its course by the time of the Armistice in 1918, to be replaced by the more streamlined genre of variety' (2013: 15). But it was within music hall that the origins of the double act as still seen today were forged: the cross–talk, the punctured dignity of the straight man and their duet to conclude the act. Benny Green saw the process of various clubs evolving into the music hall as one of moving from:

Eating and drinking, to eating and drinking to the incidental distraction of a singer or comic, to eating and drinking challenged as the main entertainment by singers and comics, to professional entertainment where food and drink were readily available, to professional entertainment patronised purely for its own sake. (1986: 1)

Its roots date to the eighteenth century when chaps would frequent taverns which eventually established rooms that were devoted to 'free and easy' musical evenings. These were popular across the UK, and there is a correlation between their use of a chairman, the calling-up of artists on to the stage and the communal singing and the later halls (Maloney, 2003: 40). The penny-gaff, a form of ad hoc entertainment staged in back rooms or above warehouses, had the organiser of the event shouting the various turns on offer for a most reasonable fee, and when Henry Mayhew visited one such show, he was decidedly unimpressed. The comic singer was:

> Received with deafening shouts. Several songs were named by the costers, but the 'funny gentleman' merely requested them 'to hold their jaws', and putting on a 'knowing' look, sang a song, the whole point of which consisted in the mere utterance of some filthy word at the end of each stanza. Nothing, however, could have been more successful. (Mayhew, 1851: 89)

Music hall also has its origin in the supper clubs of the capital city, which attracted the middle and upper classes. They featured professional entertainers, paid 20s per week plus food and drink, who would often battle to impose their personalities over the inebriated diners. 'Some set a bawdy tone, and as the wine flowed and inhibitions fled, customers would join in to perform the rudest song in their repertoire' (Major, 2012: 24). The establishment that represents the first purpose-built music hall was the Canterbury Hall in Lambeth, established by Charles Morton, the publican of the Canterbury Tavern, in 1852. He had taken over the venue as manager in 1849 and by 1851 had applied for a music licence, thereby bringing an end to the free and easy amateur sessions that were staged in a room of the original pub. The new, far more elaborate, building marked a definite break with past entertainment traditions as did 'Ladies' Thursdays', which marked a change from the all-male audiences of the supper clubs.

James Ewing Ritchie described the Canterbury in his 1858 book *The Night Side of London*, writing approvingly of how 'the majority present are respectable mechanics or small tradesmen with their wives and daughters and sweethearts'. Furthermore, 'the presence of the ladies has also a beneficial effect; I see no indication of intoxication, and certainly, none of the songs are obscene' (1858: 70). His experience of the audiences at the older Cyder Cellars club was markedly different. In the 1840s and '50s it was famed for the standards of its cuisine and the entertainers it attracted (Major, 2012: 29), but during Ritchie's visit, he found that 'even the men about town do not go there much' (1858: 110).[1]

By the end of the 1870s, there were over 300 halls in London, while outside of the capital many taverns were adapted into new venues. On stage the entertainments might take the form of mocking:

> The police, the rent collector, the bailiffs, mothers-in-law, the drunken husband and the shrewish wife, the spendthrift who had gambled away his pay before he got home Friday night – such were the dragons slain by these seedy St Georges. (Leslie, 1978: 48)

The comic songs would typically contain 'patter' that formed the main part of the number (Baker, 2014: 187) and Roger Wilmut suggest that one major influence on the early form of the double act during the late nineteenth century was 'the American "Nigger Minstrel" type of show' (1985: 53). Dan Emmett's the Virginia Minstrels were the first of such shows to be seen in the UK, arriving in Liverpool in 1843. 'The Artistes were Frank Brower as bones; Billy Whitlock, banjoist; Dan Emmett, fiddle and Dick Pelham, tambourine ... the tour was a failure. From this crude beginning sprung all the bands of later days' (Keynote, *The Star*, 10 November 1885: 10). In that same year Edwin Pearce Christy established the Christy Minstrels with its formula of a line of

---

1   Compare this with his impressions of *A Costermongers' Free and Easy*: 'Just look at the people in this public-house. A more drunken, dissipated, wretched lot you never saw.' (1858: 200)

musicians in 'blackface' make-up presided over by 'Mr Interlocutor', the authority figure who engaged in cross-talk banter with the two 'end men', 'Mr Bones' (percussion) and 'Mr Tambo' (tambourine).

1857 saw Raynor & Pierce's Christy Minstrels, a variant of the original troupe, making their London debut at the St James's Theatre. The critic of *The Morning Chronicle* considered their burlesque dancing as 'scarcely suited to the latitude of St James' although he admitted that 'singing is of a high class, and all the ballads, pathetic and comic, are well rendered' (29 July 1857: 5). J.W. Raynor returned to the USA in 1860 and the act divided into various troupes (Major, 2012: 179), which remained popular until the end of the Victorian era. One double act in 'blackface'[2] was the Brothers Courtney, with Jack as the comedian and his sibling Will as the straight man; the historian J.S. Bratton contends that it was from the minstrel shows that the music hall, and subsequently Variety, cross-talk act emerged (1981: 138). The pioneering duo was the Dublin-born Joe O'Gorman who formed an act with Joe Tennyson in 1881 (Kilgarriff, 1998: 253) The pair were smartly attired – their bill-matter was 'The Two Irish Gentlemen' or 'The Patter Propagators' – and in place of the 'Mr Interlocutor' routines of the Minstrel Shows, O'Gorman and Tennyson stood centre stage, Joe as the comic, Dave as his foil.

The act broke up with the retirement of Tennyson in 1902. In 1955 the music hall enthusiast W.H. Potter wrote to O'Gorman's sons Joe and Dave:

> I was a boy at the time, and my father took me to see them at the Empire. And what an act. I have never forgotten them. 'The Two Irish Gentlemen.' Box Hats, Frock Coats, Spats, sticks, light boots with twinkling feet inside them. They had everything. I saw them whenever they came to Bristol. Their repartee was very humorous and your father Joe, led Tennyson in a dance. He teased and cajoled him. Joe found a small hole in the stage and after a lot of business got Tennyson to stand over it, when a stream of water shot up into his face.

---

2   Major also points out that 'the British public drew clear distinctions between black performers and "burned cork" performers' (2012: 179).

They must have been amongst the first with what became known as Simultaneous Dancing and could give points to many such acts today.

By the 1890s a bill might also include The Two Mikes ('The Inimitable Irish Comedy Purveyors'), Michael Ford and Michael McCarthy, who formed a comedy team in the 1870s. Their antics included a trapeze performance, pretending to bury axes in each other's heads and a self-penned playlet '*The Murder of Murphy The Piper*' (*London and Provincial Entr'acte*, 8 November 1884: 12) and they enjoyed great popularity in the UK and overseas. Fred and Joe, the Brothers Griffith, had a weightlifting routine which involved 'Sansom' (dressed as a 'swell') emerging from the audience to accept the £500 challenge of his on-stage sibling – 'the burlesque … is bound to be one of the great attractions of the day' (*Music Hall & Theatre Review*, 30 November 1889: 7). Sweeney and Ryland were an American duo who first came to the UK in 1885. Sweeney was the straight man, while the tall, thin Ryland was the comedian, and by the 1890s they were lauded as 'genuine comedians with the wildest and funniest dialogue, they stand unrivalled. The appearance of vacuous imbecility assumed by the imperturbable Ryland is alone sufficient to convulse a steam-roller apart from his humorous whimsicalities of conversation with clarion-voiced Sweeney' (*Music Hall & Theatre Review*, 18 July 1891: 8–10).

In the Edwardian era, one of the most popular double acts was Sam T. Poluski and his brother Will, who played theatres of the Continent, the USA, Australia and South Africa. Sam was the authority figure, referring to his irritating brother as 'boy', and their stock in trade was the 'interrupted act' and the straight man being trapped into agreement with the comic (Wilmut, 1985: 54–5). One of their routines was a cricketing sketch entitled 'Flannelled Fools', which was 'pronounced by the press and public an instant success' (*London and Provincial Entr'acte*, 22 November 1902: 13).

Such duos performed in bills that were markedly different from the pioneer halls of the mid-nineteenth century. Benny Green believed that after the end of the First World War 'slowly, inch by inch, theatre by theatre, the music hall was fading into the past' (1986: 276), but its decline had been set in place many years previously. The penny gaff visited by James Ritchie, where the young audience seemed to resolve to 'as soon as they had the chance, to drink their quarter of gin and to whop their wives' (1859: 111–16), was already far removed from the Canterbury Hall. In 1885 the London Pavilion became the first such venue with tip-up seats (Barfe, 2013), marking the beginning of the end to the days when a trip to 'the hall' was a social occasion, to eat, drink and talk with one's friends as much as watch the acts.

By the 1890s the chairman had largely vanished from the proceedings; replacing the music hall bill, which might last for over three hours was the 'twice nightly' system of fixed Variety bills. The double act was now a part of a more formalised entertainment, often appearing in venues that were intended to create a sense of awe among the audience. The architect Frank Matcham had created an elaborate new Elephant and Castle Theatre on the site of a venue that burned down in 1878, and it was to be the first of over 200 such buildings (Major, 2012: 74). His works 'combined function and ornate opulence' although Matcham 'was considered by gentlemen architects to be not quite *comme il faut*, too "commercial" to be entirely respectable' (Aldous, *History Today* 2002: Vol. 2. Issue 5. May.)

The issue of architectural 'respectability' was ironic given that there were those who decried the chains of plush halls, stating that they could not hope to compete with the art and community spirit of earlier days. Walter Besant observed in 1884 how it was 'a thousand pities that among the "topical" songs, the break-downs and the comic songs, room has never been found for part-songs or for music of a quiet and somewhat better kind' (2004: 31),[3] but by 1912 there was the first Royal Command Performance, possibly the ultimate seal of Establishment approval to the popular entertainment. A 1913 article in *The Era* decried pleas for 'the ancient music hall, with its torpor of monotony, its dingy surroundings, its chairman, and even its music. Such eccentric writers seem to ignore

---

3   Besant also refers to how free and easy evenings could still be experienced.

the existence of conditions in the old days that paralysed the better impulses of the artiste and degraded his art' (16 July: 13). Furthermore, one of the axioms of Stoll's code of management was that 'the music hall should rise on stepping stones of dead traditions to higher things'.

After the end of the First World War, Variety suffered from the popularity of intimate revue, with its acts appearing within the context of a show with a finale – 'the word "revue" almost ousted "variety" in the lexicon of the halls' (Bevan, 1952: 45). Talking pictures and wireless made further inroads into the genre's traditional audience base in the 1930s. It was also during this decade that Variety saw a plethora of double acts. They were an established aspect of the bill of a show, either opening or taking the second spot (Midwinter, 1979: 167). A speciality act, often one with a dance routine, would open the show, followed by the 'second spot' comic who would typically perform a twelve-minute routine before a backcloth covered with advertisements. Tommy Trinder remembered that in the 1930s it might 'depict a street scene. There would be an airship with McDougall's self-raising flour painted on the side; a bus siding extolling the virtues of Ted's Night Powder; and an old man with a sandwich board urging you to eat at Barney's' (quoted in Pilton, 1976: 38). Both parties within the double act would have to move around the stage; if they occupied a fixed spot that happened to be in front of a particular advertisement, the business concerned would refuse to pay for the space. The first half of the bill would culminate with the second-billed attraction. After the interval the bill would work towards the headliner, who was frequently a comic act.

One reason for the popularity of the cross-talk comedians may have been that the audiences were becoming more acclimatised to rapid speech patterns via exposure to US cultural influences in Variety. Bud Flanagan reflected that in the 1910s:

American acts had been coming over to play the Halls for some time now, and they fascinated me with their new style and approach to the public and especially by their way of talking. They were always rehearsing, either polishing up old bits or trying out new bits of

business. They brought a novel style of singing to a new type of song
… British artists soon cottoned on and before time there was a spate
of imitators of American-style acts. (1961: 24–5)

And so, a Variety bill of the 1920s or '30s might feature Will Collinson
and Alfie Dean, 'The Argumentative Comedians', where the irate
straight man was nearly a foot and half taller than the impish comic; or
Dave and Joe O'Gorman – 'a pair of genuine fun makers' (*The Stage*,
15 April 1937: 3). One act of this era who abides in the folk memory
is Murray and Mooney (Harry Church and Harry Goodchild) for
routines that they did not originate but certainly became associated with
– Murray would be interrupted by Mooney with 'I say, I say, I say!' to
receive the humourless response, 'I do not wish to know that – kindly
leave the stage!'

The duo had met in 1909 and, after disbanding the act during the First
World War, resumed in 1920. Wilmut is palpably un-keen on their legacy
– 'awful jokes delivered at high speed' (1985: 56) – while Midwinter saw
Murray and Mooney as 'the classic double act' who were 'the guardians
of a tight and restricted format' (1979: 167).[4] The inherent problem
with any act that applies a strict formula is the risk of ossification –
in later life, Jimmy Jewel of Jewel and Warriss reflected that 'we were a
bit like dinosaurs. We couldn't adapt or alter our image as Morecambe
and Wise did' (1982: 148). But the critic who caught their routines of
Murray and Mooney at the Chelsea Palace in 1935 reported that they
'caused so much mirth as to interfere with their business' (*The Stage*,
31 October: 3). Their names are now virtually forgotten but even in the
twenty-first century Howard Moon would forever wish to inform Vince
Noir to 'kindly leave the stage' – but would never dare to do so.

---

4 Such acts were not always comprehensible to visiting acts from overseas. When
appearing in the UK Duke Ellington referred to 'seven Royal Hindustans, the real
openers, go through a whirlwind of tumbling, setting a pace which is slowed down
by the next act, Murray and Mooney, comedy patterers, with a line of chatter dating
back to the flood' (1999: 82).

Bud and Ches

Bud in raccoon coat and old straw hat, his high lamenting cantor's wail soaring to the back of the gallery, and Ches, dapper and deadpan, emphasising the words in a mellow croak. (Dixon, *The Guardian*, 30 December 1972: 10).

The act who will forever be associated with interwar Variety is Bud Flanagan and Chesney Allen. Bud was born Chaim Reuben Weintrop, his parents having emigrated to London from Poland. They intended to relocate to the USA, but in Hamburg, a crooked shipping agent had taken virtually all their savings for a £2 10s ticket to New York only to provide a 7s 6d passage to England (Flanagan, 1961: 18–19). Before teaming with Allen, Flanagan had temporarily relocated to the States to try his luck on the Vaudeville circuit, had worked as a taxi driver and, as was evident from beneath the genial tones of his memoirs, possessed a sense of unceasing drive and self-belief. He derived his stage name from an anti-Semitic Irish sergeant major whom Weintrop had encountered during the First World War: 'I shall use your name on stage, you horrible bastard' (1961: 72).

Flanagan had first met Chesney Allen, then an officer in the Royal West Kent Regiment, in a café during the war but the two would not form a double act until 1926. The straight man hailed from Brighton, where his father was a master builder, and before entering show business he was articled to a solicitor. But in 1910 Allen gave up a future of provincial middle-class sobriety – mowing the lawn at the weekends, attending the Rotary Club during the week – to become an actor. When he first worked with Flanagan in *Here's To You*, a revue headed by Florrie Forde, Allen was also manager to the Australian singer.

Flanagan and Allen were professionally associated with Forde until early 1931, and it was an appearance at the Argyle in Birkenhead, supporting D.J. Clarke, that consolidated their fame. Nine months later, the producers Val Parnell and George Black established 'Crazy Week' at the London Palladium in November 1931, with a bill consisting of

Jimmy Nervo and Teddy Knox, Charlie Naughton and Jimmy Gold, and Billy Caryll and Hilda Mundy. 'These periodical little outbursts of irresponsibility cannot fail to give a fillip to variety in general,' said *The Stage* (24 December 1931: 3). Flanagan and Allen were included in the bill of 'Crazy Month' in 1932 – the term 'Crazy Gang' would not be employed until 1937 – and they would come to be regarded as first among equals within the group.

A staple of Bud and Ches' routines was the latter correcting the former's malapropisms; the cross-talk delivered with speed and clarity. John Fisher makes the argument that such humour was relevant when so many members of London's immigrant community would have struggled with the new language (2013: 64). Across the Atlantic, Lou Costello similarly battled with the nuances and mysteries of the English language, but his innocents had the misfortune to be guided by the ever-unsupportive Bud.

The straight man of Abbott and Costello was one of the finest in Vaudeville and burlesque, but whether the routine was 'Who's On First' or 'Loafing', his characters were ever-poised to mock, deride and exploit the comic. His approach was sharp and aggressive – the archetypal 'huckster' – while the softly spoken Ches is tolerant and even complicit of his eccentric partner's foibles. At the end of their routines, Flanagan would mock his partner – 'I would be thanking the audience, and Bud would be pulling my hair and saying, "Just a wig you know"' (quoted in Dixon, 1972: 10), but they were ultimately friends in a troubled world. It was in those moments when they concluded their routines with 'Dreaming' or 'Underneath the Arches' that their stage personae coalesced. Bud had never known better days but was hopeful that they might still be attainable; Ches had the manners of a white-collar professional now down on his luck but never deprived of his dignity.

Gert and Daisy

Fisher contends that 'the variety stage knew few women with the attack and ruthlessness essential to the comedian to break down the inhibitions into uncontrollable laughter' (2013: 245). However, Midwinter notes that female double acts led much of music hall and Variety – in the last years of the nineteenth century, there were the Sisters Levey, the Sisters Cuthbert, and the Richmond Sisters (1979: 166–67). By the 1920s there were Ethel Revenell and Gracie West, the former standing about 6ft 2ins and the latter at barely 4ft 6ins. Their careers began in the concert party circuit before they devised routines centred on 'The Long and The Short of It – Two Cockney Comedy Kids'. In Scotland, one of the most famous double acts was the Houston Sisters: 'In the days of varieties' last flowering, there were several famous sister acts, among them the Dolly Sisters, the Trix Sisters and the Duncan Sisters but none endeared themselves to the public throughout the country as much as the Houston Sisters' (Marriott, *The Stage*, 4 August 1966: 8).

Renee Houston was the comedienne of the pair, her sibling Billie the straight woman who always dressed as a boy; their double act lasted from 1920 to 1936, when illness forced Billie's retirement (Hudd with Hindin, 1998: 85). Renee's solo career as a great character actress continued until the mid-1970s, even creating a believable character of one Agatha Spanner in the appalling *Carry On At Your Convenience* (Gerald Thomas, 1971). Their on-stage characters were so convincing that they were sent toys by their fans and the world that they evoked was one that was self-contained and convincing to the audience:

> The power of personal presences seems especially high after a further meeting with the Houston Sisters, whose charm and humour remain so thoroughly unexplained. Perhaps there is no reason why any frigid theory of comedy should be out to their precious and intimate quarrellings, the fragmentary burlesque of their elders, and the extramural asides which appear to take us so deeply into the home life of Billie and Renee. (*The Guardian*, 5 November 1929: 14).

Another female double act who bridged the gap between Variety and character acting were Elsie and Doris Waters. Their creations Gert and Daisy will forever be associated with Britons of a certain age with Ministry of Information (MOI) shorts about the best ways to prepare Wotton pie. In fact, their career began in the aftermath of the First World War, and if you paid a visit to Bournemouth during the summer of 1976, you had the opportunity to see Freddie Starr at the Winter Gardens ... or the Waters sisters at the Pavilion. At first sight, Gert and Daisy did not seem to belong in the same timeframe as Elton John and Kiki Dee singing 'Don't Go Breaking My Heart'; they are an act that is very difficult to envisage in colour, let alone in the same time frame as the Vauxhall Cavalier and *The Sweeney*. But by that time, 'Gert and Daisy' had entered popular consciousness to the extent that they were also the nicknames for Reggie and Ronnie Kray, although it was probably wiser not to inform the brothers of this fact.

Elsie and Doris had both studied at the Guildhall School of Music and formed a polished cabaret routine comprising musical numbers interlinked with patter. The act attracted critics' note, and the Waters became full-time entertainers in the following year. Their intimate approach seemed better suited to cabaret and radio; Elsie later reflected that 'we were heard by Parlophone when we were broadcasting from Birmingham. The company thought our voices were suitable for recordings and so we made six records, which seemed to be doing all right' (quoted in Dixon, *The Guardian*, 13 September 1972: 9). After disc number five, the duo believed they had exhausted their musical material and so they devised a character sketch. The Waters had attended a fashionable wedding when they overheard the proceedings being discussed by two Cockney girls, who inspired the first Gert and Daisy routine. The subsequent disc was a vast success, and its impact surprised the duo, who were unaware that it had received considerable airplay on the radio. They were performing their standard act at a restaurant in Holborn when a guest requested 'The Wedding Sketch', prompting costumes improvised from a hat turned back to front and a silk handkerchief (Lelliott, *The Age*, 30 August 1952: 7).

Gert (Elsie) and Daisy (Doris) would come to define the careers of the Waters for the next forty-five years. Their off-stage lives were as far removed from Stratford and Leyton as William Hay, the Fellow of the Royal Astronomical Society, was from his fraudulent schoolmaster. The sisters favoured Norman Hartnell gowns and resided in a villa in Sussex, but there was no hint of caricature with their creations. The travails with Daisy's idle husband Bert and Elsie's equally unseen fiancé and their termagant neighbour Old Mother Butler were delivered in laconic East End tones that are still far removed from the current Dick-Van-Dyke-meets-Sid-James drama-school patois for soap-opera villainy. Certain *EastEnders* characters would have been quite at home as music hall grotesques, but the Waters reflected that 'cockneys don't shout unless they're selling something – they just say what they think in a nice quiet way' (quoted in Wilmut, 1985: 148). The Waters sisters did employ scriptwriters over the course of their career, but they were more than capable of devising their own material, unlike many male comics of this period. Neither of them was the straight woman per se, but Elsie, who was the principal writer, often allotted the lion's share of the material to Doris, who was the more ebullient performer of the two. They also possessed a remarkable facility for improvisation (Banks and Swift, 1988: 58).

Throughout the 1930s and '40s, Gert and Daisy were frequent guests on radio concert parties and Variety bills. In 1956 their radio comedy *Floggits* began, written by Terry Nation, John Junkin and Dave Freeman with a supporting cast that included Ron Moody, Ronnie Barker and Anthony Newley. Doris died in 1978, Elsie in 1990 and they continued to perform live into the late 1970s. Their act never transferred to television, although in later life they believed 'if the BBC had any sense we could have been the original *Coronation Street*-style show' (Dixon 1972: 10). The heirs to Gert and Daisy are both Ena Sharples and her cronies in the snug of the Rovers Return, fulminating about the evils of 1960s life over port and lemon and *The Liver Birds* (BBC, 1969–79), especially with its finest duo of Nerys Hughes as Sandra and Polly James as Beryl in the 1971 to 1976 period.

The Comedy Playhouse pilot for Carla Lane's creation was not universally well received. Stanley Reynolds became positively splenetic: 'I wish someone would take it and limp to a mercy killing' and 'rooted in the endearing faith that any regional accent will somehow resuscitate a limp joke' were merely two of his observations (*The Guardian*, 15 April 1969: 8). But at its best, *The Liver Birds* was more about the characters than any self-consciously 'Scouse Humour' with Carla Lane creating a partnership in which neither the genteel Sandra or the more outgoing Beryl was the straight woman. Nor would they have endured the treatment meted out to Olive in *On The Buses* and perhaps the main limitation was the characters' ages. *The Liver Birds* were meant to be in their 20s, and as the series progressed, it became harder for the actresses to play such characters. Gert and Daisy were forever aged about 45 and always completely believable. Their feature films, their wireless appearances and their MOI shorts reflect a lost world the sisters created the Waters are both of and transcend their era.

Variety after the Second World War

With almost any form of entertainment, the signs of its time passing are not always apparent. Sometimes the age of a film is demonstrated in those seemingly insignificant details; the moment in *Victim* (Basil Dearden, 1961) where a police car extends a trafficator arm to make a left turn or the steam locomotive in *A Hard Day's Night* (Richard Lester, 1964). By the end of the Second World War, Variety had been fighting the picture houses and wireless for the loyalties of the audiences for more than two decades. In 1945 Flanagan and Allen were still presiding over the bill at the Victoria Palace but it was to be one of the straight man's last outings as a full-time entertainer. Years of ill health had caught up with Chesney Allen, and at the age of 51, he was forced to retire from the stage on medical advice (Flanagan, 1961: 181).

Many of the traditional Variety acts were now well into their middle age at the very least, and although television was not yet a factor – the BBC service would not resume until 1946 – the medium would overtake radio in popularity by 1958. The Variety Artists' Federation, which had been formed in 1906, still had over 6,000 paid-up members in 1951, but fourteen years later this number dwindled to a little over 1,100 (*The Guardian*, 21 November 1966: 3) and the organisation would merge with Equity in 1966. At the end of the 1950s rants such as Jimmy Wheeler's claims that 'Variety is utterly, irreplaceably dead' (quoted in Carthew, *The Daily Herald*, 14 March 1959: 2) were commonplace in the media and by 1960, the capital had just four Variety halls that were still functioning (Double, 2012: 70). The Crazy Gang made their farewell performance from the Victoria Palace on 19 May 1962 and by this time even Bud Flanagan was aware of how his stage attire now appeared to a younger audience – 'tastes have changed so much in popular entertainment' – that he wore a lounge suit rather than his traditional costume (*TV Times*, 20–26 May 1962: 3).

One of the double acts to emerge via the twilight of the Variety circuit after the Second World War was Kenneth Earle and Malcolm Vaughan, 'a highly experienced witty inventive comic' and 'an excellent straight man and superb tenor' (Hudd with Hindin, 1998: 50). They teamed in 1954, and their eighteen-year career demonstrates how an act could adapt to a changed landscape: solo records from Vaughan, who was probably one of the best British crooners of his era; guest appearances on television; six seasons at the Jersey Watersplash holiday resort. As a further indication of the changing times at the tail end of Variety, in 1957 Earle and Vaughan were the support acts on Bill Haley's first British tour, together with the bandleader Vic Lewis and the pipe player Desmond Lane.[5] The surviving venues in which young double acts such as Earle and Vaughan

---

5   The worlds of Variety and skiffle or rock and roll did not always blend successfully. Tommy Steele described in his 2007 memoir *Bermondsey Boy* how a uniformed fireman had to appear with him on stage in 1956 as the authorities were afraid of the risk from an electric guitar.

performed were increasingly entering Archie Rice territory, and in 1962 Tony Hancock wrote in his sadly unpublished memoirs how:

> It is sad to think that most of the theatres where I used to die have since died themselves. The obvious thing to blame is television but I think the trouble with variety goes deeper than that. There is a strain of suicide in the murder. Whenever I go back to the halls, I am appalled by the defeatist spirit surrounding the managements, the deadly take-it-or-leave-it approach to artists and audience alike. (Quoted in Fisher 2008: 234)

The only consolation – and it was an exceedingly cold one – was that during this same period many cinemas were also closing. In the early 1960s, the 1920s picture house and the late Victorian music hall were both easy prey for the property speculator arriving in his Jaguar Mk X to oversee the destruction of the capital's landscape. When the Metropolitan in the Edgware Road finally closed its doors in 1963 the writer Norman Shrapnel reflected on how remote it seemed from the post-war concrete office blocks and how the stars who had returned for this last night were 'light years distant!' from Lenny Bruce:

> We were back in the world of George Robey, George Formby, Dan Leno, Marie Lloyd and Little Tich. Most of the audience looked like grandparents, yet there were a surprising number of young people, too, and they seemed fascinated. (Shrapnel, *The Guardian*, 13 April 1963: 4)

The act who did provide a bridge between the gas-lit music hall and the charcoal suited business executive were Eric and Ernie, of whom we will hear more in the final chapter. For the ambitious performer, one alternative to the Variety theatres was pantomime, playing the Brokers' Men to the latest pop sensation, a development of the late 1950s that was regarded as either great or deplorable by those in the profession (Frow, 1985: 182). There was the holiday-camp circuit and the option of 'clubland', which provided 'a good source of income for refugees from the collapsed theatre circuits' (Double, 2012: 207). In 1862 the Club and Institute Union (CIU) was established by Rev. Henry Solly and an initial ban on alcohol was lifted in the 1870s, a move that proved very profitable for many clubs, as the income from beer would comfortably exceed their rent. By the 1950s Richard Hoggart noted:

> There seems to be a great shadow-world of semi-professional entertainers, men and women who make a comfortable addition to their normal wages by regularly performing at club concerts, moving from club to club in the city as they become known, and if they are particularly good, building up a circuit in the industrial towns for thirty miles. (1957: 178–79)

One such semi-professional was Ken Dodd, then a merchant who in the evenings might find himself on the same bill as a police Superintendent who was also a singer. Clubs would also run coach trips to the seaside or even charter special trains, while the opening of Rotherham's Greasbrough Variety Club in 1961 marked a stage toward more professionalism in the presentation and artist booking. The club had seating capacity for 600, and its bills included Bob Monkhouse and even Johnnie Ray; by 1965 the committee was making a bid to hire Sammy Davis Jr. It was all far removed 'from the days when the "Sunday night entertainment" was an amateur comedian who performed for a pound or two with beer' (*The Guardian*, 15 January 1965: 6). Two years later Jimmy Corrigan opened the Batley Variety Club, which cost £100,000, had the capacity for 1,500 guests and whose early attractions included Val Doonican, The Bachelors and Jayne Mansfield (*The Stage*, 12 January 1967: 6).

Some acts loathed working on the club circuit, Jimmy Jewel referring to them as 'terrible bloody places where there was no space for production sketches' and the material 'dreadful stuff … short, sharp gags with a laugh in every line. We split the act up and never stayed too long'

(1982: 144–45). October 1967 saw the introduction of the breathalyser, a development which was viewed with some alarm by the licensed trade.[6] Louis Barfe considers that the end to the golden years of clubland began in 1968 when the Gaming Act dictated that there had to be a separation between gambling and entertainment (2013). It was the licence of the former that often subsidised the latter. By 1978 the Batley Variety Club had been transformed into a disco with the less than enticing name of 'Crumpet' while Eric Midwinter was of the opinion that:

> The club circuit seems to prefer the harder hitting, less ceremonial quick-fire stand-up comedian, and there are now no more than three or four double acts which the ordinary citizen could name, as opposed to a dozen or twenty back in the 'forties. (1979: 70)

It is a compelling argument, although one could make the equal claim that the double act had evolved into a television sitcom format – q.v. – and that of the 'three or four' names, Cannon and Ball, Little and Large, were continuing the formula of the Variety double act via the working men's club. They came to national prominence; at their summit the star attraction might be Cliff Richard, where chicken in a basket cost £1.05 and where the backing musicians 'often had to enter the stage from kitchens slippery with cooking oil' (Turner, 2008: 264).

Worse still were those venues with club secretaries who made Colin Crompton in *The Wheeltappers' and Shunters' Social Club*[7] look like James Mason and the depressing spectacle of Diana Dors being paid in cash to perform patter numbers before beer-sodden audiences who requested that she remove her clothes.[8] At least many of the supporting acts could have hailed from the early days of music hall and Neil Anderson's *The Dirty Stop Out's Guide to Working Men's Clubs* pays tribute to Shag

---

6   A representative of the Milk Marketing Board recommended starting and ending a drinking session with a half-pint of milk. It didn't work.
7   Granada TV 1974–77.
8   They would soon regret such heckles.

Connor's Carrot Crunchers ('Country Comedy Musical Act')[9] and Crick's Canine Wonders ('Featuring a boxing match with dogs').[10] Another, and frankly unmissable-sounding, attraction might be Madame Charmaine ('The world's greatest clairvoyant hen').[11]

Syd Little (Cyril Mead) and Eddie Large (Edward McGinnis) met when Syd, clad in his best Teddy Boy regalia, was playing the guitar in a club – 'I was a one-man karaoke machine!' – only to encounter heckles from Mr McGinnis. The musician eventually invited this loud party on to the stage, and the two formed an act. They turned professional in 1962: 'One of our earliest routines was Bobby Vee's "Rubber Ball"; I'd play, and Eddie would bounce around the stage to the refrain "bouncy bouncy".' They adopted the name 'Little and Large', and after a televisual diversion on to *Crackerjack* ('that didn't really suit us; we did not want to be typed as "children's entertainers"') their mainstream career began in 1977 with *The Little and Large Show* on Thames Television.

The show transferred to the BBC in 1978 and ran for another thirteen years. It was at its strongest, not during the sketches, but with the act's routines in which the large, ebullient comic plagues Syd as he attempts to complete a song. Little states in a 1978 interview that 'we are nothing like Morecambe and Wise … We are great admirers of theirs, but our act is totally different' (quoted in McGarry, *Coventry Evening Telegraph*, 12 October: 16). Ernie was a self-assured character, forever writing his plays, grovelling at the guest star or issuing orders to Eric, but with Little and Large the fact that the straight man did not speak for the first ten minutes was quite deliberate; the joke was as much Little's increasingly disgruntled expression as Eddie's succession of impersonations. Each serves as the best audience for the other – the diligent musician and the show-off – and footage from *The Wheeltappers*

---

9   Gloucestershire's answer to Adge Cutler and The Wurzels.

10 Billed as 'the only dog fight in Britain played to Queensberry Rules', and the act which held the top score on *New Faces* for one week in 1976. By 1980 they were 'a howling success at the weekend family lunchtime shows at Cesar's nightclub Luton' (advertisement in *The Stage*, 31 January 1980: 88).

11 Which does beg the question as to whether there were any others.

shows how effective this on-stage relationship could be as Syd valiantly tries to complete at least one verse of 'Till There Was You'.

Little and Large's near contemporaries were Tommy Cannon (Thomas Derbyshire) and Bobby Ball (Robert Harper), who began as a musical duo ('The Harper Brothers') before forging a comic double act. Their dynamic was centred on the unbreakable bond between two old friends, even if the straight man's image is now of flashy self-confidence and, again, *The Wheeltappers* provides an illustration of how effective the formula was. Bernard Manning announces Cannon as a crooner, and he arrives on stage with a convincing version of 'Summertime', and when Ball, in the guise of his one-time workbench mate, begins calling out his name, some audience members take him for a real heckler. London Weekend Television gave them their first TV vehicle in 1979. They are still touring to this day, proof that a double act cannot be manufactured – in Cannon's words, 'we weren't two separate acts who met up in a club one night and were thrown together' (quoted in *The Stage*, 30 August 1979: 16).

A second route to sustaining a career was in the seaside resorts. In 1934 J.B. Priestley described Blackpool as 'this huge mad place, with its miles and miles of promenades, its three piers, its gigantic dance-halls, its variety shows', and how its visitors were conveyed by 'seventy special trains a day'. Compared with the wonders of the Lancashire resort, Brighton, Margate and Yarmouth were 'merely playing at being popular seaside resorts' (1968: 265–66).

The major seaside towns were also subject to a post-war decline; albeit at a slower rate, with a sixteen- to eighteen-week booking representing a professional lifeline for many a performer. Louis Barfe points out that as recently as the 1980s, 'away from the television and the clubs, the best performers were guaranteed bookings in the highly successful summer shows that each major seaside town offered' (2013). By the 1960s visitors were increasingly likely to arrive by car instead of by train or coach, and in 1965 the Butlin empire reported its first loss (Ferry, 2009: 62), as the happy campers began to tire of the quasi-National Service atmosphere.

The impact of television inevitably began to shape the entertainments, and in the 1970s a holidaymaker would be able to see a stage version of *George and Mildred* or *Nearest and Dearest*. The medium also affected the audience in their reaction to live entertainment. Double points out that the concept of 'The Fourth Wall' was largely alien to Variety audiences, even with sketch comedy (2012: 130), but entertainers were now encountering patrons who had little or no memory of regular outings to Variety halls, and so they would view the acts as via the small screen. Mike Winters remarked in 1978 how people would attend summer shows and frequently 'just stare. It's very unsettling, and you have to chip the wall down' (quoted in Doncaster, *Daily Mirror*, 26 July 1978: 15).

By the 1960s the entertainments and publicity officers of major resorts were often engaged in booking conferences (Walton, 2000: 186) when they were not arranging PR for an extremely eclectic entertainment bill. Stanley Reynolds observed of Blackpool in 1963 that 'most of the shows derive from their television counterparts of the past year; the main difference being that they are live, go on longer, and we have to pay to get in ... oddly enough, the BBC's *TWTWTW* has not had the impact we might have expected'.[12] The emphasis with the pier-end shows was not on modern jazz, square-bottomed ties and quips about Reginald Maudling but a show where 'there is always some man who puts on lingerie' (*The Guardian*, 27 July 1963: 5).[13] It was further along the coast in Morecambe that the unimpressed Mr Reynolds found 'the missing dimension necessary for real music hall' with a performance in the Winter Gardens of Jimmy Jewel and Ben Warriss.

At first, it seems rather dismissive to consider Jewel and Warriss in the twilight of their career as a double act, one that John Fisher considered to be 'raucous yet brilliant' (2013: 462). They were cousins who formed

---

12 *That Was The Week That Was*, 1962–63, was known for short as *TWTWTW* or *TW3*.
13 A film which captures seaside entertainments of this period is Val Guest's *The Beauty Jungle*, which was partially shot in Weston-super-Mare and Bognor Regis in the summer of 1963. Tommy Trinder plays Charlie Dorton, a fading Variety comic now reduced to pier-end shows; a morose Sid James is a judge at a holiday camp beauty contest; our heroine Shirley (Janette Scott) takes part in 'Cheltenham's Miss Banana Yogurt' and other stellar events.

an act in 1934 and enjoyed their major period of success in the late 1940s with their radio show *Up the Pole* (1947–52). The partnership broke up in 1966, Jewel noting that they were never comfortable on television where they lacked the ease of Morecambe and Wise (Jewel, 1982: 148). The surviving recordings of Jewel and Warriss reveal an act with the brisk manner of two travelling salesman planning their day's patter at a seaside boarding house – possibly one that is presided over by Meg with her limited array of breakfasts. Michael Billington argues that in *The Birthday Party*, 'the lonely lodger, the ravenous landlady, the quiescent husband; these figures, eventually to become Stanley, Meg and Petey sound like figures in a Donald McGill seaside postcard … if the play had been tried out at seaside rep in Bournemouth or Torquay, I bet audiences would have loved it' (2009: 131). He also proposes that one template for Goldberg and McCann might well have been Jewel and Warriss and they might have indeed rubbed shoulders with a young actor named David Baron:[14] 'Ben Warriss, sleek and sharp-suited, with patent-leather hair, was always the bullying straight man, Jimmy Jewel, nervously apprehensive was the comic fall guy. Their act was a classic study in domination and submission' (2009: 132).

A third route was, of course, television itself; although for a while some older entertainers decried 'the idiot's lantern', it had thoroughly absorbed many of Variety's tropes. This did not just apply to *Sunday Night At The London Palladium* but also to a seemingly endless parade of 'Seaside Specials' and the format of television comedies which, as Dick Fiddy remarks, 'up until the early 1960s often seemed to end with an elongated sketch'.[15] If the best British situation comedies focused on the life behind the bright lights, these were the shows that brought the best of live entertainment to your front parlour (Briggs, 1995: 210). Some comics followed Tony Hancock and made a transition into situation comedy: *Double Cross* (BBC, 1956) starred Jewel and Warriss as two MI5 officers whose doppelgangers were a Variety act; Francie (Jack Milroy)

---

14 The older quietly dignified Jewel would have made the ideal Petey
15 The first programme to be broadcast from the BBC's new Television Centre was a variety show entitled *First Night* starring Arthur Askey and David Nixon (Barfe, 2013).

and Josie (Rikki Fulton), Glasgow's most ambitious Teddy Boys, had commenced as a sketch in the 1958 review *Five Past Eight*.

Milroy was a comedian who enjoyed vast popularity in pantomime and who staged shows at Aberdeen's Tivoli Theatre. Fulton was a character actor of immense versatility, and on the BBC's *Show Band Show* he served as the mid-Atlantic toned compere in addition to taking part in self-penned sketches. The act transferred to television with *The Adventures of Francie and Josie* (Scottish Television 1962–65) and the series was broadcast across the north of England. Josie (a Ted of intellectual pretensions), was forever ordering Francie – who had none – to 'dry up', using words that sounded impressive.

Others adopted the roles of quiz show hosts, smiling with a Colgate grin at the human traffic as they failed to win 10s–worth of nylon stockings (1950s) or an Austin Mini Metro City (1980s). This was not a position that encouraged the formation of a double act but lurking in the memory is a duo of sorts that could be seen in the pages of the *TV Times* and your local theatre: Hughie Greene and Monica Rose. The former was London born with a Canadian passport and accent, and was the genial compere of ITV's *Double Your Money* (Associated-Rediffusion, 1955–68); the latter was a contestant on the show in 1964 who became a hostess for the next three years.

There was also an influx of acts that had primarily attained their fame via the small screen and were now embraced by a medium that would previously have liked to see them deported to the Antarctic regions. Benny Hill made a return to the halls in the wake of his first shows for BBC Television, and there was also the opportunity to see a provincial bill containing a live version of *What's My Line* (BBC, 1951–63). The cult of personality had already begun, with audiences paying their 3s 9d to learn if Gilbert Harding really was as irate as he appeared on the screen. In 1966, by which time Variety had already entered the history books, you might have felt the inexplicable urge to book tickets to see Hughie Green (as 'Baron Batman') and Monica Rose in the pantomime *Babes in The Wood*.

Fame on the small screen did not always translate into live fame. Mike and Bernie Winters arguably made their breakthrough on television as the resident comic relief on *The Six-Five Special* (BBC, 1957–58) at a time when the surviving Variety theatres were having to book teenage acts to survive. The success of the pop show and combined with the effects of tours in 1956 and 1957 with Tommy Steele and The Steelmen – 'TV's Crazy Funsters' who were 'Just Nuts' – prompted them to create their own roadshow. It proved to be a disaster. When writing about the brothers, it is essential to ignore the fact that they were the butt of many cruel jibes – 'the only double act with two straight men' – and the story of their notorious debut appearance at the Glasgow Empire: 'There's two of 'em!' Many an English entertainer had died there before them.

Michael and Bernard Weinstein first began performing as musicians in the Canadian Legion, and during the immediate post-war years, they slowly evolved a double act under the stage name of Winters. Their partnership lasted, on and off, for over thirty years and in 1954 the Winters were described by *The Stage* as 'a most promising act … Bernie is a real goon, Mike being his straight man. Mike is also a fine clarinettist and does an amusing take-off of a crooner' (21 October 1954: 5). By the mid-1950s, the partnership had already dissolved on several occasions, and Bernie reflected of his brother's decision to enter the garment business, 'how do you walk away from all that money for the opportunity of struggling in fleapit theatres' (1976: 74). The act gradually evolved with Mike, who was originally the comic, deciding to become the straight man before one performance when he placed the 'funny' hat on his brother's head (Hudd with Hindin, 1998: 198). By 1955 they had come to the further realisation that their identical lounge suits did not sufficiently differentiate their on-stage personae, so Mike commissioned an ill-fitting Teddy Boy suit to emphasise Bernie's dim-witted stage persona.

It was via *The Six-Five Special* that they first enjoyed national fame. The BBC devised the programme in 1957 as a mean of filling the former 'Toddler's Truce', when television went off air between six and seven in the evening. The solution, as devised by Jack Good, was a youth programme and as Mike was then aged 31 and Bernie 27, they could both adapt television age with greater ease than older Variety artists and fit with the ethos of the show rather more convincingly than the resident hosts. The limited amount of footage that exists shows Jo Douglas and Pete Murray presiding over the show in the manner of two determined youth club leaders.[16]

The Winters left *The Six-Five Special* in May 1958, but the pathway from a skiffle and rock and roll show and starring in their own programme for ABC Television was not straightforward. In 1959 Bernie was offered a solo contract with Warwick Films, the production company that served as the British division of Columbia, and the act dissolved once more. The resulting films were often very odd – *Jazz Boat* (Ken Hughes, 1960) had Anthony Newley moodily crooning as he mooched along the banks of the Thames, wild music from Ted Heath and His Band, David Lodge as a biker (!) and Bernie as the comic relief playing 'The Jinx'. *Johnny Nobody* (Nigel Patrick, 1961), a murder drama with religious overtones, was shot in Ireland and was possibly the last film where you might expect Bernie Winters to appear in the semi-straight part as a newspaper photographer. 'I suppose they (Warwick) didn't know what to do with me' (1976: 153). The act reformed and received a second television breakthrough in 1963, hosting the ABC series *Big Night Out*, the first series featuring a bill of guest artists that perfectly encapsulated the era: Petula Clark, David Nixon, Dickie Valentine, Susan Maughan, Gerry and The Pacemakers, Vera Lynn, Marion Ryan and the Beatles.

From 1965 to 1973 the Winters had their own TV show, five years before the act broke up in acrimonious circumstances. There are, of course, difficulties in judging the comedy routines of any act from the past. Television footage survives of the brothers Winters, as do comic records such as the LP *Mike and Bernie Winters in Toyland*. One challenge, according to the writer Eric Geen, was that Mike 'was jealous and it made it very difficult to write sketches. He didn't like other people on the show getting laughs' (quoted in Barfe, 2013), but another challenge

---

16 The programme was treated with some suspicion by the BBC, in case the wild beat of skiffle incited washboard-crazed youths to revolution.

is the brothers' sometimes downbeat attitude to their career. Their very readable memoir, *Shake a Pagoda Tree*, is charmingly self-deprecatory ('the theatre was about a quarter full, and we got a one-clap applause' (1976: 52)) as was their oft-quoted response to Morecambe and Wise: 'An act like that only happens once in a lifetime, but why did it have to happen in ours?' Their anecdotes from the 1950s often read like an early draft script for *Expresso Bongo* (Val Guest, 1959), two quick-witted and faintly desperate young men haunting Denmark Street and the various milk bars of the West End on their circuitous route to success.

One of their last routines as a double act was on *The Good Old Days* in 1977, their cross-talk routines adapted with ease to the players setting. The faded colour footage shows what used to be referred to as a 'good standard act' that was ideal for the transitory period between the twilight of Variety but consisting of elements that were not so much disparate as completely individual. Mike was the smooth straight man addressing the audience in the tones of a prosperous restaurateur who is not to be crossed, and it is a wonder why he never made the transition into straight acting. It is certainly possible to envisage the older brother as a saturnine London heavy in the Lee Montague/George Sewell tradition while Bernie was a childlike clown whose best work was playing Bud Flanagan in the stage revue *Underneath The Arches*.

As for the inevitable comparisons of the Winters with Eric and Ernie, perhaps Nancy Banks-Smith best described this as being Mike and Bernie's misfortune but not their fault (*The Guardian*, 1 October 1970: 13). Michael Grade also opined that the act 'was excellent but never had quite the same instinct for the right material that Morecambe and Wise always demonstrated' (Grade, 1998: 48).

However, their cover of the 1961 Peter Scott Peters novelty single 'Fallout Shelter' remains a work that only the Winters brothers could have created. Nothing that the Bonzo Dog Doo Dah Band ever recorded could ever equal the impact of Mike (cod-American) and Bernie Winters (New York meets Islington and is already regretting it) singing, 'Twenty megatons is the size of the boom – and if they let it go, I'll feel no doom'. Music hall began with comic songs and now a satire of American paranoia – which was originally recorded by a Canadian – was transformed now by the Winters into a bizarre form of sing-a-long. The Victorian traditions of popular entertainments certainly died hard.

With thanks to Dick Fiddy, Chris Gidney and Syd Little.

Bibliography

Books

Anderson, Neil (2017), *The Dirty Stop Out's Guide to Working Men's Clubs*. Sheffield: ACM Retro.

Baker, Richard Anthony (2014), *British Music Hall: An Illustrated History*. Barnsley: Pen and Sword.

Banks, Morwenna and Swift, Amanda (1988), *The Jokes On Us: Women in Comedy from Music Hall to The Present*. London: Pandora.

Barfe, Louis (2013), *Turned Out Nice Again: The Story of British Light Entertainment*. London: Atlantic Books.

Besant, Walter (1884), 'The Amusements of the People', in Polley, Martin (ed.) (2004), *The History of Sport in Britain, 1880–1914: The Varieties of Sport, Vol. 1*. Abingdon: Routledge.

Bevan, Ian (1952), *Top of The Bill: The Story of The London Palladium*. London: Frederick Mueller.

Billington, Michael (2009), *Harold Pinter: New and Updated Edition*. London: Faber and Faber.

Briggs, Asa (1995), *The History of Broadcasting in the United Kingdom. Vol. 5: Competition*. Oxford: Oxford University Press.

Cannon, Tommy and Ball, Bobby with Gidney, Chris (2001), *Rock On, Tommy!* London: Harper Collins.

Double, Oliver (2012), *Britain Had Talent: A History of Variety Theatre*. London: Palgrave.

Ellington, Duke and Vail, Ken (ed.) (1999) *Duke's Diary: Part One*. Lanham: The Scarecrow Press.

Ferry, Kathryn (2009), *The British Seaside Holiday*. Oxford: Shire Publications.

Flanagan, Bud (1961), *My Crazy Life*. London: Frederick Muller Ltd.

Fisher, John (2008), *Tony Hancock: The Definitive Biography*. London: Harper Collins.

Fisher, John (2013), *Funny Way To Be A Hero*. London: Preface Publishing.

Frow, Gerald (1985), *'Oh Yes It Is': The Story of Pantomime*. London: BBC.

Grade, Michael (1998), *It seemed Like a Good Idea at the Time*. London: Pan.

Green, Benny (1986), *The Last Empires: A Music Hall Companion*. London: Pavilion.

Hoggart, Richard (1957), *The Uses of Literacy: Aspects of Working Class Life*. London: Allen Lane.

Hudd, Roy with Hindin, Philip (1998), *Roy Hudd's Cavalcade Of Variety Acts, 1945–1960*. London: Pavilion.

Jewel, Jimmy (1982), *Three Times Lucky – An Autobiography*. London: Enigma Books.

Kilgarriff, Michael (1998), *Grace, Beauty and Banjos: The Peculiar Lives and Strange Times of Music Hall and Variety Artistes*. London: Oberon Books.

Leslie, Peter (1978), *A Hard Act to Follow: A Music Hall Review*. London: Paddington Press.

Little, Syd with Gidney, Chris (2004), *Little by Little*. Norwich: Canterbury Press.

Major, John (2012), *My Old Man: A Personal History of Music Hall*. London: Harper Collins.

Maloney, Paul (2003), *Scotland and the Music Hall, 1850–1914*. Manchester: Manchester University Press.

Mayhew, Henry (1851/1970), *Mayhew's London: Being Selections from 'London Labour and The London Poor'*. London: Spring Books.

Midwinter, Eric (1979), *Make 'em Laugh: Famous Comedians and Their Worlds*. London: Allen & Unwin.

Pilton, Patrick (1976), *Every Night at The Palladium*. London: Robson Books.

Priestley, J.B. (1968), *English Journey*. London: Heinemann.

Reynolds, Harry (1928), *Minstrel Memories: The Story of Burnt Cork Minstrelsy in Great Britain from 1836 to 1927*. London: Alton Rivers.

Ritichie, James Ewing (1858), *The Night Side of London*. London: William Tweedie.

Ritchie, James Ewing (1859), *Here and There in London*. London: William Tweedie.

St. Pierre, Paul Matthew (2003), *Song and Sketch Transcripts of British Music Hall Performers Elsie and Doris Waters*. New York: Edwin Mellen Press.

Steele, Tommy (2007), *Bermondsey Boy: Memories of a Forgotten World*. London: Penguin.

Turner, Steve (2008), *Cliff Richard: The Biography: 50th Anniversary Edition*. London: Lion Books.

Walton, John K. (2000), *The British Seaside: Holidays and Resorts in the Twentieth Century*. Manchester: Manchester University Press.

Wilmut, Roger (1985), *Kindly Leave The Stage: The Story of Variety 1919–1960*. London: Methuen.

Winters, Mike (2010), *The Sunny Side of Winters: A Variety of Memories*. London: J R Books Ltd.

Winters, Mike and Bernie (1976), *Shake a Pagoda Tree*. London: W.H. Allen.

Journals and Periodicals

Advertisement: Crick's Canine Wonders (1980), *The Stage*, 31 January, p. 88.

Advertisement: Poluski Brothers (1902), *London and Provincial Entr'acte*, 22 November, p. 13.

Advertisement: The Two Mikes (1884), *London and Provincial Entr'acte*, 8 November, p. 12.

Aldous, Tony (2002), 'Frank Matcham, Theatre Builder', *History Today* 52(5).

Banks-Smith, Nancy (1970), 'Television Review' in *The Guardian*, 1 October, p. 13.

'Batley's New Club' (1967), *The Stage*, 12 January, p. 6.

Bratton, J.S. (1981), 'English Ethiopians: British Audiences and Black-Face Acts, 1835–1865', *Yearbook of English Studies* 11.

Carthew, Anthony (1959), 'I'm Sick of Earning Peanuts, says Jim, the Mayfair Man', *The Daily Herald*, 14 March, p. 2.

Doncaster, Patrick (1978), 'Mike and Bernie: End of The Pair', *The Daily Mirror*, 26 July, p. 15.

Flanagan, Bud (1962), 'Farewell, Gang!', *TV Times*, 20–26 May, p. 3.

'Gert and Daisy Talk To Stephen Dixon' (1972), *The Guardian*, 13 September, p. 9.

'Keynotes' (1885), 'The First Negro Minstrels', *The Star*, 10 November, p. 2.

Lelliott, Eileen (1952), 'Gert and Daisy Off Stage', *The Age*, 30 August, p. 7.

Marriott, R.B. (1966), 'Renee Houston Celebrates Her Golden Year', *The Stage*, 4 August, p. 8.

McGarry, Pete (1978), 'We're NOT like M & W', *Coventry Evening Telegraph*, 12 October, p. 16.

'Opera in The Halls' (1913), *The Era*, 16 July, p. 13.

Review: Ardwick Empire (1929), *The Guardian*. 5 November. p. 14.

Review: The Brothers Griffiths (1889), *Music Hall & Theatre Review*, 30 November, p. 7.

Review: The Chelsea Palace (1935), *The Stage*, 31 October, p. 3.

Review: The Christy Minstrels (1857), *The Morning Chronicle*, 29 July, p. 5.

Review: The Holborn Empire (1937), *The Stage*, 15 April, p. 3.

Review: The Palladium (1931), *The Stage*, 24 December, p. 3.

Review: Sweeney and Ryland (1891), *The Music Hall & Theatre Review*, 18 July, pp. 8–10.

Reynolds, Stanley (1963), 'Don't Bother To Applaud', *The Guardian*, 27 July, p. 5.

Reynolds, Stanley (1969), 'Television Review', *The Guardian*, 15 April, p. 8.

'Round The Halls' (1954), 'The Balance of The Bill Was Wrong', *The Stage*, 21 October, p. 5.

'Sammy Davis Jnr May Not Be Far Behind' (1965), *The Guardian*, 15 January, p. 6.

Shrapnel, Norman (1963), 'The Met's Final Night', *The Guardian*, 13 April, p. 4.

'Stephen Dixon Interviews Chesney Allen' (1972), *The Guardian*, 30 December, p. 10.

Television Today (1979), 'An Adventurous Double Act – Not Manufactured', *The Stage*, 30 August, p. 16.

Online resources

O'Gorman Brothers Website http://ogormanbros.co.uk/

2

Films and the British Double Act

One tall, one short, one fat, one thin. A comedy team is more easily arrived that than a comedy star working solo, because the double act instantly suggests the prevalence of what is deplorable in the human condition. (Kerr, 1967: 177)

'Get in the back of the van!' (Policeman No. 2 in *Withnail and I*, Bruce Robinson, 1987)

Introduction

A proposition that might have devotees of music hall eating their flat hats in rage is that a cinematic double act may have an impact greater in just one picture than a hard-working second-tiered duo who spend decades working the halls. Richard E. Grant and Paul McGann only worked together once, but those 107 minutes granted their screen partnership immortality. Many of the most famous double acts of British cinema were not the filmed antics of Variety comics but actors whose relationship was never formally billed, or even lasting beyond one picture but whose screen relationship abided in the affections of the public. Nor were all cinematic partnerships always intended to reassure. One of the highlights of *The Green Man* (Robert Day, 1956) was the attempt of Alastair Sim's contract assassin to prevent the infuriatingly persistent George Cole from calling the police. With *The Lavender Hill Mob* (Charles Frend, 1951) Henry Holland (Alec Guinness) and Alfred Pendlebury (Stanley Holloway) find liberation in each other's company while in *Kind Hearts and Coronets* (Robert Hamer, 1949) Dennis Price is faced with the hydra-headed embodiment of privilege as represented by the D'Asycoyne family. Guinness played eight roles but, as is so often the case, it was the straight man who anchors the narrative.

Sixteen years later, Dennis Price – sad, prematurely aged and in the throes of alcoholism – would appear in the BBC's adaptation of *The World of Woodhouse* as Jeeves, opposite the Bertie Wooster of Ian Carmichael. The double act was popular with the public over twenty episodes,[1] but they could not equate with the high comedy of *Kind Hearts and Coronets*. Ten years later, the censorship of the day dictated the apprehension of *The League of Gentlemen* (Basil Dearden, 1960) but the double act of Lt Col Hyde, played by the almost permanently irascible Jack Hawkins, and his impishly dangerous 'adjutant' Major Race, played by Nigel Patrick ('old darling'), more than compensates.

Regardless of whether the picture was a vehicle for a Variety double act, a B-feature, a major production backed with Hollywood money or even that nadir of British cinema, the 1970s 'sex comedy', one factor remains consistent. The chemistry between the two parties on screen may be indefinable but it is immediately recognisable by its absence and it cannot be artificially created. Peter Vaughan and John Carson were so entertaining in the low-budget comedy-thriller *Smokescreen* (Jim O'Connolly, 1964) as to make one wish they had featured in their own television series, while Rita Tushingham and Lynn Redgrave in

---

1   Only one complete story now survives in the BBC archive.

Woodfall's adaptation of Edna O'Brien's *Girl With Green Eyes* (Desmond Davis, 1964) were a vibrant and wholly believable pair of friends. The two actors and the same director were reunited for 1967's *Smashing Time*, but it suffered from wishing to celebrate 'Swinging London' as much as satirising it – and from an air of artifice in place of that much-overused word 'chemistry'.

A film need not be a critical masterpiece to establish a team in the memory. It could be Reg Varney and Bob Grant desperately trying to bring a modicum of humour to an *On the Buses* spin-off film or Anthony Booth reacting with 'you stupid bleeder' as Robin Askwith suffers once more from malfunctioning trousers. It could even be Cannon and Ball in a prop Mini Metro Panda car in a picture with longueurs to rival *L'Année dernière à Marienbad* (Alan Renais, 1961).[2] A team need not appear in a major production to be accepted as such; as with the best of Britain's cinematic double acts the public would recognise an authentic comedy duo.

Music Hall

If you grew up in the 1970s or '80s you were too young to have directly experienced music hall or Variety, but its shades could still be encountered – on *The Good Old Days* (1953–83) on the BBC, in interviews on various nostalgia programmes or in faded copies of *Film Fun Annual* that you might still find in a charity shop. There might also be the airing on BBC2 or pre-*Celebrity Z-List Bus Station Challenge* Channel Four of one of the many products of minor studios somewhere in the outer London suburbs. One problem faced by the younger viewer was that the pictures devised as vehicles for comedians of the 1930s and '40s are often almost resolutely anti-cinematic. Unlike the finest work of Laurel and Hardy,

---

2   *The Boys In Blue* (Val Guest, 1982) might well have been improved by Bobby Ball informing Tommy Cannon 'These whisperings, worse than silence, that you're imprisoning me in.'

the camera is rarely complicit in the antics of the lead comedians, but for every ten pictures shot with a camera virtually cemented to the studio floor, there might be one sequence or even moment that encapsulates the act's very essence. These are the films where the immediacy of the talents broke the 'fourth wall' of the screen, celebrating the Donald McGill postcard world famously described by George Orwell:

> Marriage is a dirty joke or comic disaster, where the rent is always behind ... where the lawyer is always a crook and the Scotsman always a miser, where the newlyweds make fools of themselves on the hideous beds of seaside lodging houses and the drunken red-nosed husbands roll home at four in the morning to meet the linen-nightgowned wives who wait for them behind the front door, poker in hand. (1998: 30)

Pathé newsreels would film the antics of Variety double acts for their pictorial series, allowing the chance to see Collinson and Dean's aggressive interplay or the cynical Harry Haver and Frank Lee. The former was aggressive, bespectacled and spoke in an American accent with undertones of the comic's native Liverpool; his foil was short, moustachioed and resigned to his position in life. There were also those directors whose scope and ambition transcended budgets; the documentary maker John Grierson praised John Baxter as one of the few film-makers who 'can put the authentic hallmark of the British character into a film' (quoted in Richards, 2010: 299). He was responsible for one of the most indelible moments of any screen double act with *Dreaming* (1944), one of two separate vehicles made by Bud Flanagan and Chesney Allen, and even some quite superfluous cutaways cannot quite dispel their power as they perform one of their signature tunes.

The variety film was in part a product of the Cinematograph Films Act of 1927, created to make it a legal requirement for exhibitors to screen a larger percentage of domestically made pictures. The quota was raised from 7.5 per cent to 20 per cent in 1935, and three years later the act was modified to exclude films shot within the British Empire.

UK-based subsidiaries of Hollywood majors and a network of domestic production firms churned out material without over-spending. Some features were elevated from B-picture status to the main attraction. The two screen vehicles for Elsie and Doris Waters, *Gert and Daisy's Weekend* (Maclean Rogers, 1941), and *Gert and Daisy Clean Up* (Rogers, 1942) were just two of the pictures that were elevated to main feature status by public demand. It is easy to understand why the films were so popular, such were the talents of the Waters sisters, who could transcend the primitive studio conditions and the lack of a live audience. A further element to Variety hall double acts on the silver screen is that until the 1950s, it was economically viable to make comedies for regional markets. The Mancunian Film Company was operated by John E. Blakeley and specialised in comedy films for picture houses that were situated north of the Tees–Exe line. As C.P. Lee points out:

> John E. appreciated how the simple, uncomplicated, feel-good quality of his movies was as down to earth as their viewers. It is instructive to remember that he had an imitate knowledge of rental and distribution in this area and would have had a fairly shrewd idea of what his punters wanted to see. (2012: 55)

For a younger viewer catching sight of a Mancunian film on afternoon television,[3] they could often be an extremely strange experience, with the cast sometimes acting as though they were rooted to their chalk-marks. Most importantly, the audience was missing, and the routines exist in a vacuum.

Rather more ambitious were the quartet of pictures made by The Crazy Gang for Gainsborough Studios: *O-Kay for Sound* (Marcel Varnel, 1937), *The Frozen Limits* (Varnel, 1939), *Gasbags* (Varnel, 1941) and *Alf's Button Afloat* (Varnel, 1938). It is the last-named that is the only one of their films that captures their ethos as described by John Fisher: 'one of hoax and mayhem on both sides of the footlights, the whole theatre a

---

3   It is sometimes forgotten just how eclectic a British television schedule could be during the 1970s and 1980s.

vacuum for lunatic exuberance' (2013: 72). Putting comics in uniform and having them barked at by a moustachioed NCO was a familiar trope of British cinema comedy for decades – having the Crazy Gang confronted by Alastair Sim's genie, who makes them look reasonably sane by comparison, was a masterstroke.

Even that arch-curmudgeon Leslie Haillwell regarded *Alf's Button Afloat* as the 'supreme achievement of the *Crazy Gang*, perhaps an extravaganza rather than a comedy but still perfectly controlled by director Marcel Varnel' (1987: 106). In later life, the writer-director Val Guest recalled that 'we had six people to deal with at any one time. We used to keep a chart in front of us while we were writing so we didn't leave one of them out for more than seven pages at a time' (quoted in Macnab, *The Independent*, 4 September 1997). As a footnote to *Alf's Button Afloat*, it is very hard to dislike any film in which the then-obligatory juvenile leads are eaten (offscreen) by a bear somewhere in the Home Counties.

Arthur Askey made a quartet of films with his radio partner Richard Murdoch of which *The Ghost Train* (Walter Forde, 1941) is by far the best. The narrative is updated for a Second World War audience and cleverly expanded from the original stage play, while the device of having the central character divided into two roles for Askey and Richard Murdoch is extremely effective. The former's inmate approach, forged via years of touring with concert parties, meant that he was far more suited to cinema than some of his Variety contemporaries who were prone to bellowing their lines. Askey also possessed a talent for acting that allowed his Tommy Gander to be just the right side of the dividing line between 'eccentric' and 'supporting characters all plotting to strangle him'.

Murdoch was equally on form as the genial ass who is more than he initially appears, but he appeared in only one more picture with Askey, *I Thank You* (Varnel, 1941) before he joined the RAF. After the Second World War, Askey was teamed with the tall, thin and amiably moonstruck Glenn Melvyn in *The Love Match* (David Paltenghi, 1955). Melvyn had written the original stage play about two football-obsessed steam locomotive drivers and the film was partially on location in the north of

England, capturing the landscape celebrated by Richard Hoggart in *The Uses of Literacy* when on a Sunday evening, 'the middens up the back had a fine topcoat of empty salmon and fruit tins' (Hoggart, 1957: 24).

Raymond Durgnat saw *The Love Match* as capturing 'something of the drive, the bickerings, the warmth of working class idioms' (1970: 53) and one scene in particular merits a place in the pantheon of British comedy moments. Bill Brown (Askey), in the company of his wife Sal (Thora Hird) and his friend Wally (Melvyn), nervously awaits the arrival of Alf Hall, the latest boyfriend of his daughter Rose (Shirley Eaton). Danny Ross played Alf and for any BBC2 viewer of the 1970s who had only previously heard Ross on *The Clitheroe Kid*, it was immediately apparent that his appearance perfectly matched his nasal Odham-inflected voice. Ross possessed legs that were probably formed of India rubber; even his hair was unkempt, and for several seconds Askey and Melvyn, subsequently joined by Hird, just stare in disbelief at this grinning apparition. *The Love Match* may be a minor production, but it is still a masterclass in how less is more in any comedy.

By the 1950s the low-budget musical hall comedies were as much on the wane as the stage tradition from which they had sprung. Second feature comedies did not vanish from local picture houses – as late as 1962 Hylda Baker and Cyril Smith appeared in *She Knows, Y'Know* (Montgomery Tully). But the dominant image of the B-feature was now the crime drama, a formula which had the budgetary merit of requiring a police Wolseley, a leading actor in a trilby and a villain in a natty black shirt/white tie combination. During the post-war years the Hammer/Exclusive company made screen versions of radio and, subsequently television, comedies. To an extent the sitcom spin-offs that commenced in 1969 may also be seen as an heir to the tradition of placing variety comics in cheap films.

The early 1980s saw an odd postscript to this cinematic subgenre in the form of *The Boys in Blue* (Val Guest, 1982), a remake of *Ask a Policeman* fashioned as a vehicle for Cannon and Ball. I.Q. Hunter, who was clearly not a fan, wrote that it was 'a uniquely dreadful hold-over from another era' and would have 'benefitted from some gratuitous bad taste ... As it is, *The Boys in Blue* is a film stranded in time' (2012: 1958–59). Guest was one of Britain's most versatile film directors, but here a combination of limited budget and a visibly disinterested supporting cast (this is one of the few times when Roy Kinnear telegrams in a performance) prove fatal to an enterprise that must have had a limited appeal. Cannon and Ball were one of the major attractions on ITV and *The Boys in Blue* cannot quite mask their likeability, the latter aggressively enthusiastic, the former long-suffering and proud of his sergeant's stripes. But, despite Ball's terrier-like stage persona, there is none of the aggressive anarchy of its 1939 predecessor or, with Cannon's self-possessed Sergeant, of Will Hay's justifiable fears that he is only one step removed from the Establishment discovering his total lack of qualifications or integrity.

The main failing of the picture is that it captures little of the strange blend of aggression and pathos that was central to Tommy and Bobby's stage relationship. As the narrative meanders to a conclusion with one of the most pitiable car chases in the history of the medium, the question remains as to who represented the intended audience. In the early 1980s those in search of entertainment could enjoy a dreadful film rented from their local video library as opposed to a cinema, which appeared to have been last decorated when Alec Douglas-Home was the Prime Minister. When Cannon and Ball's sole cinematic vehicle went on general release, some long-established picture houses were being converted into branches of McDonald's. To this day *The Boys in Blue* remains essential viewing for enthusiasts of 1982-vintage British Leyland cars but for all others it remains a cinematic enigma.

Old Mother Riley

Of the Variety acts on screen, Daphne Bluebird Snowdrop Riley merits an individual mention. This was the full stage name of the drag character played by Arthur Lucan, commonly known as Old Mother Riley. She and her daughter Kitty (played by Arthur Lucan's wife Kitty McShane) formed a double act in 1934 and they made their cinematic debut in the revue *Stars on Parade* (Oswald Mitchell/Charles Sanderson, 1936). By 1942 Lucan and McShane were the third most commercially popular British film stars – Leslie Howard was second and George Formby the first (McFarlane, 1999: 48). Despite this, an Old Mother Riley film would not receive a West End premiere until 1949 (Fisher, 2013: 97) and, looking at the pictures today, two factors are very obvious. Firstly, Kitty McShane is marginally talented at best and it is easy to appreciate why, during her musical numbers, people were known to seek refuge in the auditorium. Secondly, Lucan was an actor of genius, for no matter how shambolic the production values, how inept the direction, how truly bizarre the supporting cast,[4] Lucan's commitment to the character was absolute: 'Old Mother Riley is to all intents and purposes real – watching her, we are not witnessing an impersonation but rather participating in the life of a foolish, garrulous old lady. She is "she" and will remain so' (Slide, 1998: 84).

Mrs Riley was also entirely at ease with her milieu and contemptuous of almost any middle-class authority who has the misfortune to enter her orbit. Dave Russell argued that to many characters of the music hall, life simply happened to them and they had no control over their destiny (1997: 126) but while Bud and Ches dreamed, Mrs Riley was perpetually fighting against fate, the local authority bank managers and even Nazi agents. Eric Midwinter has suggested that 'part of being a great comedian lies, consciously or unconsciously in being attuned to the refrains of society, in hearing its melodies, in orchestrating them, and in playing them back' (1979: 13). That would certainly apply to Arthur Lucan.

Lucan's final film *Mother Riley Meets the Vampire* (George Minter, 1952) deserves a special mention, both for the circumstances of its production and its co-star. The relationship between Lucan and McShane eventually descended into the very stuff of nightmares – Kitty was eventually barred from the studio. She toured in a separate act, 'Old

---

4   Katie Boyle appears in *Old Mother Riley Headmistress* (John Harlow, 1950).

Mother Kelly' – and the former, as Barry Cryer was keen to note, in a picture with no mention of the 'Old' – the pair would work together on stage only one more time after the film's completion. Lucan may have lost his prefix, but he had gained a new screen partner in the fairly unlikely form of Bela Lugosi, even if it is debatable whether this film was an improvement on a professional future that involved starring in the works of Ed Wood. There are several moments in which Lugosi seems truly bemused by Lucan's very appearance[5] and *Mother Riley Meets the Vampire* was at least partially the result of Lugosi needing to raise the funds to return to the States after a British theatrical tour of *Dracula* failed (Cryer: My future wife saw that in Brighton. He had a coughing fit on his first entrance). At least, unlike Kitty McShane, Bela did not feel the need to sing at people who had done him no harm.

Vampire is a picture to make the viewer doubt their own concept of reality; Lugosi really does not belong in a comedy featuring a man from Lincolnshire in a dress, a moustachioed Richard Wattis and song-and-dance numbers featuring Dandy Nichols and Hattie Jacques. But even in a film as misguided as *Vampire*, Old Mother Riley always does her utmost to fight against the fates. This is a key element of her films, be her opponent a recalcitrant landlord's agent or, in *Old Mother Riley Detective* (Lance Comfort, 1943), a police inspector named Cole: 'I wish you'd tell your fiddlers to keep their hands off me!' Even when confronted by a mad scientist with a scheme to flood London with some very sub-par robots and a palpably uncertain grasp of his lines Daphne Riley remains ever resourceful, determined and self-reliant.

At the time cross-dressing was often associated with *pagan rites and rituals*, and many of the performances of Lucan convey a sense of unease. Arthur Askey's screen characters were kept reasonably near ground level by Richard Murdoch or Glenn Melvyn, Bud Flanagan's excesses were tempered by the courtly Chesney Allen, but Mrs Riley is a human dervish with a Liverpool-Irish accent and a relationship with the audience that not even the most limited of budgets can quell. She is

---

5   The same applied off set as Lugosi apparently was genuinely nonplussed by Lucan's habit of arriving and departing from the set in full costume.

also, to quote David Robinson, 'vulgar, comic, touching and true to working-class life' (1969: 120), even if the role of her partner remains obscure. To quote one of the great lines of cinema: 'If I wasn't a lady, I'd give them a slap in the gob.'[6]

Two Respectable Chaps

As well as filmed Variety double acts, many of the cheap comedies took the form of drawing-room farces. The adaptions of the Aldwych farces (twelve farces staged at the Aldwych Theatre between 1923 and 1933, nine of which were written by Ben Travers) were commercial hits, conveying the essence of the relationship between the bounder and the naïf. Michael Balcon had a dim view of Walls' ability as a director, in that he 'did not understand films in any technical or creative sense' (1969: 92) but this straightforward approach to the cinematic versions of the farces was not quite enough to mask the genius of the cast – or to prevent Tom Walls from being the most popular British star at the British cinema box office between 1932 and 1937 (Richards, 2000: 102). Farce was a theatrical form that often employed double acts and their and associated comic 'business' (Smith, 1989: 175) and in both the theatrical and film versions of Ben Travers's works both the naïf and the bounder are often forced to unite against a threat from an outside party. Travers took care that the troubles and embarrassments suffered by Lynn's characters were accentuated by reasonable and acceptable motives (1978: 92). In the eighth film of the Aldwych farces Lynn's characters would typically, and for the best of motives, find themselves in trouble where they would be variously confounded and helped by the man about town of Tom Walls, the owner of the most salacious moustache in British cinema. 'Five of my parts were old or elderly men, irascible colonels

6 We could mention that *Mrs Brown's Boys* is very much in the tradition of Old Mother Riley, but that would involve actually having to re-watch the show.

or old soaks, or as Ralph once put it, "wet accumulators"' (Self profile in *The Tatler*, 20 November 1946: 10).

> When they have their backs to the wall, pinned there generally by a middle-aged woman, the male characters talk very strangely. They speak before they think, which is a characteristic of people in farce, and the reason why farce can be played faster than any other form of theatre. Speech propels speech, almost without mind intervening. (Gilliatt 1973: 177)

Towards the end of the decade, this cinematic tradition of eminence had been largely assumed by two actors, as opposed to comedians, Naunton Wayne and Basil Radford, a.k.a. Charters and Caldicott. The characters were created by Frank Launder and Sidney Gilliat for *The Lady Vanishes* (Alfred Hitchcock, 1938), two English gentlemen whose courage in times of real crisis could be completely relied upon by the film's leads. Radford's Charters is their bluff leader, while the genial Caldicott of Wayne sometimes has his faint doubts – 'Are you sure that is wise, old man?' – and beneath their stereotyped obsession with cricket they are quick wits of considerable resourcefulness. 'Rotten shot; I only knocked his hat off'.

Unlike Ralph Lynn and Tom Walls, Charters and Caldicott are about the same age and neither is a lubricious man about town or a 'silly ass'. They have clearly been an inseparable pair ever since Oxford, presenting to the world the air of utter decency combined with the excitement of first-formers who have embarked on a thrilling adventure – albeit one populated with untrustworthy types who neither dress for dinner nor speak English. Radford could be bracketed with Lionel Jeffries or John Thaw as an actor who would be near impossible to imagine as 'young', but he was able to convey a boyish enthusiasm (usually when England were going to bat) while Naunton Wayne could be positively impish at times. They were comedy actors of such timing and verve that they could dominate a scene containing Michael Redgrave and Cecil Parker. During the 1940s they appeared together on radio and in eleven subsequent films, although a dispute with Launder and Gilliat concerning their billing in *I See A Dark Stranger* (Launder, 1946) meant that they could no longer be known as Charters and Caldicott.

Intriguingly, the characters crossed genre boundaries; Ealing Studios used them in The *Next of Kin* (Thorold Dickinson, 1942) as a demonstration of how eccentricity could be self-indulgent and even lethal in times of war. Wayne and Radford also served as the comic relief in *Dead of Night* (Alberto Cavalcanti/Charles Crighton/Robert Hamer/ Basil Dearden, 1945) – but they are still part of Walter Craig's recurring nightmare. *It's Not Cricket* (Alfred Roome/Roy Rich, 1949) is not only one of their finest screen outings – an everyday story of Otto Fisch (Maurice Denham), a mad Nazi scientist who enjoys subverting cricket matches – it also has our heroes encountering an early incarnation of what was to become known as 'youth culture'.

The recently demobbed Major Bright (Radford) and Captain Early (Wayne) have formed a private detective agency where after advertising for a secretary they are simultaneously baffled and terrified by the 18-year-old Diana Dors, who was demonstrating how, even in the early stages of her career, she was one of British cinema's best young character actresses. Sadly, Radford and Wayne were now suffering from a problem that was to bedevil the *Carry On* team: the erroneous assumption that their personae were now so well established that they would not require carefully tailored scripts. By 1949 the latter was openly complaining that:

There seems to be a popular belief – not only among the film going public – but in the film world too, that the characters we portray on the screen are more or less the same as the ones we use in private life. I can assure you that's pure fallacy. Therefore, when we get scriptwriters outlining a story, suggesting treatment and more or less leaving us 'to be ourselves' and get on as well as we can it's not surprising that their efforts get us nowhere. (Quoted in Peregrine in *Picturegoer*, 10 September 1949: 10).

It is to be much regretted that a planned appearance in *The Third Man* (Carol Reed, 1949) was eventually replaced by Wilfrid Hyde-White's Crabbitt. It is easy to envisage how Captain Carter (Radford) and Captain Tombs (Wayne) would have caused great bewilderment to Holly Martins (Joseph Cotton) without detracting from the film's mood. Basil Radford died in 1952 and Naunton Wayne in 1970, and this writer's favourite memory of Charters and Caldicott is of their Englishmen abroad in 1939 Germany, with Radford purchasing a copy of *Mein Kampf.* You never know, it might shed a spot of light on all this 'how do you do'.

Transferring from Television

As we have seen, the 1950s was the decade that saw the inexorable rise of television and decline in picture house attendances:

> Whereas in 1950 there were less than 400,000 licences, by 1959 this had grown to over 9m ... During the same period, the cinema audience and the number of cinemas both fell sharply. In 1950 an audience measuring 1,396m visited 4,483 cinemas. By 1959 this had diminished to about 600m attendances and only 3,414 cinemas. (Armes 1978: 239)

With those comedy acts who either made their names or redefined their careers in the medium of television there often remained a sense that cinematic stardom was the pathway to 'international' – i.e. US – fame. Of the double acts in the book, Denis Goodwin never appeared on the big screen with Bob Monkhouse, while Mike and Bernie Winters did their best with a profoundly unfunny script when they cameoed in the film of *The Six-Five Special* (Alfred Shaughnessy, 1958). The brothers then temporarily split and on resuming their partnership had the profound misfortune to find themselves in *The Cool Mikado*

(Michael Winner, 1962), a musical bearing the hallmarks of a young director with financing from Harold Baim, some studio space and a limited budget. Mr Winner was also possessed of the brave, if quixotic, belief that what the nation's teenagers really wanted to see was a twist version of Gilbert and Sullivan.[7] Ironically, the one British comedian who did achieve major US success was neither part of a double act nor one whose comic film vehicle *Who Done It?* (Basil Dearden, 1956) was a major success.

In the 1960s, the most determined and ambitious attempts at cinematic stardom made by British double acts were the vehicles for Morecambe and Wise, and Peter Cook and Dudley Moore. The performances of the former in summer season were appreciated by the producer Hugh Stewart when he was making the Norman Wisdom vehicle *The Bulldog Breed* (Robert Asher, 1960) on location in Weymouth and four years later Morecambe and Wise signed a three-film contract with the Rank Organisation. This was a logical development in their attempt to appeal to audiences in the USA – by 1963 they had already started the first of several appearances on the *Ed Sullivan Show* (1948–71) – but their first picture *The Intelligence Men* (Asher, 1964) shoehorned the comedians into the Wisdom slapstick formula that, ironically, that comedian was already tiring of (quoted in Dacre, 1991: 47).

Unlike the works of Butcher's Film Services, *The Intelligence Men* may have been shot in colour and possess the cheap flashiness of a Ford Cortina GT, but it was also inflicted with a spoof-Bond storyline, which made it appear derivative virtually from the outset. A further problem was that the team's regular writers Sid Hills and Dick Green had created of a cinematic narrative and more of a collection of sketches and it is hard to disagree with the fulminating critic of *The Monthly Film Bulletin*, which ranted about how the dinner party scene was 'an almost classic example of how not to amuse while apparently trying' (1965: 75). Kenneth Tynan rather snidely referred to Morecambe and

---

7 Surprisingly, they didn't, even if the 'Tit-Willow Twist' by The John Barry Seven and performed by Lionel Blair and his Dancers will haunt all those who see it.

Wise as 'a clever professional team, though well below genius level'[8] but he brilliantly summarised the fundamental problem of their first film outing – they rushed 'headlong into the familiar trap of trusting British film-makers' (*The Observer*, 28 March 1965: 25).

The duo's last Rank film was *The Magnificent Two* (Owen, 1967), and the overriding impact is not of the less-than-golden moments nor the extensive Pinewood's all-purpose 'Mediterranean/African/Latin American' sets;[9] it is the incredibly uneven tone. The plot has Eric and Ernie as travelling salesmen in 'Parazuellia' and the film belongs in the ranks of those productions in which moments of 'comic' violence go far beyond the film's remit.[10] On the release of *The Magnificent Two* in July 1967 several critics observed the quite remarkable body count for what was ostensibly a comedy. The postscript to Morecambe and Wise's attempts at a cinematic career was *Night Train to Murder* (Joseph McGrath, 1983), a made-for-television special shot on harshly lit and flat video-tape. This was the project that lured Morecambe and Wise from the BBC to Thames, whose Euston Films division did produce shows of real cinematic flair.[11] Instead we are offered lingering shots of 'period' cars and a pace that is not so much slow as sloth-like.

Had Eric not succumbed to a heart attack in 1984 and had *Night Train to Murder* been produced in the late 1980s as a Film Four production, been made in black and white in homage to *The Cat and The Canary* (Elliott Nugent, 1939) and directed by Stephen Frears, it could have been cinematic magic. But the story of British cinema is suffused with 'if onlys' and *That Riviera Touch* (Cliff Owen, 1966) remains the finest Morecambe and Wise picture. It works as a film narrative, has a sense of ambition with its overseas locations and because of an air of polish,

---

8   Ten years later his opinion of Morecambe and Wise was far higher.

9   Ernie Wise famously discovered that the budget for the volcano set of *You Only Live Twice* (Lewis Gilbert, 1967) on an adjacent sound stage exceeded the total cost of *The Magnificent Two*.

10 Think of the scene where Reg Varney is attacked by an irate Italian chef in *Holiday on the Buses*; it lasts for much too long and is shot in a manner that makes you think of a Mike Hodges gangster film rather than a comedy.

11 Just look at the skill that went into almost every edition of *The Sweeney* (1975–78).

from Otto Heller's cinematography to Suzanne Lloyd as the enigmatic Claudette and Ernie's Jack Jones-style ballad over the opening credits. Most importantly, it is the only one of the Rank trio to capture their essence. As Eric Midwinter put it: 'What Morecambe and Wise have done is to created characters from the unpromising profiles of the funny man and the straight man' (1979: 171), and with *Riviera* we are already far removed from the templates of Wheeler and Woolsey or Abbott and Costello. The film does convey a sense of two innocents abroad who stray out of their depth, with Ernie at least starting to understand that they are in real danger as Eric delights in his 'casino winnings'.

That Riviera Touch also immeasurably benefits from the supporting performances from Armand Mestral as a world-weary police inspector and Paul Stassino's menacing villain hinting at another, more ambitious picture. As it was, the reviews were not universally flattering – 'Messrs Morecambe and Wise can be extremely funny; here they are not' (Richard Roud, *The Guardian*, 25 March 1966: 11) and the team's cinematic ambitions were to remain unrealised. In the 1970s Eric remarked that 'If we had Neil Simon writing for us and Billy Wilder directing, I know we could be international stars' (quoted in McCann, 1998:). He was right.

The film career of Peter Cook and Dudley Moore achieved greater heights and far more unwatchable lows than that of Morecambe and Wise. Of the latter, *The Hound of The Baskervilles* (Paul Morrissey, 1978) must rank alongside *Lisztomania* (Ken Russell, 1975)[12] and *I Don't Want to Be Born* (Peter Sadsy, 1975) as one of the most unwatchable British films of the 1970s. Their first outing as the caddish Morris and the not quite as caddish John Finsbury in *The Wrong Box* (Bryan Forbes, 1966) – 'Respectively raffish and runtish' (Kenneth Tynan, *The Observer*, 29 May 1966: 20) – suffered from being trapped within a self-consciously arch 'comic' reconstruction of Victorian England. These were also supporting roles, as were the Inspector and the Sergeant in the United Artists'-backed adaption of Spike Milligan's play *The Bedsitting Room* (Richard Lester, 1969). Here, the police officers survey a post-nuclear

---

12 Ringo Starr appears as the Pope, but the film could not have been any worse had Ken cast his fellow Sotonian Benny Hill in the role.

holocaust England from their wrecked Morris Minor patrol car that floats from a hot air balloon, as they constantly order the survivors to 'keep moving'. It was more of a series of routines than a cohesive narrative and Peter and Dudley are merely two more cartoon figures, even if Cook's Inspector did contribute a memorable speech at the conclusion – 'The earth will burgeon anew, the lion will lie down with the lamb, and the goat give suck to the tiny bee. At times of great national emergency, we often find that a new leader tends to emerge. Here I am – so watch it!'

The principal cinematic legacies of Cook and Moore lies with one of the most ambitions comedies to hail from Britain during the 1960s and a surprisingly delightful contribution to an 'international' feature. *Bedazzled* was a re-working of the Faust legend with a script from Cook, Moore's musical score[13] and directed by Stanley Donen for 20th Century Fox. Stanley Moon (Dudley) works as a short order chef in a Wimpy, lacks the confidence to make overtures to the waitress Margaret Spencer (Eleanor Bron) and is so dissatisfied with his life that he attempts to hang himself, only to be approached by a sinister individual named George Spigott (Peter). The latter is the devil himself, who offers Stanley seven wishes in exchange for his soul.

As with so many of the male double acts in this book, there is that sense of the playground, with Spiggott as a Flashman-style bully who secretly regrets the loss of his prefect's status and Stanley as his scholarship acolyte. Lucifer is currently at a low ebb – 'There was a time when I used to get lots of ideas ... I thought up the Seven Deadly Sins in one afternoon. The only thing I've come up with recently is advertising' – his earthly base is a London nightclub that is underperforming largely because his employees have been recruited from the ranks of the Seven Deadly Sins – 'What terrible sins I have working for me. I suppose it's the wages I pay them.' His latest exploits have been very sub-par – scratching records, setting a swarm of wasps on some early hippies – but in the final reel Lucifer positively scampers towards Heaven (which, appropriately enough, looks like Kew Gardens), hoping that his one self-aggrandising

---

13 Surely one of the finest of any British film of the 1960s, ranking on a par with Mike Vickers's score for *Press for Time* (Robert Asher, 1966).

act of kindness towards Stanley will restore him to glory. The plot is undoubtedly episodic but *Bedazzled* boasts eminently quotable: 'This is the club room. Quite nicely decorated and painted – early Hitler.'

Throughout the film George and Stanley do form an odd parasitic bond that reflects some of the tropes of their television appearances, including that of time slowly passing and Satan (in the guise of a traffic warden) explaining his downfall to Moon while sitting atop a pillar box: 'Here, I'm getting a bit bored with this – can't we change places?' 'That's exactly how I felt'. Both crave attention. In the stand-out scene of the *Ready Steady Go* spoof Stanley attempts to impress Margaret by becoming a pop singer who literally screams 'Love Me!' But his number is followed by Cook as the uber-cool crooner Drimble Wedge (and The Vegetations) who informs his fans 'you fill me with inertia'.

Though *Bedazzled* was made during the 'Swinging London' era, it is not of it, Spigott surveying its tropes with the boredom that often afflicted Cook himself and many of his characters.[14] In *Not Only But Also* and *On The Braden Beat* Sir Arthur Streeb-Greebling, E.L. Wisty and even The Glidd of Glood are pre-occupied with the enemy of Time itself, and in *Bedazzled* George's relationship with Stanley serves as both distraction and the vehicle for social elevation. Lucifer may assure Stanley that there is 'nothing personal' in his cruel treatment but at the conclusion Moon decides to ask Margaret out without any infernal assistance. As a consequence, she notices him for the first time – there is a wonderful double-take from Bron – and Satan threatens to cover the earth in the mass-produced abominations of 1960s Britain – 'I'll cover the world in Tastee-Freez and Wimpy Burgers. I'll fill it full of concrete runways, motorways, aircraft, television and automobiles, advertising, plastic flowers and frozen food, supersonic bangs' – in retaliation. But it is too late. Stanley has escaped for he is no longer a victim.

The film received mixed reviews; Penelope Mortimer, in the great tradition of British critics ignoring filmic quality in their midst, thought

---

14 When watching *A Clockwork Orange* (Stanley Kubrick, 1971) in the cinema Cook became so bored that he jumped from his seat and urged his fellow audience members to go home (Thompson, 1997).

that 'Stanley Donen makes the whole bag of tricks look lovely, which somehow makes it worse' (*The Observer*, 24 December 1967: 18). It was almost as if there was a sense of resentment at Cook and Moore for daring to transcend their television format and Thompson notes how 'the results were excellent, but they weren't recognisable as anything Pete and Dud had done before' (1997). In the USA Roger Ebert referred to 'this magnificently photographed, intelligent, very funny film' that 'is also often dry and understated, permitting the audience to find the humour without being led to it. In films of this sort, too often the camera records the fun instead of joining in it' (*The Chicago Sun-Times*, 30 January 1968).

20th Century Fox was dissatisfied with the box returns of *Bedazzled* to the extent that a follow-up film was cancelled and Cook and Moore's final major celluloid outing of the 1960s was *Monte Carlo or Bust!* (Ken Annakin, 1969), a semi-sequel to *Those Magnificent Men in Their Flying Machines*.[15] Amid an expensive cast led by a relentlessly over-acting Tony Curtis, the film is stolen by Terry-Thomas and Eric Sykes, and by Cook and Moore as Major Dawlish (tall, dim and ultra-patriotic) and Lieutenant Barrington (short, eager and long-suffering).

Harry Thompson makes the argument that Cook as a film actor was 'not sufficiently engaging when playing himself (as he was, to all intents and purposes) to attract the sympathies of a mass audience' as he was afraid to show his real vulnerable self to the audience (1997). With Major Dawlish, he could parody the sort of chap his education and background had equipped him to become and aside from an interesting support role as a camp-sinister MI5 official in *A Dandy in Aspic* (Anthony Mann/ Laurence Harvey, 1968), Cook was best used on screen as a seemingly self-possessed authority figure. Dawlish and Barrington channelled the spirit of Charters and Caldicott, except they were of equal status while the major was born to lead men into chaos just as his lieutenant was born to obey him without question. The pair are also exceptionally likeable, readily lending a hand to a fellow competitor in a screen moment that captures the ethos of Charters and Caldicott some thirty

---

15 The film was released as the not-very-catchily titled *Those Magnificent Men in their Jaunty Jalopies* in the USA.

years earlier. Indeed, there are those of us with the unfashionable view that Cook and Moore are better showcased in *Monte Carlo* rather than the cry of alcohol infused despair that is *Derek and Clive Get the Horn* (Russell Mulcahy, 1979).

The Horror ... The Horror

Many cinematic historians might tell you that the *Confessions* series – *Window Cleaner* (Val Guest, 1973), *Pop Performer* (Norman Cohen, 1975), *Driving Instructor* (Cohen, 1976) and *Holiday Camp* (Cohen, 1977) – came about because of the producer Greg Smith obtaining the backing of Columbia-British to make films based on Timothy Lea's series of comic erotic novels. In the early 1970s the policies of the National Film Finance Corporation were that only pictures that stood a reasonable chance of box office receipts would gain financial support and a further alleged reason was the relaxation in British film censors' regulations after the departure of most US major studios from the UK at the end of the 1960s. The age of admission to an X-certificate film was raised from 16 to 18 by July of the following year, paving the way for a new generation of 'adult films'. But there are those of us who have long sensed a reality not dissimilar to *Bedazzled*. It took the form of a pact signed one drab afternoon in the foyer of the Southampton Classic cinema circa 1972 and the parties to this dark contract were a dirty raincoat-wearing Faust, and Mephistopheles, a cinema manager clad in an Oxfam-reject dinner jacket:

Dirty Raincoat (Kenneth Connor): I'd like to see nudie ladies on screen at my local picture house please. Not just the odd glimpse, *Carry On Henry* style, but full frontals.

Mephistopheles (Peter Sellers): Very well. I shall fulfil your desire to see dispirited-looking peroxided blonde actresses in their full glory but there are certain conditions attached ...

DR: Name them!

M: Cinematography that looks though the film stock was acquired in a fire-damage sale, locations that make you think you are watching a BBC2 documentary on social deprivation in North London and supporting roles played by brilliant character actors all bearing the defeated air of ones reduced to appearing in shod. There shall also be any number of music hall comedy routines that Archie Rice would have rejected and at least one of these pictures will look as though the director has his back to the camera. Plus …

DR …?

M: Robin Askwith's bottom making regular appearances.

DR: That's a bit much, even for me. (Thinks) Tell you what – throw in a Strawberry Mivvi and you have a deal.

M: (Lighting crashing over Above Bar Street) Done! Ha! Ha!

And thus, the four *Confessions* films did come to pass, each more rancid than the last. And the people did forget that Mr Askwith had once worked with Lindsay Anderson (the film *If …* in 1968) and Pier Paolo Pasolini (Rufus in *The Canterbury Tales*, 1971) or that Tony Booth as his brother-in-law and side-kick had once inspired a record by the Monkees and had starred in the agreeable 1963 crime film *The Hi-Jackers* (Jim O'Connolly, 1963). All they recalled was RADA graduates stripping off as if by rote, Booth's performance mainly consisting of his saying 'you stupid bleeder' every five minutes and Robin's trousers falling down.

Apologists for the *Confessions* series often like to note that they are in the tradition of low-budget comedy in British cinema. As we have previously seen, the Aldwych farces were not exactly masterpieces of directorial flair, and some of the vehicles for Lucan and McShane, Elise and Doris Waters or Brian Rix and Ronald Shiner looked as though their budget was 10*s* 6*d* and a suitcase full of co-op dividends. But to compare the Group 3 production *The Love Match* with its crisp black and white cinematography and Arthur Askey/Glenn Melvyn double act with the misadventures of Booth and Askwith is on a par with trading in a beautifully preserved Morris Minor tourer for the latest Austin Allegro.

Indeed, the cynicism of the *Confessions* series is on a par with the consumer goods of quite remarkable shoddiness that were churned out with such lack of flair during the 1970s. The message – be it a TV set that fused within a week, a British Leyland (BL) car that broke down within 12 hours of taking delivery or a film starring Robin's bottom – was that this was all the consumer deserved, so just be grateful. If the *Confessions* films did enjoy major commercial success, this could well have been out of a national sense of glum apathy. Back in his lair, Mephistopheles laughs manically as he counts the ticket receipts and reads the review of Derek Malcolm in *The Guardian*: it was 'difficult not to keep a straight face' and 'the fact that this could well become the first of a series positively sets the jaw solid' (22 August 1974: 10). Still, it cannot be denied that Robin Askwith was indeed an adroit comedy performer. Val Guest began his film career at Gainsborough Studios writing for Arthur Askey, a fact that was observed by the film historian Geoffrey Macnab; 'Askey and Askwith even seem like distant cousins – a pair of diminutive, cheeky chancers or "funny little men", as Guest calls them without much evident affection.' (*The Independent*, 4 September 1997).

Leaving aside the truly nightmarish vision of Arthur Askey appearing in a 1970s British sex comedy,[16] Askwith's performance in *Window Cleaner*, with his awkwardness and eagerness to please, actually infer a younger version of Norman Wisdom,[17] variously helped and hindered by Booth's Sidney, and the two do make an engaging double act in the face of cinematic adversity and the female gender. As I.Q. Hunter wisely points out, in these films 'sex is a source equally of nervous laughter and outright fear' (2012: 157) but although it would be easy – in fact a relief in many respects – to dismiss the *Confessions* series, the adventures of Timmy Lea and Sidney Nogsmith were a major box office success. *Window Cleaner* became Columbia Pictures's most profitable non-American film of all time.

---

16 This cinematic abomination actually came to pass with *Rosie Dixon – Night Nurse* (Justin Cartright, 1978).

17 Wisdom did make an erotic 'comedy' *What's Good for The Goose* (Golan, 1969), which is so unspeakably awful that it merited a burial at sea.

For all its (many) faults, the first *Confessions* film did benefit from a tight narrative structure and the charming ingenue of Linda Hayden and a believable Lea family headed by the patriarch of Bill Maynard. The two next films in the series did at least have our heroes working towards a well-defined goal; Sid and Timmy might have engaged in their regulation nude scenes with the passion of a meter reader on duty in the middle of October but there was indeed a discernible plot. By contrast, *Holiday Camp* was a comedy of a quite unique nature as our heroes act as hosts in an out-of-season rain-sodden Mill Rythe Holiday Village on Hayling Island. If only the narrative had followed its logical pathway:

The setting: a country road. A tree. A washing line with a pair of pants on it.
Enter Timmy Lea and Sid.
TL: Let's go.
S: We can't.
TL: Why not?
S: The screenplay has scheduled another badly executed slapstick routine in which all participants look positively mortified … you stupid bleeder.
TL: (despairingly) Ah!
His trousers then fall down for no reason whatsoever. Back in Portsmouth ABC the ice-cream girl weeps on to her Cornettos while the few members of the audience desperately think of happier times and pull their trilbies over their ears to drown out the sound of Askwith and Booth struggling with the dialogue.

After *Holiday Camp* there were to be no more adventures from the brothers-in-law, for in 1978 Klinger declined to fund *Confessions From A Haunted House* and by then the British sex comedy film was already on the decline. One problem was that, unlike the sitcom spin-offs, their content merited X-certificates. This meant that they could not encourage the family audiences to return to their local picture houses in a decade when the habit of regular cinema-going was fast waning. The 1980s would see the *Confessions* films occupy the 'Adult' section of video libraries where the patrons were promised erotic comedy in exchange for a modest £0.50 daily rental but the reality, in *Driving Instructor* at least, was plentiful shots of the Askwith derriere through the sunroof of a second-hand Ford Cortina Mk II. The following day the ashen-faced customer returned the cassette, mentally vowed to pay more attention to revising A-level economics and opted for *Augirre: The Wrath of God* (Werner Herzog, 1972) for some light relief.

The Carry On films

At first sight, the *Carry On* series does not belong in this book at all. Surely, they were 'gang show' comedies and, furthermore, another challenge is their sheer familiarity which has not been assisted in recent years by a spate of docu-dramas or documentaries concerning the 'dark side' of the series. Typically, there would be a portentous voiceover, doom-laden background music and some of the more despairing extracts from *The Kenneth Williams Diaries*. You might well be left with the impression that the average *Carry On* was akin to a Strindberg drama; albeit with the addition of the occasional flying bra. But within the regular cast were several delightful pairings that transcended the limitations of both script and direction with apparent ease. With *Screaming* (Gerald Thomas, 1966),[18] Kenneth Williams and Fenella Fielding took it in turns to out-camp each other, as guest star Harry H. Corbett can only gurn in amazement while Jim Dale and Peter Butterworth, one the most wonderfully understated talents of the genre, stole every scene from a very out-of-place Phil Silvers in *Follow That Camel* (1967). Butterworth was also teamed with the formidable Hattie Jacques in *Abroad* (1972) to great effect, even if his 'Spanish' accent sounded vaguely Croydon, while the

---

18 And all *Carry On* films.

middle-aged couple of Terry Scott and Betty Marsden were a saving grace of *Camping* (1969).

Each of these pairings light up the screen to the extent that they make you wish that they had featured as a formal team within subsequent *Carry On* films. Despite the popular mythology that each film had the same plot but a different set of costumes, the format allowed for more variation than is popularly imagined. *Cruising* (1962) was very close in form and content to a middle-class Rank comedy of the previous decade and *Jack* (1964) could not quite balance the elements of costume parody and farce.

The *Carry On* films were produced by a man who was wont to say that it was the title that was the star. It was a claim that Peter Rogers would trot out on a regular basis, especially when the issue of his cast's fees was aired – and it was palpably false almost from the outset. As early as 1958 the producer stated in a letter to the National Film Finance Committee that 'it has become increasingly evident that the *Carry Ons* will depend more and more for their success on a handful of feature players' – ones who were in more demand 'than so-called stars'. Furthermore, his bill for the lead performers was 'low for artistes who virtually carry a film' (quoted in Webber, 2009: 54). Given that Peter Rogers was a producer who could arrange for product placement from Saxo Table Salt in a film,[19] it was increasingly evident that the art of acting and of furthering careers was of lesser consequence than an over-run of shooting meaning paying costs from your own pocket. Besides, the formula was a box office bonanza, and in the words of Penelope Gilliatt:

> The comedy is appallingly laborious and planted, but it makes more millions of people laugh than a first-rate, free-wheeling wit like the Goons' or a first-rate piece of plot-making like Feydeau's. It is enough to make high-minded reformers want to give up. (1973: 284).

---

19 In *Camping*, Hawtrey pays for his coach ride with a box of the same.

The first six entries, scripted by Norman Hudis, are gentle-mannered farces where authority is seen to be human and in need of support. The headmasters, senior surgeons, caravan site proprietors and factory owners of the later films were often sad, infantile figures, much given to snivelling and blustering, but in the early *Carry On* films they gain the support of their loyal teams. With the third in the series, *Teacher* (1959), there was also the first sighting of one of the double-acts within the films – Charles Hawtrey and Kenneth Williams.

In the late 1950s, the screen image of Hawtrey was that of a camp and faintly psychotic middle-aged schoolboy, one that had been established by his work with Will Hay in the 1930s and '40s. He also co-starred with Patricia Hayes on the BBC Home Service in *The Adventures of Norman and Henry Bones: Boy Detectives* but a look at the 1956 edition of *Spotlight Casting Directory* provides evidence that he perceived his film career in more elevated terms. There in the 'Leading Man' section stands Laurence Harvey bearing his habitual expression of dashing narcissism while the still on the opposite page shows the arguably less dynamic figure of Charles in a 'comic' pose.

There is something both poignant and defiant about spending a week's broadcasting fees on such a folly and that the actor's listed contact details are his home address – 217 Cromwell Road, Hounslow – and telephone number. Hawtrey may currently be 'between agents' but in his mind at least he is a star as he sits in his front parlour, indulging in cooking sherry and shouting at the cat. Today will hopefully be a day when someone at Pinewood or Shepperton dials HOU 0636 to request his services. At last, a ring of the black Bakelite phone promises work from that chap who made the B-film *Time Lock* (Gerald Thomas, 1957).[20]

Roger Lewis has observed how Hawtrey's characters were 'always lit up and eager to please' (2002: 2) and in *Sergeant* this served to distract from the fact that he was already aged 44 and thus 18 years beyond the maximum call-up age for National Service. Private Peter Golightly has the appearance of someone who has blithely wandered into the barracks

---

20 Set in Canada but very obviously shot in Buckinghamshire. It also featured Sean Connery as a young welder with a quite indefinable accent.

and who is going to enjoy this strange world with aplomb, with all its strangely bellowing uniformed authority figures. In *Nurse*, Humphrey Hinton blithely exists in a world of his own, virtually welded to the radio and eagerly imparting knowledge to his completely disinterested fellow patients, but in *Teacher* Michael Bean is a believable denizen of Maudlin Street Secondary Modern. His principal sparring partner in the staff room is Williams's Edwin Milton; equally idealistic but younger, worldlier wise and somewhat more acerbic.

Over the past three decades 'the Kenneth Williams Story' has become almost as familiar as 'the Tony Hancock Story' thanks in large part to his published diaries and letters. But in that same 1956 edition of *Spotlight* is the photograph of a 'Younger Character Actor' of remarkable versatility. By 1959 Williams's CV encompassed Hancock and Kenneth Horne on the wireless, Orson Welles and Alec Guinness in the West End, playing the Dauphin in *Saint Joan*, a 12-year-old schoolboy newspaper editor in *The Buccaneer* and co-starring with Maggie Smith in the revue *Share My Lettuce*. Milton was the creation of a much in-demand performer and while Hawtrey theatrically moans and wails, flapping his academic gown in the manner of a suburban vampire in danger of missing his afternoon tea, Williams essays a low-key performance of a young English master.

This is not to infer that *Teacher* is lacking in the badly executed slapstick that would become a *Carry On* trademark – 'labourious establishing shots about ha-ha accidents that are going to happen in three minutes' time' (Gilliatt, 1973: 287) – but the waspish Hawtrey/Williams banter was a highlight of the film and of the series in general. The double act was repeated in *Constable* (1959), *Follow That Camel* (1967), *Doctor* (1967) and *Matron* (1972) and Hawtrey always seemed to be the same: the pedantic diction, glasses that where becoming dated even when *Sergeant* was released, and a jet-black toupee. He was, as Lewis points out, a figure who 'seemed always to be delightfully oblivious of his effects' (2002: 3) while in the later films Williams's performances were becoming progressively less disciplined. His confidence had suffered in the wake of theatrical misadventures and a 1967 BBC TV interview in the company of Maggie Smith displays a palpable desperation to be taken seriously as an actor that was now increasingly at odds with his film career. That same year saw him described in a profile in *The Observer* as 'a genuine clown. He can't help being funny about unhappiness – his own and the unhappiness basic in humour' (19 March 1967: 23).

By the end of the 1960s Williams's *Carry On* acting now seemed to consist of any amount of face-pulling – appallingly so in *Camping* but to better affect in *Again Doctor* (1969) and *Matron* where he was counterbalanced by the drily eccentric Hawtrey. The latter film was to be their last pairing – Hawtrey was sacked from the series in 1972 either for drink-related reasons (Webber, 2009: 129), for spurning a television special on the grounds of his billing, or a combination thereof. His professional future was one of end-of-the-pier shows and the occasional truly unlikely guest appearance, his personal future one of sadness.[21] Williams remained with the *Carry On* films, stating in public his regard for the tradition of bawdy humour: 'If they think our comedy is all tits and bums,' he once wrote in the *Telegraph Sunday Magazine* about the prospect of being interviewed for a French documentary about the British cinema, 'I'll point out the precedents set by Aristophanes as well as Plautus' (Montgomery-Massingberd, *The Daily Telegraph*, 16 April 1988).

In private he would write how the script for *Dick* lacked any merit whatsoever and conclude his latest diary entry with the bleak phrase 'it is a *Carry On*'. The 1970s was the decade in which the series fell prey to hyper-inflation and a fall in box-office receipts, but a third factor must be the palpable weariness of the surviving cast members. Peter Rogers, probably contemplating his latest Aston Martin, remarked that 'Kenneth was worth taking care of because, while he cost very little – £5,000 a film, he made a great deal of money for the franchise' (quoted in Butters and Davies, 2008: 224). But he wasn't taken care of; neither was Hawtrey, and maybe that is the key to their tragedies. Better to think of Williams and Hawtrey in terms of Roger Lewis's description of 'England's

---

21 In 1981 Hawtrey appeared as 'Count Dracula' in *Runaround*, the Southern TV children's quiz show hosted by Mike Read, in the manner of a *Sweeney* villain desperately awaiting the arrival of his getaway Jaguar.

Never-Neverland, that demi-paradise and secret garden where you can side-step growing up' (2002: 3–4) and perhaps that is why the pair are so enjoyable in *Teacher*. They are two grammar-school types, the swot and the insecure prefect, now grown to adulthood and still bickering within the safe confines of the staff room.

The second form of *Carry On* double act stemmed from the theatrical tradition of the romantic juvenile lead; Bob Monkhouse in *Sergeant*, the laconic Terence Longden in *Nurse* and the ever-magnificent Leslie Phillips in *Teacher*. To re-watch the films is to be reminded of the high standards of light comedy these pairings could achieve: Ian Lavender and Adrianne Posta in *Behind* and both Richard O'Callaghan and Jackie Piper and Terry Scott and Imogen Hassall in *Loving*.[22] With *Matron*, Barbara Windsor and Kenneth Cope are a delightful couple, she no longer the quasi-Jayne Mansfield human cartoon as established in *Doctor*, he wry and put upon – 'and we do actually get married in the end,' remarks Cope.

Perhaps the actor who best coped with the potentially deadly role of the juvenile lead was Jim Dale, one of the figures within this book who wears his myriad of talents lightly.[23] He was a stand-up comedian and former skiffle bandleader who was also a dancer, a song-writer and the most appealing naturalistic young actor to feature in the series. Even in the 1958 film version of *The Six-Five Special*, in which a bequiffed Dale was obliged to mime to a BBC Light Programme style version of 'The Train Kept a Rollin'', his charm was palpable. *Cowboy*, his fourth Carry On, was his first with star billing. It also may be the only Western with extensive footage of Chobham Common but, as Gilbert Adair famously wrote in *The Nautilus and the Nursery*, 'the producers had only to crown the green and gently undulating English countryside with a sheriff's office, a saloon bar and a livery stable, like a schoolboy wearing a Stetson hat, and the trick was done' (*Sight and Sound*, Spring 1985: 130–32).

---

22 Scott's tea party scene is a highlight of both his screen career and the series in general.
23 Mel Smith, Julian Barratt, Fry and Laurie, and Armstrong and Miller are some others.

Dale had the clear but classless speaking voice and the non-threatening good looks of the period with a nervous manner and angular body language. His partner was Angela Douglas as Annie Oakley, winsome yet determined and distractedly noticing Sid James' attentions in the manner of someone who really must finish her thesis. Dale and Douglas were teamed again in *Screaming* and *Follow That Camel* and in 1967 the actor was very effectively partnered with Anita Harris in *Doctor*. By that time, he was already Oscar nominated (Best Song: *Georgy Girl*) and his performance as Bottom in Frank Dunlop's production of *A Midsummer Night's Dream* was hailed by one critic as marking 'the emergence of a major comic star' (Bryden, *The Guardian*, 27 August 1967: 16). His final *Carry On*, aside from the dire *Columbus* (1992), was *Again Doctor*; a revival of the Dale/Douglas teaming in that perennial favourite of Christmas television *Digby: The Biggest Dog in The World* (Joseph McGrath, 1973) reminded cinemagoers of the potential that Rogers, once again, had failed to capitalise on.

Their departures from the series were appropriately well timed, as *Camping* was a watershed for the *Carry Ons*, the first with a non-institutional contemporary setting since *Cabby* (1963) and the first to display real paranoia towards everyday life. This was noted by some critics at the time: 'An unpleasant sequence in which The Gang brutally destroy a harmless hippie rave-up. If this is vox populi, we are in worse shape than we know' (Penelope Mortimer, *The Observer*, 6 July 1969: 23). *Camping* anticipated the following decade of threadbare scripts, increasingly snide treatment of certain team members and the increasingly cheap look of a series that had often managed to belie the paucity of its budget. Jim Dale and Angela Douglas were just too likeable a screen couple to endure the series in its declining years.

Finally, we have the *Carry On* films' continuation of the Donald McGill postcard tradition of husband and nagging wife or girlfriend:[24]

---

24 That said, the Great (i.e. dismal) British Holiday was not really explored by the *Carry On* films until as late as 1969 with *Camping*. *Cruising* was set aboard a cruise ship but that is probably the least recognisable of the series.

Sidney James with Joan Sims in *Up the Khyber*, *Camping* and *Abroad*, or with Hattie Jacques in *Loving*, *At Your Convenience* or *Cabby*. It is the last-named that provides one of the most plausible screen marriages in the history of the series in one of the few *Carry On* films that may be said to possess the elusive element of charm. In many respects it marks a milestone of the series – the first to be scripted by Talbot Rothwell and the last to use James as the straight man and Jacques as a human being rather than as a grotesque. Better to think of Peggy Hawkins, a monarch of all the Ford Consul Cortina 'Glamcabs' she surveys, rather than 'Matron' pursing Kenneth Williams, with the increasingly uncomfortable sensation that the life-threatening eating disorder and the sexuality of an actor were being mocked. Perhaps that is why the James/Jacques partnership in *Cabby* is the finest in the series – it conveys genuine affection.

The Great British Sitcom Spin-off Film

The year is 1975. The month is August. The place is a caravan site somewhere in Dorset where a group of desperate holidaymakers are completing the escape tunnel started four days ago under a derelict Bedford CA. The rain, the UHT milk and the prospect of dining off Frey Bentos pies for a week all conspired to drive them to plan this rash act, but the final straw was the film show scheduled for this Saturday in the entertainment hall – a revival of *Mutiny on the Buses*.

No chapter on the British sitcom double act would be complete without a reminder of a form of British cinematic life that flourished between 1969 and 1980. It was one that was generally loathed by most film critics and one that, in the wise words of Mr Barry Cryer, was a fundamental flaw. 'The greatest British sitcoms have always been about entrapment – think of Hancock and Sid – but the films felt the need to open out the narratives; the characters always seemed to be going on holiday.' And indeed, *Holiday on the Buses* (Bryan Izzard, 1973) was just one of several sitcom spin-offs to employ the plot device of sending the central characters on vacation.

The sitcom spin-off is a type of film that could only really hail from the pre-Multiplex era, when a picture house visit meant lethal hot dogs and faded velour upholstery that reeked of old Woodbines. Following advertisements for the local car dealer promising a great deal on the new Morris Marina 1.8 TC and a restaurant offering 'a taste of the east' would be the main feature: a 'big-screen' version of a television sitcom. The roots of this genre date back to the 1940s when Hammer Films specialised in churning out low budget film features based on BBC radio shows. However, by the end of the 1960s, Wardour Street faced the prospect of the withdrawal of virtually all the main American production companies from the UK. To save more ABCs and Gaumonts from being transformed into a branch of Victor Value, a cinematic version of a television series would be cheap to make, and, from a sales perspective, it would star actors who were instantly familiar to their potential audience.

Till Death Us Do Part (Norman Cohen, 1969) was the first of such pictures while *Bless This House* (Gerald Thomas, 1972) was very rudely referred to by Derek Malcolm as having 'all the aplomb of a drunken ostrich' (*The Guardian*, 5 July 1973: 10), but from a twenty-first-century perspective it is the *Citizen Kane* of sitcom spin-off films. There is the delightful father/son pairing of Sidney James and Robin Askwith,[25] the former long suffering and infinitely good hearted, the latter petulant, deadpan and a wholly believable teenage art student. There is also the bonus of Terry Scott and June Whitfield as the next-door neighbours, with Ronald Baines pompous but clearly highly professional – that is, he does not utter the phrase 'Cor!'

Four years later, *The Likely Lads* (Michael Tuchner, 1976) is both a comic road movie and a film about encroaching mid-life crisis. Rodney Bewes was arguably at his finest as Bob Ferris, now trapped in 1976-vintage suburban apathy as he moans about the stolen wing mirrors from his new Vauxhall Chevette and life in general. Should you

---

25 Replacing Robin Stewart from the television series.

want a precis of the Bob Ferris/Terry Collier dynamic, it is in the moment when Bewes declares 'in the chocolate box of life, the top layer's already gone – and someone's pinched the orange crème from the bottom' – only to receive the stunned reply of 'bloody hell!' For once the plot device of a holiday trip does not seem extraneous as this is a weekend trip as opposed to an elaborate vacation – and because caravanning is a further form of confinement that highlights the mannerisms of our heroes. *Porridge* (Dick Clement, 1979) was shot on location in Maidstone prison, emphasising the desperate existence of inmates and guards alike, with Fletcher and Godber savouring each and every small victory. *Dad's Army* (Norman Cohen, 1971) is a coarsened version of the BBC show but the moment when Captain Mainwaring – that sad, vulnerable and incredibly brave man – faces possible death at the hands of the Germans is very moving.

In the main, the British sitcom film soon became synonymous with utter grimness, and from a twenty-first-century perspective the relentless levels of tat on display often has a warped fascination of its own. The previously mentioned sitcom duos were usually at their best when squabbling in a living room or café, while the combination of cinematography in the full spectrum and low budgets was not a happy one. To see one of these epics rescreened on a wet Sunday is to be reminded of ill-lit and ill-stocked supermarkets, litter-strewn streets and houses that are a testament to the power of buff-coloured wallpaper. When Hammer returned to their old format with *On the Buses* (Harry Booth, 1971), the budget was under £100,000, which was low even for the period, but it earned over £1 million in the UK alone within just six months, in addition to becoming second to *The Aristocrats* as the most popular cinematic attraction in the country (Walker, 1985: 114). The film was not given a general press launch, which was probably a wise idea; in more recent tines Sinclair McKay wrote in unflattering terms:

> The screenplay entirely revolves around loud people hurling witless insults at each other while Blakey shakes his fist and falls off the bus's

rear platform. It is gob-smackingly mortifying. And it makes any one of the *Carry On* films look like Richard Brinsley Sheridan. (2007: 146)

But the audiences already knew and indeed loved this, for if the average sitcom spin-off made *The Seventh Seal* look like a *Carry On* offering this was all par for the course. Cinemagoers knew as soon as Stan Butler drove through a safari park in *Mutiny on the Buses* (Booth, 1972) that a chimpanzee would eventually take the wheel. The sequence also features a lioness who is clearly depressed on missing out on the lead role of *Living Free* (Jack Couffer, 1972) and, being reduced to co-starring with Reg Varney, muses on the indigestion consequences of eating the leading man. Likewise, when audiences saw Michael 'Mr Bronson' Sheard inspecting the engine bay of a Ford Zodiac Mk IV in *Holiday on the Buses* it was an inevitability that (a) his head would soon be trapped beneath the bonnet and (b) his car would be struck by a double decker that was driven by a total incompetent. If the viewer could endure the next few reels, they would be rewarded with the never-to-be-forgotten spectacle of various 'dolly birds' falling for Jack and Stan, the latter now fetchingly clad in woollen swimming trunks.

But with *Holiday* the effect of placing our undynamic duo away from the studio – some of the picture was shot in a real Pontins holiday camp in Wales – makes them appear less the lotharios of the bus depot and more comic grotesques who have strayed from a provincial Variety theatre circa 1948. By the end of the decade the genre was really on its last legs and after the films of *Rising Damp* (Joseph McGrath, 1980) and *George and Mildred* (Peter Frazer Jones, 1980) the great British sitcom spin-offs was largely no more. The latter is an especially bleak experience, Dick Sharples's script lacking almost all of the Thames TV series nuances. Asides from the transport café scene with Dudley Sutton as possibly the world's oldest ton-up boy, it was a highly dispiriting piece of work – 'not a patch on the series' in the succinct opinion of Brian Murphy – and I can vividly recall my disappointment when it aired on Christmas Day 1980. By that time Yootha Joyce had been dead for four months and this lovely actress deserved a far better epitaph than low-rent shoot and 'comic' Morris Minors.

Thus, there was never to be a major big screen *Terry and June* (which is to be regretted) or *Bread* (which is not) and during the 1980s a VCR was becoming as much a symbol of suburban affluence as owning a Soda Stream. One side effect of this growing phenomena was *That's Your Funeral* (John Robins, 1972) or *Never Mind the Quality, Feel the Width* (Ronnie Baxter 1973) gathering dust on the Betamax section of your corner video library. Long after a comedy's master tapes were stored in the studio shed or even wiped, the cinema version would continue to haunt viewers, especially on afternoon television.

Above all, a true double act film should look as though it has been sellotaped together, and boast lighting that makes the watcher wonder why the producer couldn't top up the meter. But for some enthusiasts the sight of Stephen Lewis moaning 'Like a moon coming over a mountain' in *Holiday on the Buses* instantly conveys the taste of flat Kia Ora and a Strawberry Mivvi. Followed by 'an exotic meal only ten minutes from this cinema'. Meanwhile, our escapees have redoubled their efforts after they receive the news that next week the film show will feature *Nearest and Dearest* (John Robins, 1972).

The Decent Chaps of the 1950s and '60s

Leslie Halliwell once argued that in terms of British cinema 'none of the pre-war comedy stars were still around in the late forties, not least in top recordable form, and it would be a long haul before they were replaced, if ever they were' (1987: 187). Their place was taken by character actors with a gift for comedy, and by the late 1950s the formula appeared thus – our hero (hair pomade, well-cut tweed jacket, Singer Gazelle Convertible, prone to saying 'gosh') wishes to marry the daughter (twin-set, sensible hair, sensible shoes) of a judge/senior surgeon/captain of industry who is (a) bearded and (b) more than somewhat of a curmudgeon. Daddy regularly berates our hero for being a nincompoop and a miserable worm in general but in their final reel all will be resolved in a car chase involving at least one black police Wolseley with a clanging bell.

Within this almost hermetically sealed realm, one popular theme of comedy duos was the division between age and comparative youth. Raymond Durgnat points out that the 1950s British cinema was rich in father figures (1970: 174–75) although in the productions featuring George Cole and Alastair Sim, they were not always reassuring. With *Laughter in Paradise* (Mario Zampi, 1951) no less a critic than C.A. Lejeune believed that 'it may well be that his long theatre association with George Cole has taught the younger man many useful tricks; at all events, young Mr Cole is not far short of the master in Sim's own impeccable style' (*The Sketch*, 20 June 1951: 36). In *The Belles of St Trinian's* (Frank Launder, 1954) Millicent Fritton is stately, possessed of an innate dignity and with secret *joie de vivre*; there is a treasurable moment in which she is delighted to discover that she can whistle. Cole's Flash Harry moves like a metronome on legs, dresses like every music hall spiv there ever was and has clearly acquired his patter from the avid study of British film noir. In a film concerned with retaining social status with the bare minimum of means, and with even less justification, the headmistress and the former boot boy understand the character and motive of the other.

Another major figure to emerge in British films of the 1950s is not automatically associated with double acts, but many of the felicitous moments in the screen career of Terry-Thomas involved a partner. His screen persona was an extension of his stage and variety act – the former wartime temporary gentleman turned peacetime rotter. He was one of the last of the great cads of post-war cinema, far less menacing than the saturnine Eric Portman, the angry self-loathing Rex Harrison of *The Rake's Progress* (Sidney Gilliat, 1945) or the feline Dennis Price but less naïve than the younger Leslie Phillips. The comic himself hailed from the ambiguous outer regions of the middle classes: raised in Finchley, educated at Ardingly, his father the director of a firm of meat importers at Smithfield. If the characters he depicted on screen were recognisable as a parvenu by those in the know – Thomas once pointed out that Robert Morley, David Niven or Wilfred Hyde-White could instantly see through his various bounders – anyone who was even remotely naïve stood rather less of a chance. This was demonstrated by a trio of Thomas's unofficial screen partners, the first being Ian Carmichael, a RADA-trained light comedian whose breakthrough role as Stanley Windrush in *Private's Progress* (John Boulting, 1956) established his film image as a displaced Wodehouse-like hero.

A Carmichael character will often try to do their best, even as their jovial outlook is tried by circumstances and the corrupt nature of others while Thomas's first star cinematic role as Major Hitchcock revealed hitherto unused resources as an actor. *Private's Progress* is a darker film than the jovial romp of popular myth – two German officers actually commit suicide in front of Windrush – with Hitchcock less a bounder of the pre-war Tom Walls school and more of a world-weary middle-aged professional exiled to a remote concern of the war. It also set the tone for his subsequent encounters with Carmichael – the voice of experience (self-assumed or otherwise) versus eager naïvety. With the sequel, *I'm All Right Jack* (Boulting, 1959) the two share only a brief, albeit funny, scene involving a Heinkel bubble car; Thomas's best moments are opposite Peter Sellers's lonely, misguided shop steward Fred Kite. In *Happy is The Bride* (Roy Boulting, 1958), Terry-Thomas was a police officer; in *Brothers in Law* (John Boulting, 1957), he was cockney spiv with the manners of an honours graduate of the Sydney Tafler Academy of Wide Boys instructing Carmichael's pupil barrister in the realities of the law. Terry-Thomas was also ambitiously cast as Bertram Welsh in the Boultings' flawed adaptation of *Lucky Jim* (1957), for while Carmichael was palpably uneasy at bridging the gap between upper-middle-class breeziness and lower-middle-cynicism, Terry-Thomas's air of asinine superiority was remarkably adaptable to an academic milieu.

Outside of Terry-Thomas's five film contract with the Boultings, he essayed the definitive temporary wartime captain and peacetime *flâneur* in *Blue Murder at St Trinian's* (Launder, 1957). His teaming with Joyce

Grenfell's Sergeant Ruby Gates is one of those happy coincidences of British cinema that can make one forgive *Can You Keep It Up For A Week?* (Robin Gough, 1974). Romney Carlton-Ricketts almost certainly created his hyphenated name one fruitful evening in a private hotel somewhere in Bayswater before absconding one step ahead of the landlady and her unpaid bill. Sergeant Gates brings with her the ethos of the hockey team, the gawky body language of the non-academic Upper Sixth – and the promise of a substantial legacy.

Of the many sublime moments of *Blue Murder At St Trinain's* – George Cole clad in a full-dress Teddy Boy outfit informing Alastair Sim 'See You Later, Educator' chief among them – the Terry-Thomas/Grenfell double act stands tall. Just as the bounder is starting to worry if anyone could quite believe in the stories of a bankrupt who resides in an abandoned double-decker bus, for all his courtly manners and well-cut blazer,[26] enter Ruby who may have good reason to distrust the school inmates, but then she has previously encountered them in *The Belles of St Trinian's* and knows full well that the girls do not play the game. But Romney is apparently an officer and a gentleman, and you can almost see the guinea signs in the captain's eyes when he encounters Ruby. It appears that Fortune has sent him one of the few women who would actually believe his patter[27] and throughout the film the relationship between Ruby and Romney is akin to a fox[28] who quite cannot believe his prey can be that trusting.

Terry-Thomas's final picture with Carmichael was in *School for Scoundrels* (Robert Hamer/Cyril Frankel, 1960) the latter as one Henry Palfrey, a downtrodden executive in his father's firm, despised by his chief clerk (Edward Chapman), sneered at by head waiters and at a total loss to compete with the utter bounder Raymond Delauey (Terry-Thomas, naturally) for the hand of April Smith (Janette Scott).

---

26 His tailor is probably one of his many creditors.

27 In *The Happiest Days of Your Life* Guy Middleton's sports master, Victor 'Whizzo' Hyde-Brown, attempts to impress the sixth formers of St Swithin's girl's school but Terry-Thomas makes no such move in *Blue Murder*, probably surmising that they could quell him with a single blow.

28 And of course Terry-Thomas was the inspiration for Basil Brush.

The script was adapted from Stephen Potter's *Lifemanship* books, which detailed how to be constantly ahead in polite society with the minimum of effort. The production was not a smooth one, with much of the picture unofficially directed by Frankel after Hamer was incapacitated by alcohol, but Palfrey's attempts to become a modern cad are achieved with élan, especially in the scenes opposite the spivvish car dealers Dunstan and Dudley Grosvenor (Dennis Price and Peter Jones), from whom he obtains an Austin Healey 100/6 by dubious means. Nevertheless, although Henry now has the sports car and the veneer of a very 1960-style cad, ultimately, he remains the good-hearted chap. As for Raymond, he is the temporary gentleman who positively revels in his cad-dom. Any successful bounder needs an encyclopaedic knowledge of the Byzantine rules and nuances of the British class structure and Raymond is an utter rotter who revels at pushing at the very limits of social acceptability.

Terry-Thomas's last great screen partner was the almost perpetually furtive-looking Eric Sykes; they teamed up in *Kill or Cure* (George, 1962). By that time Terry-Thomas was starting to divide his time between the UK and Hollywood and their original pairing was in a farce that firmly belonged in the MGM-British realm of country house murders and wealthy dowagers, which was typical of Borehamwood's output after the late 1950s. By 1965 such gentle – and genteel – comedies, together with the black and white crime thriller and the B-feature, were under threat. As Robert Murphy noted:

> Time was running out for the small-scale black and white comedy which had been the mainstay of the British film industry since the early '30s ... in the second half of the '60s stage farces, service comedies, rural whimsy and old crock films seemed in danger of extinction. (1992:238)

One of the final screen pairings to emerge from this realm was that of Leslie Phillips and James Robertson Justice, an actor whose frequent off-screen decrials of his own talents could not disguise an inner warmth and expert comedy timing. 'There is only one James Robertson Justice, a giant of a man with an infinite capacity for living life to the full,' stated a 1954 profile (*The Sketch*, 10 February: 13) and his role as Sir Lancelot Spratt in *Doctor in the House* came about after the part was turned down by Robert Morley. Of all the memorable moments[29] the viva voce with Kenneth More's Gaston Grimsdyke stands tall as a near-perfect evocation of tradition and post-war optimism amiably clashing. For *Doctor in Love* (Thomas, 1960), the character was renamed Dr Burke and played by Leslie Phillips, the master of depicting middle-class characters who were flashy but good-hearted and constantly seeking the approval of Justice's various ogres. At his considerable best Phillips was a light comedian on a par with Cary Grant. He was a former child actor who trained at Italia Conti and his post-war adult career was varied – 'Like most young actors I everything. For three years I played old men, middle-aged men, even female impersonators. Gradually I had comedy wished upon me. Whenever a "silly ass" comedian was required, the script was chucked at me' (quoted in Richards, *The Sketch*, 6 November 1957: 28).

In addition to their appearances in the wards of St Swithin's, Phillips and Justice made three highly polished comedies for Independent Artists, all directed by Ken Annakin, of which *A Very Important Person* (1961) represents some of their finest work. Justice's Sir Ernest is a polymath who needs the assistance of Leslie Phillips' Flying Officer Cooper to escape from a POW camp to continue with his essential work. Justice takes every opportunity to take bombast to previously unchartered regions but his grudgingly paternal bond with the dim-witted but extremely brave Jimmy Cooper is a keynote to the film. The book-end sequences of the characters being interviewed after the war in a *This Is Your Life*-type programme did not quite negate the narrative's air of menace. The paterfamilias and his 'silly ass' acolyte are placed not within an idealised suburbia or hospital corridors but in very real peril.

By the mid-1960s the protagonists of such film comedies ran the risk of appearing increasingly anachronistic in a world increasingly devoid

---

29 'What's the bleeding time?'

of the familiar post-war folk devils of NCOs, majors, Teddy Boys and assistant managers. A new age of British-based comedies with US backing and ostensible 'international appeal' was represented by *Those Magnificent Men in Their Flying Machines* (Annakin, 1965). The film was another fixture of Bank Holiday television schedule for many years and during its many revivals, one began to wonder if the film lasted for years. Fortunately, Eric Sykes and Terry-Thomas are on hand to provide the few golden moments of the picture as Courtney the valet – sniggering and proletarian – and his master Sir Percy Ware-Armitage, ever keen to cheat and to flaunt his status as much as possible. Four years later Thomas played Percy's son Sir Cuthbert and Sykes his manservant Percy in *Monte Carlo or Bust!* (Davies, 1969).[30] Thomas and Sykes, together with Cook and Moore, spare the audience from the film's many and various longueurs. The careful underplaying of *Private's Progress* has now been replaced by a deliberate cartoon figure and it is notable that both films are safely set in the past, where Thomas's caddishness may be given full rein. Ware-Armitage and his servant are inseparable, largely because they know each other's foibles only too well; better that they are always in each other's sights.

Sykes and Thomas were never to be teamed again on a film; by 1971 Terry-Thomas was suffering from the effects of Parkinson's disease. The *Carry On* films succeeded for several years by avoiding the twentieth century as must as possible but *Doctor in Clover* (Thomas, 1966) has Dr Grimsdyke making a bold foray to Carnaby Street, accompanied by Kiki Dee singing 'Take a Look at Me', but ultimately seeks refuge within St Swithin's, to be safely berated by James Robertson Justice. There was to be one last outing for the duo, the sad faded *Doctor in Trouble* (Thomas, 1970), where the gimmick casting of Simon Dee and Graham Chapman, plus the sterling work from Leslie Phillips, could not compensate for a tired, ill Justice reading from cue cards. Let us not speak of it again.

---

30 In the States it was released as the not-very-catchily entitled *Those Magnificent Men in their Jaunty Jalopies*.

We've Gone on Holiday by Mistake

The final production in this chapter is one that has suffered the unfortunate fate of becoming a cult film. Art and media studies students bellow choice lines of dialogue from *Withnail and I* or, worse, engaging in the 'drinking game'. Some other British pictures have befallen the same fate but not to the extent of *Withnail and I*, its acolytes almost blithely ignoring the care that went into its creation. To quote Roger Ebert's *The Great Movies III* (2010: 394), 'it achieves a kind of transcendence in its gloom. It is uncompromisingly, sincerely, itself. It is not a lesson or a lecture, it is funny but in a consistent way that it earns, and it is unforgettably acted'. As for one half of its resident double act, if Vivian Stanshall and Laurence Harvey had a love child, it would almost certainly resemble Richard E. Grant's Withnail and as well as having more than his fair share of one-liners, he already sounds like someone whose era has already passed. Withnail is nearly 30 – 'and I've got a sole flapping from my shoe' – and if he went to drama school in the late 1950s you can easily envisage his disdain for the Royal Court Theatre and Woodfall Films. His car, a battered Jaguar Mk 2, does not quite suit his image; a Riley RM, a Lea-Francis or any other transport that once symbolised upper-middle-class security of the post-war Churchill era might have suited him better.

To our heroes, the 'Swinging Sixties' are a horrible and distant myth, and by sending them on holiday in the Lake District in the September of 1969, the remoteness from this media-created realm is only re-emphasised. Fifteen years earlier Withnail might have found himself populating a second feature as a dashing young CID officer or entering via the French windows into a well-groomed West End comedy. Now, he is reduced to shrieking down the receiver of a public call box somewhere in Cumbria; being Withnail he would probably have then thumped Button 'B', just in case. As Ben Myers pointed out in *The New Statesman*, '*Withnail and I* is framed by societal restrictions representative of the old order: policemen,[31] tutting tea room customers

---

31 'Get in the back of the van!'

and the Labour Exchange thwart the pair's lives' (20 March 2017). Add to that recalcitrant unseen landlords and London cafés that make the roadside establishment in *Hell Drivers* (Cy Endfield, 1957) look like the Savoy Grill, and it is easy to sympathise with Marwood's opinion that the duo were 'making an enemy of our own future'. Officers of the law still sport military haircuts and bearing, patrolling the motorways in their black BMC J4s. In terms of pop culture, this is the vehicle that famously adorned the cover of *Abbey Road* but here it is a symbol of mundane authority.

Outside of the capital lurk the *Cold Comfort Farm* dress extras, such as Michael Elphick's Jake the Poacher and all the while Marwood views the shenanigans created by Withnail with increasing alarm, for Paul McGann creates one of the most subtle and understated performances of a straight man in British film history. We have seen how many double acts – Hancock and James or Morecambe and Wise – resemble the squabblings of pre-adolescents but as *Withnail and I* progresses, so does Marwood's disillusionment with the games. Even their Greek Chorus, Presuming Ed (Eddie Tagoe) and Danny the Dealer (Ralph Brown) are already on the cusp of middle age and the counter-culture has been absorbed by the mainstream to the extent that hippy wigs are being sold in Woolworths.

Walter Kerr described how a double act arrived two by two, as if from the Ark (1967: 177) but this one is coming to the end of its natural cycle and the setting is not mere period nostalgia but a key detail. 'We are ninety-one days away from the end of the 1960s, the greatest decade in human history,' muses Danny. It was a period of British social history that cinema depicted in *Performance* (Nicolas Roeg/Douglas Cammell, 1968) and the deeply odd *Goodbye Gemini* (Alan Gibson, 1970), with its soundtrack by the Peddlers and array of bored swingers.[32] *Withnail and I* is indeed the archetypal 'morning after' picture, the wakening after an overlong dream to a reasonably grim reality. The character of Withnail's Uncle Monty is key in process, and not just because of the

---

32 It is entirely possible to imagine Withnail appearing in the latter, alternately being menaced by Mike Pratt or blackmailed by Alexis Kanner.

relish with which Richard Griffiths delivers Bruce Robinson's script. He is a creature of quite palpable menace – 'I mean to have you, even if it is through burglary!' – but also of utter frailty, standing along with Gilbert Harding, Godfrey Winn and all the other theatrical types who were born too late to have been affected by the Wolfenden Report. At breakfast, following his exceptionally disastrous would-be seduction of Marwood, the latter reads the old man's letter of apology – 'I do sincerely hope that you will find the happiness that has sadly always been denied me' with sympathy and resolve. 'You'll suffer for this, Withnail. What you have done will have to be paid for.'

It is now time to go home and a leading role in *Journey's End* means more than a period short-back-and-sides and a resurgence of a theatrical career; it means the end of the partnership. Earlier in the picture Danny theorises that, 'Hairs are your aerials. They pick up signals from the cosmos and transmit them directly into the brain. This is the reason bald-headed men are uptight,' but now Marwood is prepared at least partially to join the ranks of the uptight. We will subsequently encounter double acts formed of the leader and his/her acolyte – Francie and Josie – and maybe that was once a role that Marwood was happy to place – but no longer.

Few of the duos in this book cease their relationship on the screen; Tony Hancock moved from East Cheam to Earls Court with never another mention of Sid but at least we did not see them part at 23 Railway Cuttings. Eric and Ernie, Bob and Terry and Jeff and Marty all exist in the memory and in film libraries while the parting of Steed and Emma Peel was not quite rushed enough to hide the real pain felt by both Macnee and the character he was depicting. In *Withnail and I*, it is akin to Vladimir being left at the side of the road by an Estragon, who has been offered a fresh start, a parting as sad as that moment in *Billy Liar!* (John Schlesinger, 1963) when Liz smiles from the train that is leaving for London. In *Withnail and I*, even the pair's ill-fated holiday reeks of September, that month when grey clouds gather, school trunks are packed, and the beaches become de-populated. Withnail is now being put away with Marwood's other childish things – 'But I've got us a bottle open. Confiscated it from Monty's supplies. 53 Margaux. Best of the century'. The response is simple and quietly brutal, without meaning to be – 'I can't, Withnail, I'll miss the train.' *Withnail and I* has, beneath the grandiloquence and the studied mannerisms of its anti-hero, a sense of fear and timidity at a future without his best friend:

M: Withnail, why don't you go home?
W: Because I want to walk you to the station.
M: No, really, I really don't want you to.
M: I shall miss you, Withnail.
W: I'll miss you too.

The drinking and the posturing – and the 'prancing like a tit' – all now seem far away, for what we have, in the rain and iron railings, is a scenario that must have been familiar to the younger Withnail:

'Christopher?' Pooh said, looking up at Christopher as they walked hand in hand. 'You aren't coming back, are you?' Christopher looked down at the ground and took a moment before he responded. 'No, Pooh. I won't be coming back this time.' (A.A. Milne, *The House at Pooh Corner*, 1928)

You can just imagine Withnail's reaction to such a literary comparison – an intemperate one, no doubt, with liberal use of the phrase '*Children's Hour*?' 'Blank, blank *Jackanory*!' and 'How dare you? I'm star, you fuckers!' Nor has a hitherto lost manuscript of *The House at Pooh Corner* featuring our heroes vomiting lighter fluid been unearthed – but it does not mean that it lacks for truth. The bond between the two has been broken and the straight man no longer wishes to serve as the foil for Withnail. Marwood needs to part with his old friend, for if he does not, there is the very real prospect of remaining trapped in what is fast becoming a nightmare.

The original script had Withnail returning to the flat and committing suicide, but as a conclusion it is as blatant as it is horrendous. Perhaps he might borrow some more funds from Uncle Monty, and eventually take on a country pub, becoming indistinguishable from the befuddled ex-service officer he recently encountered behind the bar while going on holiday by mistake. Vivian MacKerrell, the role model for the character could both act and write, but he was ' brilliant at being Vivian' (Robinson, 2015) and in the closing moments there is a sense of real talent, of the understanding of the sheer fragility of dreams that Withnail has previously kept at bay. Perhaps he will finally arrive at a sense of peace. We can only hope so.

Bibliography

Books

Armes, Roy (1978), *A Critical History of British Cinema*. London: Secker & Warberg.

Balcon, Michael (1969), *Michael Balcon Presents … A Lifetime in Films*. London: Hutchinson.

Butters, Wes and Davies, Russell (2008), *Kenneth Williams Unseen: The Private Notes, Scripts and Photographs*. London: Harper Collins.

Chapman, James (2012), 'A short history of the "Carry On" films', in Hunter, I.Q. and Porter, Larraine (eds), *British Comedy Cinema*. Abingdon: Routledge.

Chibnall, Steve and McFarlane, Brian (2009), *The British 'B' Film*. London: British Film Institute.

Dacre, Richard (1991), *Norman Wisdom: A Career in Comedy*. London: Farries.

Durgnat, Raymond (1970), *A Mirror for England: British Movies from Austerity to Affluence*. London: Faber & Faber.

Ebert, Roger (2010) *The Great Movies III*. Chicago: University of Chicago Press.

Fisher, John (2013), *Funny Way To Be A Hero*. London: Preface Publishing.

Gilliatt, Penelope (1973), *Unholy Fools; Wits Comics Disturbers of the Peace: Film and Theatre*. London: Viking Press.

Halliwell, Leslie (1987), *Double Take and Fade Away (Halliwell on Comedians)*. London: Grafton.

Harper, Sue and Porter, Vincent (2003), *British Cinema of the 1950s: The Decline of Deference*. Oxford: Oxford University Press.

Hoggart, Richard (1957), *The Uses of Literacy: Aspects of Working Class Life*. London: Allen Lane.

Hunter, I.Q. (2012), 'From Window Cleaner to Potato Man: Confessions of a Working Class Stereotype', in Hunter, I.Q. and Porter, Larraine (eds), *British Comedy Cinema*. Abingdon: Routledge.

Kerr, Walter (1967), *Tragedy and Comedy*. New York: Simon and Shuster.

Lee, C.P. (2012), 'Northern Films for Northern People': The Story of the Mancunian Film Company', in Hunter, I.Q. and Porter, Larraine (eds) *British Comedy Cinema*. Abingdon: Routledge.

Lewis, Roger (2002), *Charles Hawtrey, 1914–1988: The Man who was Private Widdle*. London: Faber and Faber.

McCann, Graham (1998), *Morecambe and Wise*. London: Fourth Estate Ltd.

McFarlane, Brian (1999), *Lance Comfort: British Film Makers*. Manchester: Manchester University Press.

McKay, Sinclair (2007), *A Thing of Unspeakable Horror: The History of Hammer Films*. London: Amicus.

Medhurst, Andy (2007), *A National Joke: Popular Comedy and English Cultural Identities*. Abingdon: Routledge.

Midwinter, Eric (1979), *Make 'em Laugh: Famous Comedians and Their Worlds*. London: Allen & Unwin.

Murphy, Robert (1992), *Sixties British Cinema*. London: BFI Publishing.

Orwell, George (1941), 'The Comic Art of Donald McGill', in Davison, Peter with Angus, Ian and Davison, Sheila (eds) *All Propaganda is Lies 1941–1942*. London: Secker and Warburg.

Orwell, George (1998), *The Complete Works of George Orwell*. London: Secker and Warburg.

Park, James (1990), *British Cinema; The Lights That Failed*. London: Batsford Press.

Richards, Jeffrey (2000), 'Crisis at Christmas: Turkey Time, The Holly and The Ivy, The Cheaters', in Connelly, Mark (ed.), *Christmas at the Movies: Images of Christmas in American, British and European Cinema.* London: I.B. Tauris.

Richards, Jeffrey (2010), *The Age of The Dream Palace: Cinema and Society in 1930s Britain.* London: I.B. Tauris.

Robinson, Bruce (2015), *'Withnail & I': The Original Screenplay.* London: Bloomsbury.

Robinson, David (1969), *The Great Funnies: A History of Film Comedy.* Studio Vista.

Russell, Dave (1997), *Popular Music in England 1840–1914: A Social History.* Manchester: Manchester University Press.

Slide, Anthony (1998), *Eccentrics of Comedy.* London: Scarecrow Press Inc.

Thompson, Harry (1997), *Peter Cook: A Biography.* London: Hodder and Stoughton.

Thomson, David (2014), *Moments That Made the Movies.* London: Thames & Hudson Ltd.

Travers, Ben (1978), *A-Sitting on a Gate: Autobiography.* London: W.H. Allen.

Walker, Alexander (1985), *National Heroes: British Cinema in the Seventies and Eighties.* London: Harrap.

Webber, Richard (2009), *Fifty Years of Carry On.* London: Arrow Books.

Williams, Kenneth and Davis, Russell (ed.) (1993), *The Kenneth Williams Diaries.* London: Harper Collins.

Journals and Periodicals

Adair, Gilbert (1985), 'The Nautilus and the Nursery', *Sight and Sound*, Spring Issue.

Briefing (1967), 'A Sad and Laughing Life', *The Observer*, 19 March.

Bryden, Ronald (1967), 'Festival Draught of Fishes', *The Observer*, 27 August, pp.16.

Davies, Terence (2013), 'Kind Hearts and Coronets is One of the Greatest Comedies of World Cinema', *The Guardian*, 13 September.

Ebert, Roger (1968), Review: Bedazzled, *The Chicago Sun-Times*, 30 January.

Ebert, Roger (2009), Review: Withnail and I, *The Chicago Sun-Times*, 25 March.

Lejeune, C.A. (1951), Review: Laughter in Paradise, *The Sketch*, 20 June, pp. 36.

Macnab, Geoffrey (1997), 'Confessions of a Serial Director', *The Independent*, 4 September.

Malcolm, Derek (1973), 'The Moore we are Together', *The Guardian*, 5 July, pp. 10.

Malcolm, Derek (1974), 'The Lady in The Blake', *The Guardian*, 22 August pp. 10.

Montgomery-Massingberd, Hugh (1988), Obituary: Kenneth Williams, *The Daily Telegraph*, 16 April.

Mortimer, Penelope (1967), 'Films', *The Observer*, 24 December, p. 18.

Mortimer, Penelope (1969), 'Films', *The Observer*, 6 July, pp. 23.

Myers, Ben (2017, '*Withnail and I*: 30 Years On, it's the Perfect Film for Brexit Britain', *The New Statesman*, 20 March.

Review: The Intelligence Men (1965), *The Monthly Film Bulletin* 32(376), pp. 75.

Roud, Richard (1966), Review: That Riviera Touch, *The Guardian*, 25 March, pp. 11.

3

Radio: 'This is the BBC Home Service'

An idea, novel in every respect to broadcasting in this country, was approved by the BBC Programme Board today. A comedian has been selected, material will be written around him, and the New Year he will broadcast every Wednesday night for 12 weeks. Such a contract has never before been given to a radio comedian in this country. The programmes will be in serial form to the extent that the same artists and characters will be retained, but each episode will be complete in itself. (Quoted in Askey, 1975: 93–94)

A chapter that attempted to describe every double act who broadcast on the air from 1922 onwards would be the length of the *Encyclopaedia Britannica*. There would have to be references to double acts as diverse as David Kossoff and Joan Sims in the 1966 Light Programme sitcom *Sam and Janet*, or Mr Murgatroyd and Mr Winterbottom ('Two Minds with Not a Single Thought') – a.k.a. Tommy Handley and Ronald Frankau. Jimmy Jewel and Ben Warriss starred in *Up the Pole* (1947–52), an everyday story of a trading post somewhere in the Arctic circle. Jack Warner and Kathleen Harrison were *The Huggetts* (1953–62) and Canada's Bernard Braden and Barbara Kelly appeared in *Bedtime with Braden* (1950). One might also mention George Cole and Psyche the Dog (Percy Edwards) in *The Life of Bliss* (1953–69).[1]

The focus here will be the double acts that are of the very essence of the medium. Seán Street described how 'voices and music coming through the air, even now, in the second incarnation of the word "wireless" can hold a magic and a mystery' (2012: xi). This applies as much to Julian and Sandy as it does to a collaboration of Delia Derbyshire and Barry Bermange, the firm of 'Bonar Law' and the aural landscape of *The Dreams* (1964). Radio exists in the temporal dimension, and the duos in this section of the book are the comics whose broadcasts form a collaboration with the listener, as demonstrated by one of the BBC's most famous, if non-comedic, double acts. The *Paul Temple* serials ran from 1938 to 1968 with various cast changes, arriving by 1954 at the perfect combination. 'We present Peter Coke and Margery Westbury,' the announcer would intone in his most BBC tones over the strains of 'The Coronation Scot', with the two leading actors evoking without any seeming effort an atmosphere of smog, Lagondas and dubious cocktails. Two decades later, you had only to hear Simon Jones and Geoffrey McGivern to know that Arthur Dent was respectable and utterly bored while Ford Prefect was rootless and loyal.

The first double act to make their names via the wireless, as opposed to gaining fame through the halls or revue, was that of Charlie Clapham and Billy Dwyer. Both had gained their first show experience through concert parties in the First World War – Clapham while serving in the army, Dwyer in a munitions factory. They formed a comic partnership in 1925, turning professional in 1926. Clapham was the 'silly ass' comic, Dwyer was his ever-exasperated straight man and their radio popularity

---

1 Mr Cole once described the long-running show as 'Wholesome to the point of nausea' (quoted in Pettigrew, 1982: 31).

translated into stage appearances where they would make an entrance through a giant wireless set:[2]

> Clapham is a delicious comic, but he would be the first to admit that the harassed dignity of the portly Bill Dwyer is the ideal complement to his work. I cannot imagine Dwyer without Clapham or Clapham without Dwyer ... it is the injured expression that passes over Dwyer's face that tempers the audacious sallies of the mercurial Charlie. (Rose, *The Stage*, 13 August 1936: 2)

The act was ended not by a decline in popularity by through the ill health of Dwyer, who retired in 1940.

By the mid-1930s the cinema feature *Radio Parade of 1935* (Arthur B. Woods, 1934) was a testament to the popularity of several wireless double acts. The Western Brothers (the cousins Kenneth and George) made the transition from cabaret to wireless, even if the BBC was initially not keen on the title of their 1937 show *Cad's College*, as 'cad' was an insulting term. Harry Haver and Frank Lee became the resident comics on Henry Hall's radio show, and subsequently appearing in *Danger! – Men At Work* (1939–47) as the eponymous (and useless) handymen of Hotel Mimosa. J.B. Priestley unfavourably compared the 'stars who had arrived by way of amusing farmers' wives and invalids on the radio' with the music hall acts 'who topped the bill, spending years getting there, learning how to perfect their acts and handle their audiences' (1970: 85).

The first broadcast of *Band Waggon* in 1938 marked the beginning of an era of comedy programmes deliberately created for BBC Radio. The Corporation's audience research demonstrated that their output of

---

2   Radio fame did not always translate into success on the halls; Arthur Askey noted in his memoirs of his fears of how his concert party approach might not work in the atmosphere of the halls and how some radio comedians had not done well on the Variety stage (Askey, 1975: 98–99). In 1949 the performance of his partner Richard Murdoch as the Dame in Little Miss Muffett received the mild but pointed criticism that 'he will be much happier once he has settled down in his part' and 'Mr Murdoch introduces numerous radio catchphrases into his work' (*The Stage*, 30 December: 5).

dance band shows was not enjoying great popularity and so the new programme was to follow a magazine format. The compere was Richard Murdoch, a light comedian who was a graduate of the Cambridge Footlights, while Arthur Askey was a Liverpudlian with nearly fifteen years of experience on the concert party circuit. The fundamental approach of this form of seaside entertainment was to create an instantaneous – sometimes almost conversational – rapport with their audience. By the 1930s Askey's reputation in this realm was such that 'visitors to the Isle of Wight used to return to the mainland with tales of a sensational little comedian' (F.O.H., *Theatre World*, 1959–60: 26). The BBC had originally considered using Tommy Trinder, but he proved unavailable, and it was when the producers Ronald Waldman and Harry S. Pepper were visiting the Isle of Wight that they 'discovered' Askey (Took, 1981: 18).

The show was not initially a success, and so Askey and Murdoch devised, in conjunction with the production team, the idea that they lived in a flat atop Broadcasting House. Murdoch became Askey's friend, confidant and straight man and the future sitcom theme of co-existence within close quarters was established. The flat sequences occupied only ten minutes of the show, but Barry Took argues that 'those ten minutes might be said to revolutionise radio comedy in Britain' (1981: 18). The nasal clerical whine of Askey – his accent was 'Mersey' rather than 'Scouse' – and the light musical comedy tones of Murdoch blended perfectly, with the lower-middle-class comic.[3] Archive recordings reveal how Askey and Murdoch not only sound almost contemporary – by contrast, the BBC announcer sounds positively Victorian – but delivering their lines with incredible speed and clarity. At this time acts from the Variety circuit found great difficulty in sight-reading a script, Frank Muir recalling that that comic might go into a memorised routine

---

3   Barry Cryer recalls that in the late 1970s there was the opportunity for the perfect April 1st radio spoof: 'Arthur and Richard's voices sounded the same as they did in the 1940s so we were going to make a show and claim that it was a recently unearthed archive recording. And then in the middle, there would be a reference to Margaret Thatcher.' Sadly, Askey's ill health prevented the show from being made.

and rely on his straight man as the prompt. The producer would flash a warning signal when it was time to conclude the act:

(A green light starts flashing urgently)
Straight Man: (ruthlessly cutting in) Well it's certainly a funny old world we live in, but as a wise man once said …
(A note is struck on the piano and both sing romantically, in credible harmony):
'Red sails in the sunset'
(Muir, 1997: 129–30).

Band Waggon also attracted guest stars (including, on one occasion, Cary Grant), but the show ended in 1939 when Murdoch was commissioned into the Royal Air Force. In 1943, he encountered Wing Commander Kenneth Horne, a peacetime manager at Triplex Safety Glass who commissioned the radio quiz *Ack-Ack Beer-Beer* in addition to his duties at the Air Ministry. He requested Flight Lieutenant Murdoch to be his new squadron leader, and the duo created the scenario of a remote RAF station where little happened named *Much-Binding-in-the-Marsh*. Horne was the commanding officer, dim, pompous and exceptionally fond of the sound of his own voice – 'Did I ever tell you about the time I was in Sidi Barrani?' and Richard Murdoch played his second-in-command and witty straight man.

Barry Johnston saw the contrast between Murdoch's work with Arthur Askey and his routines with Horne as 'unforced, calmer and more sophisticated, and they sounded so natural together' (2007: 75). The show ran for nine years beyond the end of the Second World War, for the managerial types who enjoyed inflicting their increasingly exaggerated war memoirs on their subordinates were far from rare in the 1950s. By that time, the BBC featured two programmes made by actor-writers who delighted in exploiting the potential of radio:[4] Eric Barker and the Peters Ustinov and Jones. Phil Diak of *The Daily Herald* praised Barker

---

4   One could have also cited *The Goon Show* but that did not feature a double act per se.

as 'the cleverest and deepest British comedian' and 'an indispensable creative artist' (21 July 1959: 2). He was also a character actor of the highest order: a middle-aged shoplifter in *Z-Cars* who cannot afford a birthday present for his grandchild ('Tuesday Afternoon', 1963), a nervous driving instructor in *The Fast Lady* (Ken Annakin, 1962), a brutally dismissive bank manager in *Heaven's Above!* (John Boulting, 1963). In the days when Norman Hudis was writing the *Carry On* series Barker was the Inspector in *Constable* (1960), petty-minded and over-fond of delivering faux-genial bromides in a suburban whine.

All these characters were created without any extraneous effect. Barker worked on the radio with his wife Pearl Hackney[5] – 'a foil in a million' – and in *Just Fancy* (1951–62) dispensed with a studio audience so that his material could be directly addressed to the listeners. Peter Ustinov and Peter Jones also eschewed performing to invited members of the public with *In All Directions* (1952–55), which they improvised from scenarios devised by Frank Muir and Denis Norden. Muir and Norden would invent a situation, then Jones and Ustinov responded. The results of this ad lib session were transcribed into script form, and then recorded in a BBC studio with further ad libs contributed by Ustinov and Jones. (Took 1981:99).

The basic theme was Ustinov and Jones on a never-ending car journey not to discover the meaning of life but for the even more elusive Copthorne Avenue, encountering the spivs Morrie and Dudley Grosvenor while en route. It was, to employ a cliché, pure radio, Lionel Hale of *The Observer* noting that 'neither film nor stage could catch the fugitive Ustinov-Jones coruscations. They are airy, and of the air'

---

5   When the show was transferred to television, Ms Hackney managed to cause a scandal in one edition. To be fair, it does not seem as though it was overly difficult to cause a scandal in Britain of 1955; wearing a drape jacket during the hours of daylight or ordering two packets of custard creams from the grocers could prompt the neighbours to dial WHItehall 1212. But, in an eerie anticipation of *The Daily Mail*'s twenty-first-century approach, a headline on the front of *The Daily Herald* of 3 March 1955 informed its readers of a 'TV Slur On The Queen Mother – Viewers Protest'. In the dastardly sketch in question the writer Phillip Phillips breathlessly reported that Hackney 'bore no resemblance to the Queen Mother as far as I could see. But her voice did sound very much like the Queen'.

(17 May 1953: 15). Hales also opined that 'I am sure Mr Jones himself would agree that in every partnership there is one pre-eminence and be happy in the knowledge of his own beautiful brilliance as a foil to Mr Ustinov'. That worthy was indeed the *enfant terrible* of stage, cinema and records. In films, he would often not so much eat the scenery as create a seven-course banquet from it, delightfully so in *Quo Vadis* (Mervyn LeRoy, 1951) where his Nero gleefully subverts the MGM costume pomposity.[6] But, if a highly determined director was at the helm, Ustinov could reveal a talent for low-key wistfulness that was too seldom used by cinema – *Hot Millions* (Eric Till, 1968), more of which later; Arthur Simpson, the self-loathing Anglo-Egyptian conman of *Topkapi* (Jules Dassin, 1964) and a beautiful performance as the cuckolded Ambassador Manuel Pineda in *The Comedians* (Peter Glenville, 1967).

And if liquid gold ever achieved the power of speech, it would almost certainly sound like Peter Jones. He was a writer of pith and wit – his 1959 wireless sitcom *We're In Business* contains the sublime statement 'ninety-six million cups of tea have been drunk in the Northern Hemisphere alone; and two MPs, a bishop and a rock 'n' roll star have called British bird baths a national disgrace'[7] – he was an actor of understated brilliance. The genial suburban tones of the music society organiser in *High Treason* (Roy Boulting, 1952) and the reluctant English tourist in France in *A Day to Remember* (Ralph Thomas, 1953) could easily transform into coldly hateful diction of the contemptuous manager in *Never Let Go* (John Guillermin, 1960).

Frank Muir compared the Ustinov and Jones relationship with that of Peter Cook and Dudley Moore: 'Peter Cook and Peter Ustinov were bottomless wells of comedy invention, preferably expressed ad lib, and Peter Jones and Dudley Moore made them excellent partners, both far more than "foils" or "straight men"' (Muir, 1997: 261).[8] One essential

---

6   I.e. various elaborately costumed characters standing with the poise of a fence-post and either uttering the phrase 'ye, verily ye', or looking as though they wanted to.

7   It could almost be a line from *The Hitchhiker's Guide to the Galaxy*.

8   Peter Cook listed Peter Ustinov as one of his comic influences (Harry Thompson, 1997).

difference was that the former were more concerned with genial mockery and acute observation of character rather than a sense of subversion. Dudley Grosvenor once ruefully observed to his sibling, 'I'll tell you this much, Mowwie, if every evening after work you are hit on the head with a beer bottle with monotonous regularity mawwiage soon loses its magic.' 'But all this fun goes on in the hothouse; what we want is somebody to throw a few stones and let in some air' (*The Guardian*, 25 May 1953: 3).

Ironically, the star of the radio comedy that achieved that aim was one whose 'day job' involved issuing statements of a redoubtably uncomic and sober nature. 'Mr Kenneth Horne, Triplex sales director, said that the thickness of the gold coating will be approximately .0000002in' reported *The Coventry Evening Telegraph* about a new form of safety glass on what was probably already a fairly boring day in autumn (4 November 1953: 22). After the Second World War Horne had turned down the chance to become a full-time professional comedian and he continued his business career as the sales director at Triplex. During the late 1950s Horne would guest with Murdoch on various comedy shows, but while the latter was a full-time entertainer, the former would never allow his two personae to clash. Broadcasting and script-writing were reserved for the weekends, and the image of Horne in Barry Johnston's magnificent biography is of a kind, genial but driven figure. The student who was sent down from Cambridge for idleness became a wing commander within four years of being commissioned in the RAF, and when he recorded the pilot episode of *Beyond Our Ken* in October 1957, Horne was the chairman of Chad Valley Toys.

Kenneth Horne suffered a stroke in 1958 and retired from business to focus on his comedy career. *Beyond Our Ken*, which was written by Eric Merriman and Barry Took, ran for seven seasons, with a stellar attraction being Rodney and Charles, two self-aggrandising actors played by Hugh Paddick and Kenneth Williams. When the series was revamped as *Round the Horne* in 1964 the new writing team of Took and Marty Feldman transformed the pair into Julian and Sandy. Paddick was a fixture of West End theatre and whose aquiline profile meant that on his rare film appearances he was the ideal casting for any managerial type of instructor – he is one of the tutors of Lifemanship in *School for Scoundrels* (Robert Hamer/Cyril Frankel, 1960). By the mid-1960s Williams was suffering from a major crisis in his once-promising stage career[9] and *Round the Horne* was a watershed in his transformation from actor to 'comic personality'. With Horne it would be fair to say that he saw a paternal figure that Tony Hancock could never be; film footage survives of a *Beyond Our Ken* rehersal in 1960, and as Kenneth Williams leers into the microphone, Horne exudes the air of patrician bonhomie.

Thus, every week Kenneth Horne finds an excuse to call on the latest enterprise of Julian (Paddick) and Sandy (Williams). 'Today, many of the best films are made by the small independent film units. Recently, I visited the office of one such company. The sign on the door said Bona Prods, so I prodded and entered'. Of course, he did, for Mr Horne is forever agreeable for another encounter with Julian and Sandy. They could be managing a pop group named Ruff Trade and The Cruisers[10] or making an epic entitled *Motor Cycle Au Pair Boy*,[11] but there was always time to welcome their courteous interrogator. As we have seen in the Variety chapter, the banter between a compere and two comics was a staple of the minstrel circuit, but the relationship between Horne and Paddick and Williams was one of mutual affection and respect. He may have instructed their interior decorators to 'come in before the neighbours see you' but every week Mr Horne found himself in their company.

Had the star's performance betrayed one iota of condescension towards Julian and Sandy, or the air of the chairman of the board putting on a turn for the office Christmas party or works' annual picnic and sporting gala, then *Round the Horne* would never have functioned. Horne was the host of such events during the 1950s, presiding over a pedal car rally

---

9   *Gentle Jack* (1963), *Loot* (1965) and *The Platinum Cat* (1965).

10 Horne once reassured the audience 'I'm all for censorship. If I see a double-entendre I whip it out.'

11 If only such a film had entered production, preferably directed by Michael Winner and with Oliver Reed in the title role.

at the Austin motor works in 1955, and in the 1960s he would present the sort of advertising magazine that tactfully recommend pre-packaged goods for your new kitchen. Horne was also the quizmaster in the more remote parts of the ITA region and a presence on *Twenty Questions* – and *Round the Horne* whole-heartedly subverted his responsible BBC Home Service image.

Marty Feldman regarded Horne as 'the best straight man I had ever seen, gentle with a big heart, very still and confident but not cocky' (Feldman, 2016). *Beyond Our Ken* first aired in the twilight of broadcasting father figures[12] such as Richard Dimbleby, but Took and Feldman transformed 'Mr Horne' into a well-tailored figure of misrule who spoke in safe and reassuring tones. Their scripts, and subsequently those of Brian Cooke, Johnnie Mortimer and Donald Webster, had the star mocking his own performance and the conventions of the medium. 'Bill Pertwee was in it too, but I can't remember what he did', remains just one treasured line delivered in that calm baritone. And every week 'Mr Horne' always accepted Julian and Sandy without malice and responded to their mockery in kind:

> HORNE: Will you take my case?
> JULIAN: Well, it depends on what it is. We've got a criminal practice that takes up most of our time.
> HORNE: Yes, but apart from that, I need legal advice.
> SANDY: Ooh, isn't he bold? Time has not withered, nor custom staled his infinite variety.

Johnston's book, with great tact and sympathy, infers a troubled figure who once confessed entirely out of the blue to a junior business colleague at Triplex that 'within reason, I can have pretty well anything I want: and yet I'm not happy. Life's jolly difficult isn't it?' (2007: 141). With his visits to Julian and Sandy's latest enterprise he could be free of worry and social façade. 'Well how nice to vada your eek again, Mr Horne. What brings

---

12 Gilbert Harding was the archetypical grumpy uncle.

you trolling in here?' Kenneth Horne's passing in 1969 left a vacuum that no other radio comic could hope to fill, Williams writing in his *Diaries* that 'his unselfish nature, his kindness, tolerance and gentleness were an example to everyone' (1993: 345).

The final wireless double act within this chapter is a 'cult'[13] comedy, but *The Hitchhiker's Guide to the Galaxy* transcends this mixed blessing with ease. Douglas Adams, among his myriad of other achievements, created a double act who were destined to roam through the wastelands of time and space. Arthur Dent (Simon Jones) has the resigned petulance of a Tony Hancock who has learned that the Vogons have demolished railway cuttings and who complains that 'I don't want to die now. I've still got a headache. I don't want to go to heaven with a headache, I'd be all cross and wouldn't enjoy it'.

In a universe whose rules manage to be even more confusing and self-protective than those of your average local government department, Ford Prefect (Geoffrey McGivern) is at least predictably unpredictable. The Book itself merely adds to the chaos, despite its best intentions, for the narrator of *The Hitchhiker's Guide to the Galaxy* was played by Peter Jones in his Savile Row-tailored deadpan, wry, matter of a fact but authoritative manner. The Voice is not a standard 'Unreliable Narrator' – that would almost certainly be Zaphod Beeblebrox – and his assured tone is one that will be instantly familiar to anyone who watched Edgar Lustgarten commenting on one of many B-film murders in outer suburbia. The voiceover for the series employs much the same approach as an actor narrating a 1960s documentary about how members of the Civil Defence Corps, all Brylcreem and NHS glasses, would prepare for nuclear war by building a mock-up of a field kitchen somewhere near Bath. In 1978 this instructional approach could still be heard in Central Office of Information road safety films,[14] where the voiceover would

---

13 'Cult': a devoted following who can spend an unconscious amount of time ranting on web forums if their theories of comedy are contravened.

14 'You're driving along a country road. You are at the wheel of a ten-year-old Morris 1100. You overtake a Commer van driven by a stuntman from *Special Branch* – watch what happens!'

typically admonish the viewer, whereas Jones issued his observations in the spirit of blithe indifference.

Faced with such genial lack of support, Arthur and Ford rely upon each other. The chap who hailed from a small planet somewhere near Betelgeuse (rather than Guildford) may have named himself after a small Dagenham-built saloon car that ceased production in 1961, but he is at least a guide and mentor. Dent is half-relieved to have escaped the lower-middle-class earth-bound existence that was on the verge of becoming even duller. Ford knows that regardless of the perils and the bad poetry that may befall them, Arthur will always crave a cup of tea with the determination of the hero of *The Rebel* (Robert Day, 1961) when he is faced with the prospect of frothy coffee. And, despite the 1981 BBC TV adaptation, their journey truly belongs in the space-time continuum that only radio can create.

With thanks to Barry Cryer.

Bibliography

Books

Askey, Arthur (1975), *Before Your Very Eyes: An Autobiography*. London: The Woburn Press.

Braden, Bernard (1990), *The Kindness of Strangers*. London: Hodder & Stoughton.

Feldman, Marty (2016), *Eye Marty: The Newly Discovered Autobiography of a Comic Genius*. Los Angles: Rare Bird Books.

Johnston, Barry (2007), *Round Mr Horne: The Autobiography of Kenneth Horne*. London: Aurum Press.

Kilgarriff, Michael (1998), *Grace, Beauty and Banjos: The Peculiar Lives and Strange Times of Music Hall and Variety Artistes*. London: Oberon Books.

Muir, Frank (1997), *A Kentish Lad; The Autobiography of Frank Muir*. London: Bantam Press.

Pettigrew, Terence (1982), *British Film Character Actors: Great Names and Memorable Moments*. London: David & Charles.

Priestley, J.B. and Cooper, Susan (1970), *J. B. Priestley: Portrait of An Author*. London: Harper & Row.

Street, Seán (2012), *The Poetry of Radio: The Colour of Sound*. Abingdon: Routledge.

Took, Barry (1981), *Laughter in The Air: An Informal History of British Radio Comedy*. London: Robson Books Ltd.

Ustinov, Peter (1979), *Dear Me*. London: Book Club Associates.

Williams, Kenneth and Davies, Russell (ed.) (1993), *The Kenneth Williams Diaries*. London: Harper Collins.

Journals and Periodicals

'Christmas Holiday Shows' (1949), *The Stage*, 30 December, pp. 5.

Diak, Phil (1959), 'Tele-Parade: You Can't Kill Eric Barker', *The Daily Herald*, 21 July.

F.O.H (1963), 'Whatever Happened to Seaside Entertainment?' *Theatre World* pp. 59–60.

'From Our Radio Critic' (1953), *The Guardian*, 25 May, pp. 3.

'Gold To Beat The Cold' (1953), *The Coventry Evening Telegraph*, 4 November, pp. 22.

Hale, Lionel (1953), 'Radio – Partners', *The Observer*, 17 May, pp. 15.

Phillips, Phillip (1955), 'TV Slur on Queen Mother – Viewers Protest', *The Daily Herald*, 3 March, pp. 1.

Rose, Clarkson (1936), 'Pre-adventure – Being More Leaves from a Pro's Logbook', *The Stage*, 13 August, pp. 2.

4

'With Hilarious Consequences': The British Television Sitcom Double Act

In the early 1950s, the principal forms of popular entertainment in Britain were radio, the cinema and the variety-theatre. Since the beginning of the 1960s, the dominance of television has been almost unchallengeable. In the intervening period, television comedy became established as a recognisable entity in its own right, differentiated in form and content from its predecessors. (Goddard 1991: 75)

Hancock: What a pathetic figure must I cut!
Sid: Yes. (*Hancock's Half Hour*, 1959).

Introduction

In 1949, when the BBC television service was just 13 years old, Ray Allister, the critic for *The Sketch*, took a somewhat dyspeptic view of the medium. He bemoaned the concept of the family audience – 'a single creature with four limbs – father mother, little brother and little sister' – and believed the early entertainments were 'reminiscent of Victorian evenings' when 'a good time was had by all the performers'. Allister concluded his diatribe with the warning that television was 'no longer a wonder' and that the medium required 'professionally expert presentation of the best of entertainment' (14 September 1949: 32). By a certain irony, two of the key figures of the following decade when television expanded from a minority service that occupied just a few pages of the *Radio Times* to, by 1957, the most popular broadcast medium in the country, was a prematurely aged would-be Shakespearian and his keeper and confidant. Or, regarding the British situation comedy on TV, all roads lead to East Cheam.

If you happen to view archive television footage of a Variety act of this era on a surviving edition of *Sunday Night at the London Palladium* (ATV, 1955–67)[1] the effect is akin to viewing the routines through a prism. We are often looking at the double act through a distance.

The BBC producer Bill Lyon-Shaw once reflected of early 1950s television that 'we used to do fifteen-minute programmes from Alexandra Palace and we tried everybody. Stand-up comics just didn't work, they "didn't come through the screen"' (quoted in Lewisohn, 2002: 181). This was not always the case, and perhaps it would be more accurate to state that the sitcom was the logical development of the sketch comedies of 1930s Variety and wireless broadcasts. As early as 1954 Frankie Howerd was arguing that 'situation comedy will give me a much better chance' to display his talents (quoted by Butcher, *The Sketch*, 15 December 1954: 36)

Of course, one of the inevitable challenges of compiling such a chapter is the sheer weight of the material. Even if we discount the series that are 'Missing, Believed Wiped' to read Mark Lewisohn's magisterial work of 1998 *The Radio Times Guide to TV Comedy* is to be confronted

---

1   In the words of Dick Fiddy of the British Film Institute: 'It is terrible, just heart-breaking, how much material was either broadcast live or wiped. With *Sunday Night at the London Palladium*, there are many gaps, although we have recently recovered fragments of one show that features Morecambe and Wise. There are more surviving editions of *Blackpool Night Out* (ABC, 1964–65) and recently a lot of programmes made by Jack Hylton were discovered in the attic of one of his theatres.'

by approximately 4 million titles, some of which evoke a nightmare at which even Hammer or Amicus films would quail. So, as a form of filtration, the pairing must have evolved via the sitcom itself and not be an existing act adopting to the format such as Arthur Askey and Richard Murdoch, who appeared in *Living it Up* for Associated Rediffusion in 1958. Secondly, it must have been written 'purely as a piece of television and not as a photographed comedy sketch' (Hodinott, *The Stage*, 5 February 1959: 6).

Thirdly, it must be a comedy of narrative rather than domestic routines within a Variety format, à la Alfred Marks and Paddy O'Neil in *Alfred Marks' Time* (A-R, 1956–61), and fourthly it has to be a true double act rather than a lead comic and a regular sidekick. This rule means the exclusion of the likes of Terry-Thomas and Peter Butterworth in *How Do You View* (BBC, 1950–52) or Charlie Drake and Henry McGee in *The Worker* (ATV, 1965–70). Fifthly, it is quite noticeable that several of the established and oft-repeated examples of the genre do not follow the double-act formula. Barry Cryer remarks that the highlight of *Till Death Us Do Part* (BBC, 1965–75) was the interplay between Warren Mitchell's Alf Garnett and Anthony Booth's Mike Rawlins (the 'Randy Scouse Git'), exacerbated by the actors' off-screen antipathy ('they did not get on'). But Johnny Speight's scripts often take the form of a monologue from Alf with Booth, Dandy Nichols, Anthony Booth and Una Stubbs acting as a Greek chorus. *Only Fools and Horses* (BBC, 1981–2003) is less of a paring of David Jason and Nicholas Lyndhurst as John Sullivan created a world that was closer to the trio format of the Will Hay/Moore Marriott/Graham Moffat films.

And, most importantly, the duo must be regarded by their public as one indivisible entity, thanks to that vital combination of cast and writers, no matter their theatrical or cinematic hinterland and any glittering accolades they may subsequently gain for their screen or stage work. You might now be invited to open supermarkets, appear on comedy panel shows that made *Blankety Blank* resemble *Blithe Spirit* (David Lean, 1944) in terms of wit or be invited to inform the nation, via the pages of the *TV Times*, of your favoured recipe for apple crumble. You would also be asked, when in public, where 'your other half' was – 'people really did believe that Yootha and I were married' mused Brian Murphy of *George and Mildred*. 'Perhaps viewers were more naïve then.'

To appear as one half of a successful sitcom double act was also sometimes to alter your screen persona. When *To the Manor Born* (BBC, 1979–81) was first aired, Penelope Keith's popular image was already established with BBC audiences, but Peter Bowles had spent many years portraying 'foreign' villains for ITC; his smooth-sinister Egyptian police chief in *Danger Man* (1960–66) or KGB agent in *The Saint* (1964–67) was often the highlight of this week's thrilling adventure. In *To the Manor Born*, Peter Spence and Christopher Bond created two deceptively multi-faceted characters: if Audrey fforbes-Hamilton is brittle and vulnerable, Richard DeVere knows that for all his carefully assumed manners, the Establishment will always know that he was born Bedrich Polouvica. The programme was vastly successful – 'almost 2.4 million people watched the finale of the first series – the biggest audience for any non-live event of the 1970' (Sandbrook, 2015: 164) – because it was never about stock characters who might have populated a lesser programme. The key to the series is when Audrey is berating DeVere for not knowing what it is like to lose one's home, Bowles replies with quiet dignity, 'Yes – in Czechoslovakia in 1939.'

Alas, we will still need to find a modicum of space for those sitcom pairings that abide in the memory in the manner of lingering gout and which sane people would only view à la Malcolm McDowell in *A Clockwork Orange* (Stanley Kubrick, 1971). There are the middle- or upper-class ITV sitcoms wasting the talents of Donald Sinden, his butler to Elaine Stritch's US author in *Two's Company* (London Weekend, 1975–79) and the dreaded *Never the Twain* (Thames, 1981–91). The latter essentially consisted of antique-dealing shenanigans, face-pulling and theatrical shouting from Sir Donald and Windsor Davies. The show officially ran for ten years, but each of the sixty-seven editions seemed to have a running time of approximately two centuries. There was *Yus, My Dear* (London Weekend, 1976) with any amount of 'would-be matey condescension' (Holt, *The Stage*, 16 December 1976: 25) by Arthur Mullard and Queenie Watts.

And then there was *Love Thy Neighbour* (Thames, 1972–76), and over seven seasons of fifty-four episodes, a fine cast did their utmost to breathe life into Vince Powell and Harry Driver scripts that chiefly involved witless insults delivered at maximum volume every week. At the time of writing, the show still has its adherents, who like to cite its original viewing figures as proof that the Great British Public still craves a return to the happier times of the three-day week, power cuts and casual racism on a daily basis.[2] Leon Hunt expresses how 'there is more than a note of hysteria in *Love Thy Neighbour* – it can't begin to contain what it wants to see as harmless fun; its violent subject constantly threatens to break through' (2013: 55).[3] But long after the final episode was transmitted Jack Smethurst and Rudolph Walker, two very fine actors, are still associated with the 'humour' of warring next-door neighbours, trapped in a weekly cycle of abuse, grim workplaces, grimmer pubs, and more abuse. It is an image that continues to abide in the public memory, even if the footage is even more depressing than you ever imagined. But then whoever said that the sitcom double act was always about comedy?

Hancock's Half Hour: Setting the template

Thus, we mercifully turn to *Hancock's Half Hour* (BBC 1956–60). It established so many of the core tropes of the British sitcom for the next six decades, including that of entrapment (Barry Cryer: 'that key element

---

2 Beware anyone who claims that said show had them 'rolling around on the floor' in laughter as this might be the side effect of storing gallons of nitrous oxide in their basement.

3 'Contrary to the belief in national tolerance and in the power of laughter to defuse tension, these programmes tend to enhance prejudice and exacerbate racial discrimination. Children in schools now refer to their black compatriots as "Nig-nogs" (*Love Thy Neighbour*)' (Mahoney, *The Stage*, 2 October 1975: 10).

for a great comedy – two characters trapped in a certain situation') and mutual dependency. It 'explored existential themes of suburban torpor (a kind of Kafka with cupcakes)' (Bracewell, 5 May 2002) and it was 'organic comedy', that piquant phrase of Frank Muir that he employed to describe the work of a writer or writers whose mindset and talent could never be duplicated (quoted in McCann, 2006: 276–77). Ray Galton and Alan Simpson also created a world in which one of the protagonists both aspired to respectability and feared to plummet into a blue-collar abyss, echoing the post-war fears of the lower middle classes, as expressed by the historians Roy Lewis and Angus Maude:

> It is one thing to elevate increasing numbers of working-class folk into lower-middle-class company: this, after all, is a kind of compliment, and if the newcomers can stand the strain and establish themselves they – or their children – will be accepted. But to a process of levelling down – of forcibly merging the lower- middle class with the proletariat – resistance must be expected. (Lewis and Maude, 1950: 358)

These were also the fears of Captain George Mainwaring and of Basil Fawlty screaming about 'Proles!' in cod-David Niven tones while Bob Ferris ruefully completes the perils, as well as the advantages, of ascending the corporate ladder. Outside of the front door of 23 Railway Cuttings Hancock's attempts at social elevation are forever mocked and hindered by the other half of one of the finest double acts this country has ever produced and in the words of the comedy historian John Fisher:

> Stylistically Hancock and James were nothing like Laurel and Hardy, let alone any of the stereotyped combinations of low comedian and straight man that had crowded the variety stage since its heyday. However, in another sense the couple from East Cheam *did* correspond to Stan and Ollie. For British audiences they represented the most popular comic association to come along since the little fellow from Lancashire and the big guy from Georgia hit the big time. Not even

the soon-to-be successful combination of Eric Morecambe and Ernie Wise hit the same note. (2008: 284)

As a further sign of how the pair were inextricably linked in the minds of the public, Hancock and James even appeared in a strip cartoon in *Film Fun* magazine; by that time the 38-year-old publication had started to augment its staple diet of screen heroes with television stars. The drawings of the pair in 23 Railway Cuttings firmly placed them in the tradition of the title's previous stars – Laurel and Hardy, Abbott and Costello, Arthur Askey and Richard Murdoch or Old Mother Riley and Kitty McShane.[4]

On the wireless, Hancock was the patriarch of a retinue of characters, but the technical limitations meant that it would have been impossible for the full radio cast to make the transition to television. Bill Kerr was dropped entirely, there is only one surviving edition with Kenneth Williams as a faintly alarming-looking 'Snide' in *The Alpine Holiday* (1957), and Hattie Jacques appears in only a few editions. It was Sidney James, one of British cinema's finest and most ubiquitous character actors, one who had previously worked with Powell and Pressburger, Alec Guinness and Dame Gwen Ffrangcon-Davies, who was to become Hancock's 'friend, confidant, manager and owner'.

As Goddard points out, 'almost completely inexperienced in television comedy, Galton, Simpson (Duncan) Wood [the TV show's producer] and Hancock probably did not set out to create a comic style based on facial and reaction comedy, but all of them recognised its potential very soon' (1991: 82). The medium also allowed the viewers to appreciate the full moth-eaten grandeur of Anthony Aloysius St John Hancock, who dressed like a West End actor-manager of the previous generation, and

---

4 John Osborne wrote affectionately of the publication's 'cramped little drawings' and how the final tableau was often the comedy heroes 'sitting down in triumph to a blow-out in a posh restaurant surrounded by attentive waiters. Diamond tie-pins as big as pebbles sparkled above napkins tucked into their collars as they brandished knives and forks in front of a gorgeous mountain of mashed potatoes studded with sizzling sausages pointing outwards, like batteries of guns on a battle cruiser' (1981: 81).

of 23 Railway Cuttings itself. In the early 1950s, Frank Muir and Dennis Norden were asked by the BBC to evaluate *The Adventures of Ozzie and Harriet* as an example of 'situation comedy', and they rapidly concluded that such affluent jollity could never work with a British audience.[5]

Back at Railway Cuttings Hancock paces a mildewed living room packed with Victorian debris, his manner displaying no sense of unnecessary jolliness - and emphatically no 'hello darling I'm home!' Roger Lewis saw 'the black and white gloom and blurry tuning' as 'apt, too, for the mood' (1994: 324) but Hancock is eager to join the late 1950s as described by Harry Hopkins: 'Affluence came hurrying on the heels of penury. Suddenly, the shops were piled high with all sorts of goods. Boom was in the air' (1964: 234). Surely this brave new world required a man of Hancock's calibre, and he would at long last take his place in the haute suburbia of Cheam rather than residing in its downmarket shadow. He joins the local council, is elected the foreman of a jury, engages in amateur dramatics, plans a carnival and always does his utmost to remind the world that he is a true renaissance man. 'Sid' was often on hand to remind Hancock of his many and various limitations.

In 1955 the sociologist Geoffrey Gorer saw grumbling as to be possibly considered by the British as 'the verbal counterpart of envy and, like envy, justified and free from guilt; few observers I think would question that grumbling is not infrequent in the English scene' (290–91). It is the stock in trade of Hancock's Half Hour and is often combined by the 'strain of guileful rudeness', which is so often a feature of British national life (Gilliatt, 1990:149). This is especially to the fore when Hancock is confronted with late 1950s modernity – automated cafes, self-service laundrettes that are prone to failure – but he remains guardedly optimistic for the future while Sid is an amiable fatalist: 'Eat, drink and be merry, for tomorrow we snuff it'.

J.B. Priestley saw the screen Hancock as 'somebody close to "mass man" of today, coming out of the faceless crowd, hopeful, near to glory

---

5   The programme ran from 1952 to 1966 and it is indeed a strange sitcom in which Ozzie Nelson (a) appears to have fathered two children by osmosis and (b) has no clear professional role apart from going to the store to buy some more ice cream.

for some minutes, before the lid comes on again, before he shrugs his way back into the dark' (1975: 170). At least Sid will be waiting back home at Railway Cuttings, probably having discovered Hancock's secret store of gin into the bargain. In the 1930s and 1940s, Will Hay specialised in depictions of lower-middle-class ineptitude that forever undermined his pretensions to grandeur – the mortarboard of the latter was as essential as the theatrical Homburg of the former. But Hay's look was one of 'Dickensian fruitiness and Greenian seediness' (Durgnat, 1970: 206) while Hancock saw the world as a constant round of 'minute humiliation' (1970: 208).

If you read virtually any biography of Tony Hancock, one constantly quoted refrain is that he 'did not want a double act' with Sidney James, but to the viewing public they were just that. A letter to *The Guardian* of 7 December 1959 was headed 'James Half-Hour' and argued 'yet clever comedy team that they are, it is impossible to divide the honours; both should share star-billing' (pp. 8). In that same year, the critic of *The Stage* wrote that 'Mr James cannot be regarded as a stooge to Mr Hancock, for his place in the show is far more important than leaving openings for the principal comedian (Hodinott, 5 February 1959: 6). One can imagine Hancock's reaction to such missives and Philip Oakes, his friend and co-writer of *The Punch and Judy Man* (Jeremy Summers, 1962) reflected that 'he had the temperament and the ego of a great star. He was a perfectionist and a born worrier. Anything – or anyone – which stood between him and some so-far-unimaged goal had to be removed' (1975: 37).

Sidney James was never billed in the opening credits, but by the late 1950s, his cartoon or image in the closing titles was almost as prominent as the star. Not that the actor craved star billing either on television or in his pre-*Carry On* film career. James preferred to be listed below the title and in a 1960 interview he explained:

'Look at me,' he says, 'I'm in work all the time at the moment – I'm lucky. What happens if someone decides to shove my name up there above the title? You don't stay a star as long as you stay a character actor – and I'd much rather stay in work than be left with a "star" tag and nothing to justify it.' (Quoted in Masidlover, *The Stage*, 20 October 1960:11).

In short, James saw himself as a character actor for hire, and in *Hancock's Half Hour* his contribution to the show was augmented by straight actors – John Le Mesurier chief among them – as a part of a regular repertory company of performers. Hancock once stated to Patrick Cargill that he enjoyed working with 'real actors' as 'I'm able to rebound so much more because I've got real people there' (quoted in Webber, 2005: 166).[6] It was Sid James alone of the wireless show's supporting cast who had the opportunity to transform his character gradually; he became less the spiv of the early radio editions to the hero's cynical best friend or even brother figure. But by the end of 1959, Tony Hancock decided to dispense with James together with the East Cheam setting, and he subsequently wrote in his notes for an autobiography that:

> I must say it angered me to be asked why I had 'got rid' of Sidney James and before him people like Hattie Jacques and Kenneth Williams and Bill Kerr. You would have thought I had ruined their futures, but 'Hancock's Half Hour' was only a phase in their lives, a stepping stone to other things just as it was for me. I no more go rid of Sid than I got rid of myself. (Quoted in Fisher, 2008: 292–93).

Perhaps one of the finest examples of James' importance to Hancock's world is with 1960's *The Reunion Party*. The setting is simple – Hancock is staging an army reunion party for Second World War comrades who he has not seen in fifteen years while Sid observes in mild alarm as Hancock spends about ten weeks' wages on a party for his erstwhile wartime colleagues. By now we are far removed from the Variety format

---

6   Without undervaluing Cargill's contribution as the radio producer in *The Bowmans* and the doctor in *The Blood Donor*, it is possible to imagine the underplaying, precisely spoken Williams of *Carry On Nurse* (Gerald Thomas, 1959) in the latter role just as Hattie could have played the sister instead of June Whitfield.

of the funny man undermining the status of the straight man; we are establishing the groundwork for a clash between myth and reality. As Oakes argued:

> There was no doubt that Hancock was loved. But the character he projected was far from lovable. He was vain, he was pompous he was a bully. But the neurosis, the grumbles, the psychic warts which he displayed were common to three-quarters of the island race. He was truly representative and so he could be excused. (1975: 34)

And in 1960 there were still countless regimental reunions, with faded banners and diminished hopes of the future.[7] At Pinewood Studios Jack Hawkins was recruiting his less-than-gallant *League of Gentlemen* (Basil Dearden) so that they might rekindle their wartime professionalism by robbing a bank, but Hancock's plans are both self-aggrandising and sincere. He explains to Sid:

> It's not a question of clinging on to the past. It was the wonderful feeling we had in those days. A bunch of young chaps, thrown together from all walks of life, were joined together with a sense of purpose, mutual respect, and bound by a deep everlasting friendship that time will never erase.

Sid, in his deadpan fashion, senses the danger of this self-delusion from the outset and one of the key elements to *The Reunion Party* is his weather-beaten face looking progressively glummer as the event slowly disintegrates. Inevitably one of the guests (Cardew Robinson) is now a clergyman, but for Smudger and Ginger (Hugh Lloyd and Clive Dunn), their uniformed past was an aspect of their lives that was to be dispensed with as soon as the first de-mob suits were issued. Their military service was their sole common reference point, and now the former comrades respond to Hancock's hospitality with resigned apathy, casually

---

7   It is arguably a universal scenario. Galton and Simpson famously met in a TB sanatorium, today the equivalent would be a Facebook-inspired school reunion.

destroying the memories of past camaraderie their host had so carefully built as his defence against a grey present. As the half hour unfolds the party continues with much staring at the floor and yawning silences that Harold Pinter might have appreciated. If Hancock's attempts to convince East Cheam of his creative and professional talents have come to little, and much of contemporary life is incomprehensible – 'You're all raving mad!' – then surely, he will be able to bathe in the reflected glory of an imagined past? But Sid knows that this will only bring misery.

Perhaps the finest tribute to Sidney James is that the 1961 series *Hancock*, which featured *The Blood Donor* and *The Bowmans*, succeeded despite his absence. Galton and Simpson wrote a cameo for him in *The Rebel* (Robert Day, 1960), but Hancock spurned this idea, while one of the most memorable scenes in *The Punch and Judy Man* (Jeremy Summers, 1963) takes place in a pseudo-American ice cream parlour. Behind the counter, and presiding over the Piltdown Glories[8] is Eddie Byrne, whose sardonic grin is so reminiscent of James that one wonders if Hancock was unconsciously thinking of his former partner when he co-wrote the script with Philip Oakes. The film also benefits immeasurably from Hancock's scenes with John Le Mesurier's Sandman; for the first time, he plays the hero's friend rather than the symbol of bemused officialdom. The moment when the quiet melancholy Sandman gently advises Wally as to what is expected of a husband infers how the two could have been teamed in a series of comedies or dramas, but this was not to happen. Around this time there was a chance of a Gerald Thomas-directed vehicle for both, but Hancock turned the film down (Oakes, 1975: 54).[9] Hancock and James did temporarily reunite in 1965 for a Decca LP version of *The Missing Page* and *The Reunion Party*, but by now the former's timing was a shadow of his earlier heights.

---

8   'Two scoops of luscious vanilla, two scoops of flaky chocolate, succulent sliced bananas, juicy peach fingers swimming in pure cane sugar. Butterfat cream and a cherry!'

9   Given Gerald Thomas's approach to the art of subtle comedy, this may have been a mixed blessing.

John Fisher also describes how the comic thought that there were times 'when he felt cheated of his real identity' (2008: 105), an observation echoed by Barry Cryer, who remarks that 'Hancock wanted to prove he did not need Sid and that he existed beyond his writers. He was afraid that had no existence beyond East Cheam'. By the end of the 1950s, Ray Galton and Alan Simpson had, together with Frank Muir and Denis Norden, become rare examples of comedy scriptwriters in the public eye; their images were as prominent as that of Sidney James in the closing title sequence of *Hancock's Half Hour*. Clive James wrote of Ian Clements and Dick Le Frenais's scripts for *Going Straight* (BBC, 1978), more of which below, as a prime example of how:

> The secret of successful comedy is so often looked for in the wrong place. The actor's personality matters, but last and least. First and foremost comes the work at the typewriter. It is because people have thought long and hard through many drafts that Norman Fletcher or Basil Fawlty can be convincing with a single gesture. (*The Observer*, 26 March 1978: 27).

Post-1959 Sidney James starred in a succession of sitcoms, but none could equate with life in East Cheam and although he appeared in the *Carry On* films performing with the same degree of absolute professionalism that was his hallmark there was little evidence of his sense of inspiration in his scenes with Tony Hancock. In 1958 James wrote to the BBC that he would rather die than miss being in *Hancock's Half Hour* – it has hard to imagine the actor having the same degree of passion for *Carry On Girls* (Gerald Thomas, 1973).

It is also intriguing, albeit totally futile, to speculate how the Hancock/James dynamic might have altered over time, had their partnership not been fractured. Dick Clement and Ian La Frenais' *The Likely Lads* (BBC, 1964–66) ended with Terry (James Bolam) joining the army and when the series was revived as *Whatever Happened to The Likely Lads* (1973–74) he is aggrieved at what he has missed – and how time has changed without him. Bob (Rodney Bewes) is now on the rungs of the corporate ladder, and if his car is a second-hand Vauxhall Viva HB, it is still far beyond anything that either could have aspired to own when they were working on the factory floor. But Bob is frequently plagued with self-doubt – 'Suddenly the past seems so much larger, and the future is shrinking. And I haven't got time for the present' – and Terry sometimes appears quite lost.

As is so often the way, one of the finest summaries of *Whatever Happened to The Likely Lads* comes from Clive James. He thought that Bob's 'friendship with Terry will never cease: Damon and Pythias, Castor and Pollux, perhaps even Butch and Sundance, but never – not in a million years – *Alias Smith and Jones* (BBC2), which is typical American TV in that the buddies have no past' (*The Observer*, 11 March 1972: 8). But its nature would change over time. Dick Clement saw the sequel as exploring the nuances of the two characters:

> The Lads have become more introspective. While Bob sees himself climbing the social ladder, Terry – the lazy sod that he is – feels this is working-class betrayal. There's a great deal of hypocrisy because Bob is progressing in life and he isn't. Because he's stuck in a time-warp, he falls back on the cosy clichés of class betrayal and not seeing the need for improving oneself. But all Bob is trying to do, in a very modest way, is better himself. (Quoted in Webber with Clement and La Frenais, 1999: 91)

From the outset, both men were haunted by memories of a recent childhood and youth that now seem unattainably distant – the 1964 *Christmas Night with The Stars* sketch has the duo arguing about Rupert Bear annuals. By the 1970s Terry is equally discomfited by his friend's impending marriage to the ultra-bourgeois Thelma (Brigit Forsyth), Bob's ill-advised Jason King hairstyle and the demolition of the totems of his twenties.

It is pleasant to speculate how such a scenario might have worked in East Cheam – perhaps Sid temporarily relocating abroad only to find on his return Hancock in stable employment and about to marry Ms Pugh (Hattie Jacques) if only to avoid what became, in the words of Bob

Monkhouse, 'The Hancock Story'. Fragments of the comic's latter-day career abound; the few remaining minutes of his 1967 'Swinging London' nightclub comedy *Hancock's* is a rare example of feeling gratitude for ABC Television's policy of tape-wiping while the three episodes of his 1968 Australian television series should be shunned forever. *Hancock's Half Hour*, maybe more than any other programme in this chapter, is a fusion of indivisible elements: the writers, Wally Stott's lugubrious theme tune, Ray Cozens's creation of 23 Railway Cuttings' front parlour and the stars. *Paul Merton in Galton and Simpson's ...*(Central 1996–97), including remakes of *12 Angry Men, The Radio Ham* and *The Bedsitter*, was proof, if further proof was ever really needed, that Tony Hancock was as irreplaceable as Galton and Simpson – or as Sid James.

Steptoe and Son: 'I Can't Get Away'

As the world knows, *Steptoe and Son* evolved from the play *The Offer*, which was one of ten editions of BBC TV's *Galton and Simpson's Comedy Playhouse* (1961–62). It was aired on 4 January 1962 and for a generation brought up on the repeats of the episodes made between 1970 and 1974, the sight of Harold's desperation and his father's reaction is not so much shocking as a sight that makes you wish to turn away from the screen. There is none of Harry H. Corbett's leering, of Wilfrid Brambell's snarled Irish-cockney responses – just a growing reaction of how delusions can create snares. It is the first four series of *Steptoe and Son*, made between 1962 and 1965, that created the series legacy:

> Alan Simpson and Ray Galton have created two very funny characters. But I like the way these two have kept control of these creations and have not allowed them to dissolve into two clowns. Albert and Harold know that life is not all joviality and because they are very human, they feel the knocks and bruises of life even as you or I. (Edmund, *The Stage*, 7 October 1965: 12)

Furthermore, although the show is extremely unusual in having a complete surviving run, the black and white episodes went unrepeated for many years. The video and subsequent DVD release of the early episodes allow the opportunity to appreciate that this was a programme that employed actors as opposed to 'comedy actors' in a programme where the writers were top-billed. Corbett was an alumnus of Joan Littlewood's Theatre Workshop, although British cinema did not know quite how to best use his talents. He was a quietly menacing heavy in the sorely underrated Ealing film noir *Nowhere to Go* (Seth Holt, 1958), but his 'Maltese' gangster in *The Shakedown* (John Lemont, 1959) was a pantomime demon with a Spanish-Mancunian accent, and there are no words to describe his eponymous *Cover Girl Killer* (Terry Bishop, 1959).

Brambell was a graduate of the Abbey and Gate theatres in Dublin, and by the 1950s he was frequently seen on television playing characters far older than his age. Both actors also paid their dues at the Merton Park Studios B-film factory, Brambell playing a very Albert Steptoe-like lock-keeper in *The Sinister Man* (Clive Donner, 1961) and almost unrecognisable as the pedantic school teacher in *Urge to Kill* (Vernon Sewell, 1960). Corbett anticipated some of Harold's bluster as a devious estate agent in *Time to Remember* (Charles Jarrott, 1962), but his police Superintendent in *Wings of Death* (Allan Davis, 1961) was less successful, as the actor assumed a Scottish patois with overtones of Lord Rockinghim XI's *Hoots Mon*.

The backgrounds of neither actor anticipated the claustrophobic domestic hell of Oil Drum Lane. Albert displays a constant sense of trepidation, which pervades the first four seasons and undercuts the security of catchphrases such as 'You dirty old man'; Harold is well built and very uncertain of temper. With Old Mother Riley, there was never any physical threat from Bridget – indeed officials of all sizes quailed before Lucan's creation – but in *Steptoe and Son* it could be that Albert has taken to using psychological warfare out of a sense of fear of his adult son. There is the additional subtext that Harold once escaped into National Service – but he came back. Perhaps he had nowhere left to return to, perhaps he was already so tied to his established existence, but the result is still a comic-tragic dependency, exacerbated by the younger Steptoe's aspirations. Hancock had developed an air of resilience to stave off any self-doubt, but Harold seems lacking in even these resources.

The historian Arthur Marwick argues that the events between 1958 and 1974 'transformed social and cultural developments for the rest of the century' (1998: 5). Corbett's junkman is vaguely aware of these changes – if only he can break free of Oil Drum Lane and take part in transforming Britain. Of all the younger Steptoe's many failures to escape his prison, it is the disastrous West End night out in 'Sixty-Five Today' (1963) that shows writers and cast at their absolute peak. Steptoe *fils* celebrates his father officially becoming an OAP with a pair of leather gloves and, ominously, a night 'up West'. Throughout the evening Albert clings with a little too much malice to his avowed proletarian roots while Harold is too involved with living a Sunday Colour Supplement existence if only for one evening, to notice his father's growing irritation and eventual distress.

Throughout the series, Steptoe Senior is self-assured of his place within his realm while Junior is not so far removed from Joe Orton's Edna Wellthorpe writing spoof letters suffused with advertising terminology: 'Dear Sir, I recently purchased a tin of Morton's blackcurrant pie filling. It was delicious. Choc-full of rich fruit' (quoted in Lahr, 1987: 137). Likewise, when we hear Harold inform Albert that 'Your mere presence tends to impinge upon my aesthetic pleasures and moments of relaxation,' it is obvious he has been carefully rehearsing these rich-sounding phrases for weeks. In his lair, he almost certainly has a copy of *Queen* magazine from 15 September 1959 and can quote, word for word, from the article that urged 'We don't want you to miss it. Don't wait till years after to realise you have lived in a remarkable age – the age of BOOM!' (quoted in Walker, 1974:131). In 'Sixty-Five Today' Harold can finally experience this realm while his father may reflect in his consumerist glory, the celebration culminating in a Chinese restaurant[10] when Harold is too engrossed in ordering from a menu that

---

10 Eateries are fertile ground for the comedy of embarrassment with the often socially insecure protagonists subjecting themselves to ritual humiliation and paying handsomely for their misery.

he has learned by rote to notice his father's pride in his original gift. The gloves were more than enough by themselves, but son lacks the insight and the self-confidence to realise this.

The setting of the programme, for all its memorably seedy qualities, was never the key element of its success – compare *Steptoe* with *Nearest and Dearest* (Granada 1968–72), the sitcom about a brother and sister running a pickle factory. Fiddy believes that 'siblings give a different, interesting, dynamic' to the sitcom double act, even if James Preston of *The Stage* did not mask his disdain when he claimed the show was 'an extended music hall joke aimed at – dare I say it – a working-class audience of the flat hat and shirtsleeves variety' (21 May 1970: 17). With *Nearest and Dearest* the fascination was less the North Country urban environment and lines such as 'I haven't touched his blandishments!' and more with how Jimmy Jewel and Hylda Baker did resemble dysfunctional family members in that they so clearly loathed each other and did their utmost to step on each other's lines.

Galton and Simpson's scripts also lack much of the self-conscious folksiness of Roy Clarke's stories for *Open All Hours* (BBC, 1973–85). Ronnie Barker and David Jason's chemistry as Arkwright and Granville, and such lines as 'I hate that scrunching sound errand boys make when you have to stand on them' cannot quite mask the shopkeeper's miserable nature. Back at the junkyard, Albert is grasping, venal, sharp-witted, frail and lonely and Harold is aspirational, vindictive, incredibly vulnerable and always hopeful. Alan Simpson once pointed out that:

> We didn't sit down and decide to write a show about something that needed to be said. But if you are writing about real people in real situations, this inevitably comes into it and people say 'Ah, social significance!' But it is not deliberately socially significant. The first thing is that it's got to be funny. That's not a cop-out, it's a starting point. (Quoted in McCann, 2006: 274)

The strengths of *Steptoe and Son* were much those of *Hancock's Half Hour* before it – the writers' insight and the cast's interpretation of their work.

Albert and Harold need each other, even if the latter would rarely admit it and even if the former was prone to accompanying his bath with pickled onions.

Uniformed Comedy

There were three principal reasons why sitcoms in uniform were popular with programme-makers, the first being that the last National Serviceman was demobbed as recently as 1963. Conscription was far from universally popular: even the War Office's *A Guide for the National Service Man* dating from 1953 states that 'in this country, it [conscription] is still regarded as an innovation and interruption the normal course of life' (quoted in Weight, 2002: 108). Memories of service, of semi-insane NCOs demanding that whitewashed coal, were common to vast swathes of the male population. A second is that an institution creates its own rules within a self-contained realm and the third is that a uniform automatically creates its own assumptions, be they official or work-related. Ronald Wolfe observed that when he and his writing partner Ronald Chesney created *On the Buses* (1969–73) 'We felt the uniform would be useful; immediate recognition would tell the audience quickly about his character much of his character and background' (2003: 61). There was also the fact that even if the audience had not experienced service in the forces, they would often be all too aware of the drab authoritarianism of everyday life. In 1960 'a youth club leader in Huddersfield with six years' experience was dismissed for allowing his charges to play billiards, table tennis and darts and listen to rock and roll music' (Sandbrook, 2005:128).

Granada's *Bootsie and Snudge* (1960–63), a spin-off from the conscription comedy *The Army Game* (1957–63), took the private soldier and the bullying NCO into civilian life in a gentleman's club. The writers Barry Took and Marty Feldman saw their dramatic and comic potential

– 'more than the cardboard cut-outs earlier scripts sometimes suggested' (Took, 1990: 80) – and the writers understood that post-demob the duo needed a quasi-military setting for their relationship to flourish. The gruff NCO and the recalcitrant recruit or subordinate were familiar from countless Variety sketches but with Private Montague 'Bootsie' Biseley and Sergeant Claud Snudge, Took saw the potential beyond military parody:

> While they were in the Army the same set of rules governed them both, and both were bound by them. They could avoid them or get round them, but ultimately their actions were controlled by the greater authority of the Army. In civilian life that authority does not exist and while the Army chained them together, civvy street freed them. Why then, we asked, should these two men, complete opposites in character and temperament, stay together? (Took, 1990: 81)

The comic timing of Alfie Bass and Bill Fraser permitted the audience to overlook the fact that Private Montague 'Bootsie' Bisley had been demobbed from National Service at the somewhat advanced age of 44. The setting also allowed Took and Feldman to explore the two characters: 'Bootsie, aware of his mental shortcomings, tries his best to come up to the standard of Snudge, whose intelligence, we discover, has a thin veneer over it and who plots all the time not for it to be discovered' (*The Stage*, 27 October 1960: 10). The club is both institutional prison and safe refuge, and some of the most memorable stories have the pair squabbling within their room.

To the misadventures of *Bootise and Snudge*, one could add Paul Greenwood and Tony Haygarth in the police sitcom *Rosie* (BBC, 1977–81) and countless others, but the uniformed sitcom that has dominated the corporation's schedules for over fifty years is, of course, *Dad's Army* (1968–77). The catchphrases,[11] the two resident double acts of Frank Williams's vicar and Edward Sinclair's verger, plus Arthur Lowe

---

11 No, I'm not going to list them here. Tune into BBC2 on a Saturday evening and you are almost certainly bound to hear them.

and John Le Mesurier achieved fame to such an extent that 'like the great comic creations of Shakespeare and Dickens, these characters took on a life of their own' (Richards, 1997: 334). The platoon members are not caricatures or mere props for the writers' easy hooks for the studio audience but characters who transcended their era. Arthur Lowe, who played Captain Mainwaring, was a character actor so respected that Lindsay Anderson once stated that he would never make a film without him. Prior to *Dad's Army*, Lowe was lauded as one of the masters of comic alderman-like pomposity and hidden sensitivity, as demonstrated by his Leonard Swindley, the touchingly vulnerable haberdasher of *Coronation Street* (1960–present). He was the solicitor's clerk and prosecutor of Bill Maitland in the original John Osborne's *Inadmissible Evidence*, and by 1967 Joe Orton ranted into his diary that '*ERPINGHAM* is the best (stage) play of mine performed so far. If only Arthur Lowe were playing Erpingham they'd all be raving' (quoted in Lahr, 1984: 129). The actor took every one of the opportunities presented to him by Jimmy Perry and David Croft to create a quixotic hero and an officer of the utmost integrity.

Perry wrote in his memoirs of how during the last days of the Second World War he clashed with a cockney-accented ENSA Captain and took revenge by chalking 'NO COMMON MEN AS OFFICERS!' throughout the troop ship. The commanding officer paraded the men and after issuing a reprimand, stated that:

'Now, I just want to say one thing; the British army has no class barrier. When a man has three pips on his shoulder, he has earned that commission and he is entitled to respect, even if he is a com–'. He stopped, realising what he was about to say. There was a pause for about three seconds, then the whole deck exploded with laughter. (2002: 228–9).

That was the nightmare that was ever-present with Mainwaring, for if his bibulous commercial traveller sibling Barry (another tour de force performance from Lowe) in 'My Brother and I' (1975) shows how much Mainwaring has left his background, the captain still never quite believes in his considerable achievements. As Raymond Durgnat once wrote of the film *Sapphire* (Basil Dearden, 1959), 'respectability is not a trivial issue as its absence can have real consequences' (1997: 34) – especially for those negotiating the lower slopes of the middle classes. In films, Terry-Thomas hid his lower-middle-class background with a display of highly polished caddishness and carefully rehearsed vowels, but this route would have been unthinkable to Mainwaring. His journey from office boy to manager is the reward for self-discipline, and you can imagine the younger George quoting from Samuel Smiles: 'Progress, of the best kind, is comparatively slow. Great results cannot be achieved at once; and we must be satisfied to advance in life as we walk, step by step' (1859/1887: 44). But elevation beyond the ranks of black-coated clerks is not enough for Mainwaring, and if the Walmington-on-Sea Home Guard is a form of compensation for a barren home life, sometimes the strain is too obvious. In the 1970 episode 'Mum's Army' Mainwaring's desire for a new relationship – for which he is prepared to sacrifice everything he has strived for – displays his sheer loneliness.

When *Dad's Army* was first aired in 1968, it also attempted to capture that most remote of all eras, the recent past. Angela Moreton of *The Stage* wrote that:

> As a subject, *Dad's Army* had not the slightest appeal to me, partly because it seemed to belong to the blind spot in time, when something is not quite old enough to be history but old enough to be old hat. But this first episode by Jimmy Perry and by David Croft, who also produced it, had me in stitches. (8 August: 12).

When researching the series, Perry found little material about the Home Guard and *Dad's Army* served as a tribute to their work. It also created one of television's abiding double acts, with Sergeant Wilson serving as a fixed point in Mainwaring's circumvented universe. John Le Mesurier was an actor capable of infinite variations and patinas on middle- and upper-class bewilderment: the nervous psychiatrist in *Private's Progress*

(John Boulting, 1956) or, on television, various members of the Establishment who encounter Tony Hancock. In the 1950s he could also be found in the netherworld of the British B-feature, running the nightclub[12] *The Blue Parrot* (John Harlow, 1953) and playing the superintendent in charge of *The Drayton Case* (Ken Hughes, 1953), the first of Merton Park Studio's *Scotland Yard* series. Mention should also be made of his cat-obsessed religious fundamentalist in *Time to Kill* (Charles Saunders, 1955), although the worst miscasting of Le Mesurier's career was probably as an Italian priest in the MGM-British vehicle for Eric Sykes, *Village of Daughters* (George Pollock, 1962).

Such strange use of master character actors was par for the course with British cinema[13] and among Le Mesurier's prolific output – he made thirteen feature films in 1959 alone – were performances of insight, menace and pathos. Beneath the face of a human Eeyore lay the grieving father in *Jigsaw* (Val Guest, 1962), his rants about a wayward daughter crumbling in the face of news from a police inspector. Le Mesurier shared with Arthur Lowe a gift for creating and defining a character with mere seconds of screen time while a lesser actor would struggle with a running time of two hours – one thinks of the disdainful store manager in *Never Let Go* (John Guillermin, 1960), swatting away the inadequate commercial traveller of Richard Todd.

In short, John Le Mesurier was one of the great actors who were too often taken for granted, and when Penelope Gilliatt reviewed *The Wrong Arm of The Law* (Cliff Owen, 1962) she paid tribute to his skills:

We get so used to actors who seem to be in every home-produced comedy that we probably don't realise how skilful some of them are; John Le Mesurier, for instance. He has a marvellous wincing distaste about the rest of the world, as though it was a child making a noise when he has a splitting headache. (*The Observer*, 17 March 1963: 29)

---

12 1950s British second features seemed to be obsessed with nightclub settings.

13 Another example to stand for many – Sidney James as a 'Spanish' businessman in *Tommy the Toreador* (John Paddy Carstairs, 1959).

With *Dad's Army*, the wry smile on the face of the chief clerk signifies how well he understands his manager, but the reverse is not quite true. How could Wilson, or indeed anyone, be satisfied to coast through life when there are further social heights to scale; for Mainwaring, a directorship at the bank or, better still, promotion to major would further compensate for his disastrous marriage to the always unseen Elizabeth and quell his ever-present paranoia about his status. Wilson needs Mainwaring to stand behind just as his relationship with his sergeant is one of the aspects of his life that he believes is within his control.

Dad's Army is a comedy with an ever-present sense of danger and even foreboding. This was, in the view of the critic Stanley Reynolds, a programme in which the Walmington-on-Sea Home Guard 'has the great seriousness of the southern coast of England awaiting Hitler's invasion behind all of its jokes … the cast gives no hint that what they are doing is not deadly business' (*The Guardian*, 10 March 1969: 8). Private Pike (Ian Lavender) may think of the war in terms of Hollywood films, but the medal ribbons on the uniforms of the older members of the platoon implied otherwise. The other principal element is that of integrity, for in 1968 many viewers could recall the obverse of Second World War patriotic propaganda:

> There was the serviceman with the 'cushy number' … there was the civilian column-dodger (there were instances of famous sportsmen being driven by such criticism from the perils of civil defence into the cost haven of jobs such as physical training instructors in the forces); there were the tea-drinking civil servants, thought to be very thick on the ground; there were megalomaniac air-raid wardens and firemen found guilty of looting. (Midwinter, 1979: 75)

But in *Dad's Army* the Home Guard are soldiers of the utmost integrity with a commanding officer who would rather put his own life on the line than see one of his men at risk. Had George Mainwaring been able to serve at the front in the First World War he would have probably have been killed within minutes while defending the troops under his command.

Jimmy Perry held his next collaboration with David Croft in high esteem but looking at *It Ain't Half Hot Mum* (1972–81) it is easy to understand why Leonard Rossiter spurned the key role of Battery Sergeant Major Williams claiming, 'this part is a completely stereotyped character' (quoted in Perry, 2002: 139). Windsor Davies eventually did his utmost but lacked a partner, unless one counts Don Estelle[14] but the next Perry/Croft series *Hi-de-Hi!* (1980–88) is one of their finest creations. The opening montage is of 1959 newsreel footage, the theme song is pastiche rock and roll, but the dominant mood is one of melancholy. The setting is Maplins Holiday Camp, a form of resort that arguably dates to the first branch of Butlins in 1936. John K. Walton points out that such venues attracted greater publicity in the latter half of the twentieth century. They may never have accounted for more than one-twentieth of holidaymakers in any given year, but they were highly publicised and 'a larger proportion of the population will have passed through their doors at any one time' (2000: 38).

Such camps were also havens for acts who were young and enthusiastic – Sid Kirby and Mickey Hayes were a guitar-playing duo who were the principal comics in the Butlins revues (Hudd with Hindin, 1998: 97) – and for those whose career status fell into the 'desperate' category. *Hi-di-Hi!* is a comedy about institutionalisation where the various main double acts live for minor victories and, with one exception, have gratefully retreated behind the walls of Maplin's holiday camp. Fred Quilley (Felix Bowness) destroyed his career as a jockey through corruption and now shares quarters with William Partridge (Leslie Dwyer), a former star of the music hall reduced to be a children's entertainer. The marriage of Barry and Yvonne Stuart-Hargreaves (Barry Howard and Diane Holland) is held together by a toxic fusion of spite and desperation while the head 'Yellow Coat' Gladys Pugh (Ruth Madoc) fears her impending thirtieth birthday and spinsterhood. If she has set her sights on the new manager, a former professor of archaeology named Jeffrey Fairbrother (Simon Cadell), this is partially because he is courteous, thoughtful and well-groomed – and

---

14 Whose autobiography, *Sing Lofty: Thoughts of a Gemini* (Don Estelle Music Publishing, 1999), has already passed into legend.

because he represents her chance of escape. Fairbrother is not just the sober outsider, approaching the camp inmates with the bemused look of a newly appointed commanding officer; he also has freedom of movement.

Virtually all the inmates are aware of the taste of failure. Partridge's heyday was before the First World War, and he would have been well aware of the fate of such bill-toppers as Mike Ford of 'The Two Mikes' who, by 1913, was a boot-black.[15] Then there is Ted Bovis, the camp host, aged 45 but adopting a Billy Fury quiff that is at least twenty years too young for him and cheering the new inmates by reciting material sourced from the Dead Sea Scrolls of Variety. Outside of Maplin's empire Bovis 'dies on his feet' (Perry, 2002: 271) so it is far better to entertain his captive audience before retreating to his chalet – think early Stalag 17 only without the charm – where an illicitly stored Baby Belling can produce 'cheese on toast' and success can be celebrated with half a dozen bottles of brown ale. Not since Ronnie Barker played Norman Stanley Fletcher had there been such a British sitcom character where an ever-wary expression undermines the constant patter. Clive James praised the performance of Paul Shane, himself a former stand-up comedian, for its observation and its authenticity:

> The marvellous thing about him is that he could very well *be* a holiday camp comic, except that no holiday camp comic would have such resources as an actor. With his hair arranged in a messily glistening Tony Curtis cut that looks as if a duck has just taken off from an oil-slick, he fills the lower half of the close-up with serried chins while his trained eyes search for campers who need jollifying and his mouth unreels an unbroken ticker-tape of triple-tested patter. (*The Observer*, 8 March 1982: 26)

Ted's protégé is Spike Dixon (Jeffrey Holland), a former Inland Revenue official turned comedian who eagerly absorbs every one of the 'first rules of comedy', in a manner that is gauche but never gratingly so. But as the

---

15 'After drawing £70 a week … is now getting a poor living as a bootblack in Southampton row' (*Liverpool Echo*, 6 January 1913: 3).

series progresses, the abiding question is for how much longer will they continue to work for Bovis? Spike at least could return to the tax office and a future of polishing the Austin A40 in the driveway of the family home at weekends, but for Ted, it is tatty pantomimes and department store demonstrations in a future that would have been dreaded by countless Archie Rices across the country. Early in the series, he is turned down for an acting role in *Coronation Street*, which represented a professional lifeline to the ageing comic. The last four seasons are set in 1960, when most of the surviving halls were in the process of conversion into Victor Value supermarkets.

It is difficult to equate such a persuasive sense of melancholy with Michael Bracewell's view that Perry and Croft's works unfolded in a happy pre-modern world celebrating 'the reassurance of a simpler society in which the hierarchies of social institution protected us from our own capacity for disillusionment and disaffection' (5 May 2002). Ted was never going to be a star attraction at the Edgware Road Empire, but in the 1940s he might have found a niche lower down the bill as one of the many reliable supporting acts listed by Roy Hudd or Michael Kilgarriff. By 1960 his opportunities to be the Max Miller of the holiday camp circuit are already diminishing and by the end of *Hi-de-Hi!* Joe Maplin is remodelling his empire and if Ted and Spike have found employment in pantomime, their longer-term future in show business remains in doubt. For all its period trappings this is not a sitcom that peddles nostalgia in the manner of *Heartbeat* (ITV, 1992–2010), where it was '1969' for approximately a decade, but one with a sense of melancholy for lost opportunities. J.B. Priestley famously thought that the comedy of character was 'this humour of character, reaching its greatest height in such figures as Falstaff, is itself the richest and wisest kind of humour, sweetening and mellowing life for us. In England it ripens like an apple' (1934: 632) with *Hi-De-Hi!*, beneath the frequently brilliant set pieces was an affection for those imprisoned within the holiday camp.

Comedy of Imprisonment

Entrapment has been a key issue with British situation comedy since the 1950s, for with *Hancock's Half Hour* Galton and Simpson created a comedy where 'suburban lives might be restricted lives, petty lives, lives that prompt thoughts of escape' (Medhurst, 1997: 85). Harold Steptoe is acutely aware of his state, Terry Collier cannot really accept that his world is not immutable, and Captain Mainwaring depends to a poignant degree on his uniform as both an affirmation of status and a refuge from his domestic misery. Of the two double acts here, one is borne of a desire to escape and the other revels in virtual incarceration. Before *Porridge* (BBC, 1974–77), there was little in Ronnie Barker's screen CV that would suggest the furtive, highly intelligent and secretly regretful Norman Stanley Fletcher, save a supporting heavy in the forgotten Charlie Drake film vehicle *The Cracksman* (Peter Graham Scott, 1963).

As was their wont, the script by Dick Clement and Ian La Frenais allowed the audience to envisage the history of Fletcher; his daughter Ingrid (Patricia Brake) once reminisces that 'when I was a nipper all my dresses were made out of parachute silk'. It is a memory that both summarises Fletcher's National Service and is an understatedly poignant reminder of Norman Stanley's sad short-cuts in being a good father, with the key word being 'party'. Nancy Banks-Smith once referred to Fletcher resembling 'a Father Christmas who has come to nick the toys' (*The Guardian*, 25 February 1978: 13) and you can see the living room in Muswell Hill festooned with streamers and packed with birthday presents that all miraculously descended from the back of a lorry. What is worse is that the self-aware Fletcher realises how he has fallen short of his potential.

If Fletcher's current five-year sentence is par for the course with a habitual criminal, his latest cellmate Lennie Godber allows him a chance of reform on his terms. Richard Beckinsale was one of the rare young leading men of the period who could make naïvety seem as funny as it was reasonable and on ITV his surrogate father was Leonard Rossiter's Rupert Rigsby. Some of the most treasurable moments of *Rising Damp*

(Yorkshire, 1974–78) involved the landlord eagerly passing his invented life experience to the amiably gullible medical student Alan Moore. With *Porridge*, Fletcher guides Godber, a first-time offender, through the system; this is partially out of self-interest – he does not want a neurotic cellmate – but also out of affection. He is equal in intelligence to the prison's criminal lynchpin Mr Grout (the unforgettable Peter Vaughan) and is physically stronger than his soft, middle-aged appearance would suggest, as McLaren (Tony Osoba) soon discovers, but his 'little victories' are no longer enough. He knows that Chief Warder McKay (Fulton Mackay) is as institutionalised as most of the prisoners and that Officer Barraclough (Brian Wilde) is entirely unsuited to his role and probably only joined the service for the pension and the tied accommodation.

Aside from the Fletcher/Godber dynamic, a lynchpin of *Porridge* was the relationship between the recidivist and the senior prison officer played by the magnificent Fulton Mackay. It is fitting that the last episode of *Porridge* concludes with Fletcher remarking to his tormentor who so desperately believes in 'the System' that, 'Nobody wins, Mr McKay, that's what is so tragic'. Godber has already gained his parole and Fletcher will be released in the following year if all goes well. The opening episode of the sequel *Going Straight* (1978) has Barker and Mackay travelling by train to London, the former to Muswell Hill, the latter, now looking weary, and without his trademark bantam cock stance, facing retirement.

'You'll end up on some pathetic little charge, stealing a tin of Duraglit from Tesco's to polish up your buttons,' muses Fletcher, but they both look forward to an uncertain future outside institutionalisation, and when MacKay proffers his hand in farewell, it is an authentically moving moment. *Going Straight* lasted for just one series, but this was enough, as Fletcher's story concludes with *Going off the Rails*. He contemplates a one-off return to crime to help fund the wedding of Lennie and Ingrid. Seeking refuge in a pet shop while acting as lookout, he responds to the assistant's 'Can I help you sir?' when the line 'No. Only I can do that,' which is as affecting as it is straightforward. Fletcher knows that he has wasted his intelligence and potential for literally decades. It is time to escape being 'Norman Stanley Fletcher', the sarcastic recidivist.

Meanwhile, at the Luxton and District Traction Company somewhere in London Stan Butler and Jack Harper revel in their limited horizons. There is, on the surface, a compelling case to be made for the driver and his conductor as one of most unlikeable duos in British sitcom history with the undoubted acting talents of Reg Varney and Bob Grant only serving to make the driver and conductor even more authentically awful. They are almost criminally incompetent at their jobs, show utter contempt for their customers – and fear any signs of aspiration on the part of the other. Subtle it was not, but Ronald Chesney and Ronald Wolfe knew how to sustain fundamentally unsympathetic characters within a limited format. *On the Buses*, which was initially rejected by the BBC, became an early rating success for the new London Weekend Television franchise.

Seventy-four programmes were made between 1969 and 1973, and there were also many and various spin-offs; the comic strips in *Look-In* magazine, the sing-a-long LPs, the board games[16] – all celebrating the glorious predictability of *On the Buses*. Stan at least has a sense of family obligation that occasionally inspires him to apply for promotion, but Jack is content to lounge in the cab of a Bristol KSW and leer at bit-part actresses. For his friend to escape the driver's cab is a prospect not to be tolerated, as his lack of initiative will be further shown up. In *On the Buses*, even to aspire to a life beyond work and letching at women is seen as indicative of marked disloyalty.

A further factor in the show's popularity was its reflection of the dismalness of the everyday existence. *On the Buses* was aired in a Britain of strikes, factories churning out consumer goods of the calibre of the Morris Marina and public utilities that still believed in Atlee-era austerity. There was also the gusto that Varney and Grant invested in their lines, with Stan's authentic Canning Town accent far removed from the current Dick Van Dyke Mk II delivery of your average cast member of *EastEnders*. Of the actors tasked with portraying our un-dynamic duo,

---

16 Reg was also one of the main attractions of the 1970 LWT *Holiday Startime* Christmas special. Mercifully, the tape of a show that combines the diverse talents of Mr V, Peter Cook, Hattie Jacques and Vincent Price was not wiped.

Bob Grant was a RADA graduate who had been a mainstay of Joan Littlewood's Theatre Royal Company at Stratford East for many years. Photographs that were taken before 1969 and the actor's adoption of the trademark Jack Harper hairstyle – long sideburns and an ambitious comb-over – display an almost unrecognisable Grant. Instead of the bus conductor with the appearance of a louche Halloween mask there is a blazered individual with the bow tie, neat side-parting and practised grin of a door-to-door salesman.

As for Varney, his career after the end of his short-lived double act with Benny Hill encompassed Variety shows, playing Touchstone in a production of *As You Like It* staged by Bernard Miles and supporting Frankie Howerd in *The Great St Trinian's Train Robbery* (Sidney Gilliat and Frank Launder, 1966). He was also the world's first ever customer of a cashpoint machine.[17]

Reg Varney first worked with Chesney and Wolfe on television in 1961 when he was cast as the foreman Reg Turner in *The Rag Trade* (BBC, 1961–63) and a surprising number of episodes exist,[18] revealing an approach that very much anticipated *On the Buses*. The vision of the two writers is as distinctive as that of Galton and Simpson or Clement and La Frenais – it is just that it is almost infinitely more depressing. A typical plotline would have Peter Jones and Miriam Karlin shouting at each other, while Reg mutters 'flipping 'eck'. Meanwhile, Barbara Windsor, Judy Carne and the other factory girls variously chew gum and say, 'Cor. Here comes Mr Fenner!' approximately every five minutes.

Varney himself once pointed out that he was not a comedian but a comedy actor, and that in *The Rag Trade* there were no jokes, 'only free lines disguised by acting' (interview with Lenore Nicklin, 1969). In that Chesney and Wolfe sitcom the principal double act was Jones and Karlin, but in *On the Buses*, it was Jack and Stan, bantering the viewers into submission when they are not leering at clippies played by mini-skirted and mockney-accented drama school graduates. The depot may be dominated by an inspector (Stephen Lewis) whose demeanour

---

17 The great event took place in Enfield on 27 June 1967.
18 Twenty-one out of the thirty-six shows survive.

is halfway between a Second World War Unteroffizier and the Grim Reaper from *The Seventh Seal* (Ingmar bergman, 1957) – but at least it is a refuge from their home lives. Jack's domestic situation is mostly an enigma – one imagines a lair filled with stacks of *Mayfair* magazine and bottles of Hai Karate aftershave – but the many scenes that unfold in Stan's house reveal one that is well worth avoiding.

The first black and white season is more focused on how Stan is dominated by his mother (Cicely Courtneidge), but once the role was taken over by Doris Hare, the full misery of his situation is realised. Stan is trapped with a self-centred parent – Hare never made the mistake of playing 'Mum' as lovable – in a home packed with wartime utility furniture and 1950s electrical goods. Just to make the works' canteen offering 20 New Pence worth of lard and chips on the menu even more enticing, there is the almost constant presence of the series' other double act. The performances of Anna Karen and Michael Robbins only serve to create an on-screen marriage that Mike Leigh or Ken Loach might have rejected on the grounds of sheer bleakness. Stan and Jack may have been reasonably unlikely Lotharios, even by the standards of the day,[19] but the Rudges were a horribly convincing couple.

The married double act was a familiar trope of the Variety circuit; Gracie Clark and Colin Murray ('Mr and Mrs Glasgow') were stars of Scottish entertainment for fifty years (Hudd with Hindin, 1998: 30) while the routines of Billy Caryll and Hilda Mundy were based on an atmosphere of mutual loathing and regret. The 78rpm discs of their routine *Scenes of Domestic Bliss* capture a relationship held together by sniping and personal abuse. It could almost have been an opening scene of *On the Buses*, except that Mundy's character was never a doormat whereas Olive was framed as a 'female grotesque'. Larraine Porter contends that in British humour this was one of the two principal stereotypes of woman as comic object, the other being the 'sexually desirable busty blonde' (2004: 83–84):

---

19 To cite just two examples, Sidney James and Bernard Bresslaw in *Carry On Camping* (Gerald Thomas, 1969).

The female grotesque is well past her prime and youth is a prequisite for female desirability. Age – i.e. over 30 – makes her ripe for caricature. She's also coded as unattractive, often in the extreme, but, more importantly for the purpose of comedy, she fails to realise the lowly status of her sexuality and insists on pursuing male sexual conquests. Anne Karen as Olive in *On the Buses* with her thick spectacles, unattractive face and figure is an example of type. (Porter, 2004: 83–84)

Off screen, Karen did not resemble Olive in the slightest; a somewhat unchivalrous article in the *TV Times* of 23–29 October 1971 bore the headline 'The Beauty Inside A Fat Girl'. It was the actress's skill more than the make-up that created the illusion of Mrs Rudge. Olive craved attention while Robbins played Arthur with a morose bitterness and a pompous deadpan delivery from the Lionel Jeffries School of Petty Authority, while Olive desperately applies cold cream and wails for marital dues that her husband is unwilling to provide. Arthur's line 'I got an 'eadache' is simultaneously funnier and infinitely more depressing that Varney's constant reiteration of the phrase 'Cripes!' For all that, the character of Stan was still the show's lynchpin and when Varney left *On the Buses* in 1972 – Butler was said to have gone to work in a car factory in the West Midlands – it never recovered from the loss of its main protagonist. After Varney's death in 2008 *The Economist* wonderfully observed that he was an actor who 'kept to the end of his life the delighted glint-in-the-eye of a boy who has been paid eight shillings and sixpence for playing the accordion in Plumstead Working Men's Club' (4 December 2008).

The dissolution of the show's main double act meant that Jack Harper's ghastliness now abounded without relief and the seventh series also saw the departure of Michael Robbins. At least Olive, at long last, divorced Arthur, but the series' raison d'être had now vanished, and the last show aired on 20 May 1973. Varney was little seen on television after the early 1970s – an ATV sitcom *Down the Gate* lasted for two seasons[20]

---

20 'Reg Varney's new ATV comedy series *Down the Gate* (ITV, Wednesday July 23, 8.0) ... is unlikely to be Down the Ratings' (Sharland, *The Stage*, 31 July 1975: 13).

– and when he passed away in 2008, there is little purpose found in a description of his last days; mental illness can indeed be lethal. Instead, let us remember them on *Foggy Night* (1970), which has the winning combination of seasoned pros, a fog machine and a bus inspector struggling with a recalcitrant cow. It is a scenario which even Lars Von Trier or Werner Herzog might have approved.

Love and Marriage

The history of the British sitcom is littered with domestic sitcoms, many of which boast titles that are sufficient within themselves to induce a sense of dread. For every *Marriage Lines* (BBC, 1963–66), which paired Prunella Scales with Richard Briers, or *The Larkins* (ATV, 1959–60/1963–64) which featured the magnificent Peggy Mount and the equally wonderful David Kossoff, there are shows in which characters really say, 'hello darling, I'm home!'[21] The married couple sub-genre has a long pedigree on British television: the BBC's *Life with The Lyons*, starring the real partnership of Ben Lyons and Bebe Daniels, transferred from radio in 1956[22] and one of ITV's earliest sitcoms was *Joan and Leslie* (ATV, 1956), starring another married couple, Joan Reynolds and Leslie Randall. *The Dickie Henderson Show* (Associated-Rediffusion, 1960–68) ran for 115 episodes (many, alas, missing or wiped) establishing the lead comic and his screen wife June Laverick as a rating-topping duo. Such was the fame of Thora Hird and Freddie Frinton[23] in *Meet the Wife* (BBC, 1963–66) that John Lennon mentioned their sitcom in the lyrics for *Good Morning, Good Morning*. It was also praised by George Melly for its evocation of 'the incredulous recollection of a passionate honeymoon

---

21 Or look as though they are thinking of saying it.

22 One edition survives, according to the BFI.

23 Whose most famous work *Dinner for One*, opposite May Warden, was not actually shot in the UK but recorded in Hamburg in 1963. In the previous year Frinton had been seen on stage in Blackpool by a holidaymaking German comedian and a TV producer, who thought the sketch would appeal to their audiences.

from the viewpoint of sagging, varicated middle age' that was based on a solid relationship (*The Observer*, 1 May 1966: 25).

One could cite almost countless other titles, and while some famous duos such as Basil and Sybil Fawlty and Reginald and Elizabeth Perrin will be covered elsewhere in this tome, we will conclude with two sitcom couples who defined an era. *Man About the House* (Thames, 1973–76), written by Brian Cooke and Johnnie Mortimer, concerned one Robin Tripp (Richard O'Sullivan), a trainee chef who shared a flat with two young ladies, Chrissy (Paula Wilcox) and Jo (Sally Thomsett). For all the initial controversy about the plot and the lip service paid to the permissive society, in the great tradition of British comedy no-one probably did anything and one probable reason was that Robin already seemed too respectably middle-aged for such shenanigans. In fairness the character was not devised as especially 'hip' and indeed Robin hailed from Southampton, which remains one of the least 'swinging' cities imaginable.

O'Sullivan remains a sorely underrated light comedy actor but by the mid-1970s he appeared to have been playing a safely randy young man forever. The letter to the *TV Times* of February 1974 that claimed the actor had 'the saucy sex appeal of Leslie Crowther, with perhaps a dash of Des O'Connor' (quoted in Hunt, 2013: 50) was not being very kind but it did explain why the real stars of the programme were the landlord and landlady. At first sight, Yootha Joyce's Mildred Roper was partially of the Peggy Mount School of Gorgons and partially the sexually frustrated middle-aged woman so often seen in the later *Carry On* films – the nagging wife with frustrated petite-bourgeois aspirations (Porter, 2004: 84). Brian Murphy's George is almost perpetually grubby – his shirt collars describe various shades of grey – sniggers like Dennis the Menace and, if this were not a sitcom, you might even think of him as having faint Christie-like overtones. He was also industriously work-shy, the actor noting 'it was quite remarkable how much energy he put into avoiding a job – more than if he were actually employed!'

The final episode of *Man About the House* aired in April 1976, with Cooke and Mortimer creating two sequels, *Robin's Nest* (1976–81) as a vehicle for O'Sullivan, and the relocation of the Ropers to haute suburbia for *George and Mildred* (1976–80). In the former the landlord and landlady represented authority, and Murphy recalls that 'the head of Thames Television recognised that the characters had so much mileage'. The programme enjoyed truly vast viewing figures, and away from the flat-sharing plot, the new show, as with any good sitcom, the viewer is tempted to wonder just how the Ropers' relationship came about and how it was sustained. Did Mildred marry George partly to defy her family and partly because of her maternal instincts? Murphy observes how popular the show was with younger viewers: 'We received so much fan mail from children.'

Joyce and Murphy had first worked together at Stratford East, and they brought a wealth of nuance and timing to the show. George is furtive, puerile but with the occasional sharp insight – describing the local Tory party as staging 'whist drives in favour of the death penalty'. His sparring with the next-door neighbour Jeffrey Fourmile is a further example of the many strengths of *George and Mildred*, as Norman Eshley creates not a standard-issue snob but a sardonic professional who is ruefully aware of his own failings. Mildred dons an array of spectacularly awful outfits – most infamously a pair of banana-print trousers – and hopes for the day when George will (a) gain respectable employment and (b) finally recognise her as a woman.

Leon Hunt contends that 'we are meant to find her frustrated desires comic and occasionally mawkishly affecting' (2013: 50) but the programme has nothing of the latter quality, for Mildred is far removed from a Donald McGill postcard caricature or a Variety sketch of a nagging wife. Dick Fiddy argues that a common theme of the British middle-aged 'husband/wife' sitcom is 'why didn't we have children…? With *Man About the House*, the Ropers are only seen in five-minute bursts and are good fun'; the three youngish people upstairs are obviously Mildred's surrogate children. In the spin-off series, the mood is often 'bleaker'.

Yootha Joyce was aged 50 when *George and Mildred* first aired, and two films of the 1960s showcase her range – the bitter upper-middle-class hausfrau of *Catch Us If You Can* (John Boorman, 1965) while no-one who ever seen *The Pumpkin Eater* (Jack Clayton, 1964) will forget the depths of pain that Joyce could evoke in a five-minute cameo of a mentally disturbed woman. Mildred's vulnerability and her sheer desperation to gain acceptance with her neighbours will ring true to many people who recall the late 1970s. The tea parties, the joining of various societies and the fear of being judged as 'different' or 'unacceptable' really were a part of suburban life during that decade.

Such a theme was not restricted to *George and Mildred* during the 1970s. In the wonderful *Don't Forget to Write!* (BBC, 1977–79), created by Charles Wood, Mabel Maple (Gwen Watford) endures a scriptwriter husband George (George Cole) whose creative block is a reason but never an excuse for his self-centred behaviour. With *Butterflies* (BBC, 1978–83), Carla Lane created a virtual *Brief Encounter* (David Lean, 1945) for the 1970s, with Ria Parkinson (Wendy Craig) arguing 'We are all kids chasing butterflies. You see it, you want it, you grab it, and there it is, all squashed in your hand. I am one of the few lucky ones, I have a pleasant house, a pleasant man and two pleasant sons. My butterfly didn't get squashed,' as she contemplates adultery. Her husband Ben (Geoffrey Palmer) is acerbic, kind and lost in his realm of Lepidoptera and if an affair with Leonard (Bruce Montague) is tempting, it is because he is not a stereotypical cad but a gentleman who develops a love for her.

All the while, the villa in Cheltenham serves as a cage that is gilded by Laura Ashley for a character who, to Lane, represented one of 'a dying race who stayed with their husbands out of loyalty'. She has no career, and her lifestyle is funded by her husband, which increases the cycle of her depression. Maggie Andrews sees Ria's rejection of an affair with Leonard as being 'due to the formulaic conventions of sitcoms' (2004: 62) but it could equally be the case that the conventions of society are too strong. The tragedy, as demonstrated in the Ria–Ben double act, is that such bonds do not always create a peace of mind. She is on the verge of a breakdown, and he is frustrated in his inability to help. Of all the great television moments created by Palmer, his delivery of the line 'I can see hope running towards the sunset with his arse on fire' must rank very highly.[24]

---

24 *Brief Encounter* is one comparison, but another is *Woman in a Dressing Gown* (J. Lee Thompson, 1957); in the later film it is the husband (Anthony Quayle) who contemplates an affair as he cannot cope with his depressed wife (Yvonne Mitchell).

Back at Teddington, Mrs Roper would have probably seen the well-furnished home in *Butterflies* as the ultimate, just as she sees the tall, dark and well-spoken Jeffrey Fourmile as the epitome of the perfect husband. Instead, she dons her finest synthetic leopard coat as a show of defiance as she aims for her goal of social acceptance with its countless put-downs, stabs to the spirit and unresponsive partners. It is a formula that was often employed by Galton and Simpson for Hancock and Steptoe, except that here the one who is proud to lack ambition is a puerile but occasionally insightful husband. In the first season's 'Baby Talk', in which Mildred hopes to adopt a child only to be turned down on the grounds of her age, George hears the news and then scuttles off (Murphy's use of body language was always a highlight of the programme), ostensibly to the pub. He can cope with Mildred's mood swings and put-downs; these represent some of the fixed points by which he navigates his world, but her emotional pain is such that he apparently cannot comprehend. When he returns from the pet shop with a puppy – 'I knew you were upset', it illustrates Brian Murphy's view that 'they would be lost without each other'. They would.

Terry and June: The British Truman Show?

Many of the situation comedy double acts in this chapter are the creation of actors and writers who shunned stereotypes, that method of creating, to quote Andy Medhurst:

A shortcut to meaning, and often, due to their inability to convey complexity, a short cut to misrepresentation. Sitcom's tendency to paint social characterisation with a very broad brush in order to reach the haven of laughter as swiftly as possible makes its recourse to stereotypes virtually unavoidable. (2007: 145)

Paradoxically, we conclude with a series that makes Stan Butler and Jack Harper resemble figures of Pirandello-like complexity. The screen partnership of Terry Scott and June Whitfield commenced in 1969 when the latter guest-starred in the BBC TV revue *Scott On Marriage* and was consolidated by their supporting roles in *Bless This House* (Gerald Thomas, 1972), that Citizen Kane of sitcom spin-off films. Their first comedy series *Happy Ever After* was created by John Chapman; it commenced transmission on 7 May 1974 and, after a change of writer, became *Terry and June* in October 1979 for another nine seasons, allowing millions of viewers to regularly enjoy the following scenario:

> The Boss, who has the mysterious right to enter T&J's house at all hours, arrives for dinner only to discover that our heroes are dressed as Kings Road style Punk Rockers.
> Boss: Medford, how dare you wear a punk outfit as late as 1987? You have brought shame upon whichever business you implausibly hold a managerial role, and you are therefore fired!
> Enter a Vicar who appears to have escaped from a Brian Rix farce circa 1956. He sits on a chocolate cake that was previously placed on the sofa for no reason whatsoever.
> C/U on Terry Scott – Cor!

Matthew Coniham remarks that:

> The series was singled out for particularly fierce condemnation by the new 'alternative' generation of comedians for what they perceived its complacent gentility, outmoded social attitudes and bourgeois sensibilities. (BFI *Screenonline*)

Indeed, *Terry and June* is a programme that seems to cause problems for certain steely media types and self-appointed comedy gurus alike, with even its Ronnie Hazlehurst theme tune an apparent affront to their view of the 1980s. One problem is that British television has a dreadful habit of rolling out the same examples of news footage for ineptly researched nostalgia clip shows devoted to the recent past. For 'Swinging London' it is that 1967 *Look at Life* Rank travelogue, while the 1965 Movietone

News footage of Peter Sellers driving a customised Morris Mini Cooper S has been aired so many times that it is a surprise that the film stock has not yet disintegrated.

For the 1980s it is the same news bulletins of Margaret Thatcher and the miners' strike, usually combined with commentary from a vaguely famous person with a marginal connection to the subject – one who concentrates on nodding wisely to an off-screen researcher. According to such sources, 'alternative comedy' caused the death of all previous forms of television humour, leaving its exponents to gnash their teeth in a dark corner of Butlins or at least the outer reaches of *Blankety Blank*. But the reality is slightly different, for if you avoided BBC2 or Channel Four it was quite possible not to have seen any 'alternative' material until the late 1980s. The last series of *Terry and June* aired in the summer of 1987, one year before the first screening of *Red Dwarf* (BBC, 1988–99).

June Whitfield was Terry Scott's third screen partner, the first being Bill Maynard (*Great Scott, It's Maynard*, BBC, 1955–56) and the second being Hugh Lloyd. The surviving tapes of *Hugh & I* (BBC, 1962–67), in addition to explaining just why the programme incurred the wrath of Tony Hancock,[25] show that a strong female partner better served Scott, as his playing opposite a moon-faced innocent brought out his bullying manner. Their partnership continued with *The Gnomes of Dulwich* (BBC, 1969), a sitcom that (a) reads like a parody, (b) is hard to believe existed and (c) has been completely wiped. All that remains are stills of Scott as 'Big' and Lloyd as 'Small', two garden gnomes who were prone to grumbling about the plastic Empire-built ornaments next door.

Scott was still working with Lloyd as late as 1973,[26] but from the moment the pilot episode of *Happy Ever After* was aired on 7 May 1974 he would be forever associated with one of the most brilliant character actresses in the history of British entertainment; one whose

---

25 'He's stolen my blank blank act!' was Hancock's response to Mr Scott.

26 In the Christmas *Radio Times* for that year listed *Colour Christmas Pantomime: Robin Hood* starring the duo as the Robbers, plus Freddie Davies as Samuel Tweet, Anita Harris as Robin Hood, Billy Dainty as Nurse Trumpet and Dana as Maid Marion. Let us hope that a copy survives.

CV encompassed working with Noel Coward, Ronnie Barker, Wilfred Pickles and Leslie Phillips.

It must be said that when viewing the later episodes, the *Terry and June* devotee is confronted with a vague but nagging question, one that often arises across several TV and cinematic genres, from the *Harry Potter* films to *Two Pints of Lager and a Packet of Crisps* (BBC, 2001–11), which is, in what era is this actually set? As Penelope Gilliatt wrote of the *Carry On* series:

> Luckily, no one working on the films seems to have decided whether they are supposed to be with-it or not. This makes them strangely timeless, a dream-mixture of periods, like the language of Wodehouse; they incorporate without difficulty a lot of the pre-war flavour of beach-postcard humour, but they are also full of the 1960s. (1973: 285)

And there is a similar sense of dissonance with *Terry and June*. The suburban locations seem vaguely similar to the setting of *Ever Decreasing Circles* (BBC, 1984–89), but there the resemblance ends. The latter was one of the most accomplished works of Bob Larbey and John Esmonde, capturing the surreal mundanity of life in the provinces; the social clubs and the various genteel rituals of outer suburbia all serving to mask the loneliness and lack of confidence on the part of Richard Briers' Martin Bryce. Bracewell argues that:

> Über-suburb of suffocating order and pettiness – as neurosis made landscape, like a middle-class version of the brooding terraces and canal-side bomb sites of kitchen sink films such as *A Taste of Honey* (1961). Another shuffle of the deck, though, and *Ever Decreasing Circles* could have been a side project by David Lynch – right down to the spookily normal neighbours Howard and Hilda, who always dress in identical anoraks. This is suburbia as Munchkinland, but without the *Yellow Brick Road* to the big city. (5 May 2002)

Three points here. Firstly, the vision of suburbia as presented by *Ever Decreasing Circles* is wholly recognisable to many Britons who grew up during the late 1980s, even down to the surreal Howard and Hilda Hughes (Stanley Lebor and Geraldine Newman). Secondly, what anchors the series is the wholly believable marriage between Martin and the younger Ann (Penelope Wilton) – when she says that he appealed to her because of his kindness, it is a moment of truth.

Thirdly, Terry Medford would probably have dismissed Bracewell's words as the work of a hippie anarchist (*Terry and June* was never terribly strong on sub-cultural movements) as the show is a virtual return to the world of Leslie and Joan Randall or *The Dickie Valentine Show*, albeit with modern trappings. Yes, Terry drives a Princess 'Wedge' or an Austin Ambassador and one narrative centres on that ultra 'dated by 1990' plotline concerning a video recorder, but although *Terry and June* was set in the 1980s, it rarely attempted to be of it. The television listings of *The Guardian* once somewhat grumpily referred to 'the fantasy world of Sitcom Land, where wives don't need to work, and there's spare cash for cello lessons' (10 October 1980: 20). The Medfords do at least lack a 'comic maid' but in 1983 a 'burglar' played by Brian Hall makes jokes about Picasso that were probably last heard on the BBC Home Service. In the 1985 episode 'One Arabian Night' Terry even agrees to sell June to an 'Arab Prince' (Derek Griffiths) in exchange for some camels, and the opening episode of the final season featured June responding to 'having been called "frumpy" and "on the edge of senility" – dressed as a punk and wearing a pink wig' (Green, *The Stage*, 30 July 1987: 19).

John Chapman saw the essential difference between sitcom and farce as 'unreal people in real situations', and 'real people in unreal situations' (quoted in Wolfe, 2003: 122) but *Terry and June* were a married couple who appeared to have practised celibacy since the Suez Crisis. In the 1950s it was Whitfield's Eth Glum who, beneath her shabby genteel accent, was suffused with passions that went entirely unnoticed by a fiancé who possessed the IQ of a Ford Consul. With the Medfords, the dynamic was more akin to a mother/son relationship, and a near contemporary of *Terry and June* was *Sorry!* (BBC, 1981–88) but the focus was on the impishly sardonic Ronnie Corbett, whereas Terry is large, blustering and essentially an innocent, albeit a self-centred one.

To make such a character even remotely sympathetic required considerable acting skills, and as Brett Mills points out, 'for a comic performance to offer pleasure it must demonstrate the abilities of the person performing far more obviously than non-comic forms do' (2005: 70). Scott possessed a wider range than is often remembered. His works foreman in *I'm All Right Jack* (John Boulting, 1959) is competent and long-suffering; Ronald Baines in *Bless This House* (Gerald Thomas, 1972) is a pompous but credible senior civil servant. *Carry On Up The Khyber* gave Scott the rare chance to display pathos – the reaction of Sergeant Macnutt to the death of Private Hale (Peter Gilmore) is rather affecting – and his sardonic line delivery is a highlight of *Carry On Camping* (Gerald Thomas, 1969) but by 1979 Scott had reverted to be the overgrown schoolboy of his 1962 hit single 'My Brother'. It was a routine that he had honed to perfection and when Scott played the role of Arnolphe in Molière's *The School for Wives* one critic praised his performance as:

Terry, our old friend from *Terry and June*, who takes on this demanding role and gives a most enjoyable performance. Terry Scott always does. Yet how much of it is Arnolophe and how much the Terry we know so well from television? (Desmond Christy, *The Guardian*, 15 March 1984: 20).

Christy concluded that 'Terry Scott is nearly always Terry playing Arnolphe, so well' and in *Terry and June* he brought decades of experience and energy despite serious illness. He is frequently at his best when performing a turn – a highlight of *Happy Ever After* is the 'Hut Sut Song' (1978) opposite the great Damaris Hayman and in the *Terry and June* era he stages a hospital radio drama. Almost everything to Terry is an adventure; wine tasting, a trip to France and amateur dramatics; in many respects, the Medfords' version of *The King & I* is infinitely superior to Yul Brynner and Deborah Kerr. And although June Whitfield once stated that her job was to direct the laughs towards her co-star, this is a vast understatement. She was an actress who could ring almost infinite changes out of the line, 'yes dear,' with immaculate comic timing, and her demure head-shaking demeanour was forged by decades of coping with male inadequates. In 1961 a BBC handout cited June Whitfield as having 'worked with the following comedians; Alfred Marks, Bob Monkhouse, Benny Hill, Arthur Askey, Peter Sellers, Eric Sykes' and to that list we could add Tony Hancock in *The Blood Donor*, Leslie Phillips in *Carry On Nurse* and, of course, Dick Bentley's Ron Glum. Frank Muir thought that 'June always understands what we are getting at and gets more out of it than we put in. She is the answer to a script-writer's prayer. She is phenomenal' (quoted in Grieg, *Aberdeen Evening Express*, 27 December 1961: 2).

Miss Whitfield was indeed phenomenal, regardless of circumstance. A better film than *Carry On Abroad* (Gerald Thomas, 1972) would have played Evelyn Blunt's affair with the Spanish Lothario Pepe (Ray Brooks) with more sympathy; it was a pleasure to see Whitfield with male company other than a middle-aged inept. 'I am the girl who says loudly and clearly the unfunny line before the comedian's funny line. I prefer to leave it at that' (Grieg, 1961: 2) is an understatement from one who ranked alongside Jerry Desmonde, Chesney Allen and Ernie Wise in the pantheon of great straight men and straight women. She represents authority within the Medford household, once memorably responding to Terry's complaint that 'You can't take a joke!' with 'Well, I took you.'

Terry Scott died in 1994 while June Whitfield, now a Dame of the British Empire, will probably be forever 'and June' – for within a world that is real to them, the Medfords are indivisible. As early as 1976 some critics were referring to *Happy Ever After* as dated and by the late 1980s it was often assumed that Terry and June now mainly appealed to older viewers – 'Fortunately there are a lot of mature and elderly be-slippered viewers out there able to associate with semi-detached domesticity' (Grieg, 1961: 2). This was not entirely the case, for even beyond the charm of a sitcom that held the quaint belief that 'punk' was cutting edge in 1987 the success of *Terry and June* was due to the all-too-easily taken-for-granted major talents of its stars and their comforting predictability. Outside of the leafy avenues, nuclear bombs might be falling on Sheffield (*Threads*, BBC, 1984), the news contained bulletin after bulletin of post-industrial despair but with the Medfords, to paraphrase Orwell, everything would be the same for ever and ever.

As Andy Medhurst observed in *The Listener* on the occasion of the last season of the show, 'perhaps one of the keys to the series' longevity rests precisely with the performers and the generic types they so skilfully embody. *Terry and June* is a warm bath of a programme, soothingly anachronistic and reassuringly repetitive. (1987: 32). It was a show that made a virtue of its predictability, and if for several of the other double acts within this chapter, suburbia often formed a trap, for *Terry and June* it was one they embraced. If the final episode revealed that the Medfords lived not in Purley but in a *Truman Show* (Peter Weir, 1998) style dome this would have come as no surprise to many viewers. Although Terry would have probably reacted with 'Cor! June!'

With thanks to Barry Cryer, Dick Fiddy and Brian Murphy.

Bibliography

Books

Durgnat, Raymond (1997), 'Two "Social Problem" Films; *Sapphire* and *Victim*, in Burton, Alan, O'Sullivan, Tim and Wells, Paul (eds) *Liberal Directions: Basil Dearden and Post-War British Film Culture*. Trowbridge: Flicks Books.

Fisher, John (2008), *Tony Hancock: The Definitive Biography*. London: Harper Collins.

Gilliatt, Penelope (1973), *Unholy Fools; Wits, Comics, Disturbers of the Peace: Film and Theatre*. New York: Viking Press.

Gilliatt, Penelope (1990), *To Wit: In Celebration of Comedy*. London: Weidenfeld and Nicolson.

Gilliatt, Penelope (1990), *To Wit: Skin and Bones of Comedy*. New York: Scribner.

Goddard, Peter (1990), '*Hancock's Half Hour*: A Watershed in British Television Comedy', in Corner, John (ed.) *Popular Television in Britain: Studies in Cultural History*. London: BFI Publishing.

Goodwin, Cliff (1995), *Sid James: A Biography*. London: Century Random House.

Gorer, Geoffrey (1955), *Exploring English Character*. London: Cresset Press.

Harper, Sue and Smith, Justin (2013), *British Film Culture in the 1970s: The Boundaries of Pleasure*. Edinburgh: Edinburgh University Press.

Hopkins, Harry (1964), *The New Look: A Social History of Britain in the Forties and Fifties*. London: Secker & Warberg.

Hudd, Roy with Hindin, Philip (1998), *Roy Hudd's Cavalcade of Variety Acts: A Who Was Who of Light Entertainment, 1945–60*. London: Robson Books Ltd.

Hunt, Leon (2013), *British Low Culture: From Safari Suits to Sexploitation*. London: Routledge.

Lahr, John (1984), *Automatic Vaudeville: Essays on Star Turns*. New York: Alfred Knopf Inc.

Lahr, John (1987), *Prick Up Your Ears: The Biography of Joe Orton*. London: Penguin Books.

Lewis, Roger (1994), *The Life and Death of Peter Sellers*. London: Century.

Lewis, Roy and Maude, Angus (1950), *The English Middle Classes*. New York: Alfred Knopf.

Lewisohn, Mark (1998), *The Radio Times Guide To TV Comedy*. London: BBC Books.

McCann, Graham (2006), *Spike & Co.: Inside the House of Fun with Milligan, Sykes, Galton and Simpson*. London: Hodder & Stoughton.

Marwick, Arthur (1998), *The Sixties: Cultural Revolution in Britain France Italy and the United States, c.1958–c.1974*. Oxford: Oxford University Press.

Medhurst, Andy (1997), 'Negotiating The Gnome Zone: Versions of Suburbia in Popular Culture', in Silverstone, Roger (ed.) *Visions of Suburbia*. London: Routledge.

Medhurst, Andy (2007), *The National Joke: Popular Comedy and English Cultural Identities*. Abingdon: Routledge.

Midwinter, Eric (1979), *Make 'em Laugh: Famous Comedians and Their World*. London: Allen & Unwin.

Mills, Brett (2005), *Television Sitcom*. London: British Film Institute.

Oakes, Philip (1975), *Tony Hancock: The Entertainers*. London: Woburn Press.

Osborne, John (1981), *A Better Class of Person*. London: Faber and Faber.

Perry, Jimmy (2002), *A Stupid Boy: The Autobiography of the Creator of 'Dad's Army'*. London: Century.

Porter, Larraine (2004), 'Women and Representation in British Comedy', in Wragg, Stephen (ed.), *Because I Tell a Joke or Two: Comedy, Politics and Social Difference*. London: Routledge.

Priestley, J.B. (1934), *Four-In-Hand*. London: William Heineman.

Priestley, J.B. (1975), *Particular Pleasures: Being a Personal Record of Some Varied Arts and Many Different Artists*. London: William Heineman.

Richards, Jeffrey (1997), *Films and British National Identity: From Dickens to 'Dad's Army'*. Manchester: Manchester University Press.

Sandbrook, Dominic (2005), *Never Had It So Good: A History of Britain from Suez to the Beatles*. London: Abacus.

Sandbrook, Dominic (2015), *The Great British Dream Factory: The Strange History of Our National Imagination*. London: Allen Lane.

Smiles, Samuel (1859/1887), *Self-Help; with Illustrations of Character and Conduct*. Mumbai: The Bombay St Paul Society.

Took, Barry (1990), *A Point of View*. London: Gerald Duckworth and Co.

Walker, Alexander (1974), *Hollywood England: The British Film Industry in the Sixties*. London: Michael Joseph.

Walton, John K. (2002), *The British Seaside: Holidays and Resorts in the Twentieth Century*. Studies in Popular Culture. Manchester: Manchester University Press.

Webber, Richard (2005), *Fifty Years of 'Hancock's Half Hour'*. London: Arrow.

Webber, Richard with Clement, Dick and La Frenais, Ian (1999), *Whatever Happened To The Likely Lads?* London: Orion Media.

Weight, Richard (2002), *Patriots: National Identity in Britain 1940–2000.* London: Pan Books.

Wolfe, Ronald (2003), *Writing Comedy: A Guide to Scriptwriting for TV, Radio, Film and Stage.* London: Robert Hale Ltd.

Journals and Periodicals

Allister, Ray (1949), 'Television', *The Sketch*, 14 September, pp. 32.

Banks-Smith, Nancy (1978) Review: Going Straight, *The Guardian*, 25 February, pp. 13.

Butcher, Cyril (1954), 'Television Topics: A Pot-Pourri of Christmas Programmes', *The Sketch*, 15 December, pp. 36.

Christy, Desmond (1984), Review: The School for Wives, *The Guardian*, 15 March, pp. 20.

Edmund, Bill (1965), 'My View', *The Stage*, 7 October, pp. 12.

Gilliatt, Penelope (1963), Review: The Wrong Arm of The Law, *The Observer*, 17 March, pp. 29.

Green, Janet (1987), Review: Terry and June, *The Stage*, 30 July, pp. 19.

Grieg, Ramsden (1961), 'June Is Happy Feeding Comics', *Aberdeen Evening Express*, 27 December, pp. 2.

Hodinott, Derek (1959), 'Our View', *The Stage*, 5 February, pp. 6.

Holt, Hazel (1976), 'Styling and thoughtful – new trend in sitcom', *The Stage*, 16 December, pp. 25.

James, Clive (1972), 'Television Review', *The Observer*, 11 March, pp. 8.

James, Clive (1978), 'Television Review', *The Observer*, 26 March, pp. 27.

James, Clive (1982), 'Television Review', *The Observer*, 8 March, pp. 26.

Letters Page (1959), 'James Half Hour', *The Guardian*, 7 December, pp. 8.

Mahoney, Louis (1975), 'Racist Beliefs "Endemic" Amongst White Population', *The Stage*, 2 October, pp. 10.

Masidlover, Lawrence (1960), 'Sid James Avoids Stardom – With', *The Stage*, 20 October, pp. 11.

Medhurst, Andy (1987), 'Terry and June', *The Listener*, 118, pp. 32.

Melly, George (1966), 'Television', *The Observer*, 1 May, pp. 25.

Mike Ford, *The Liverpool Echo* (1913). 6 January, pp. 3.

Moreton, Angela (1968), 'Television Today', *The Stage*, 8 August, pp. 12.

Obituary for Reg Varney (2008), *The Economist*, 4 December.

'Pick of The Week's Programmes' (1960), *The Stage*, 27 October, pp. 10.

Preston, James (1970), 'Extended Music Hall Joke as Series', *The Stage*, 21 May, pp.17.

Reynolds, Stanley (1969), 'Television', *The Guardian*, 10 March, pp. 8.

Sharland, Mike (1975), 'The Setting Was Wasted', *The Stage*, 31 July, pp. 13.

'Tele Views' (1957), *The Stage*, 16 May, pp. 6.

'Television Listings' (1980), *The Guardian*, 10 October, p. 20.

Towler, James (1971), 'Light Entertainment', *The Stage*, 11 February, pp. 11.

Online resources

Bracewell, Michael (2002), 'Tears Before Bedtime: Melancholy in British Sitcoms', at Frieze.com.

Coniham, Matthew (1979–87) 'Terry and June', BFI Screenonline www.screenonline.org.uk

5

The Double Act in a Fifty-Minute Package: The Filmed Television Show

Mrs Peel: 'Surely you've been thrown out of places before?'
Steed: 'Only the best places.'

Any tome that attempts to capture entertainments of the past, even the comparatively recent past, inevitably encounters a sense of loss, especially with the TV programmes that now fall into that dread archive category of 'missing believed wiped'. During the 1960s, '70s and '80s the genre of filmed TV series was responsible for a quintet of double acts that were as memorable in any of this book, even if two of them did not begin in an overtly comedic vein and a third was frequently hilarious because of its po-faced scripts and acting. The shows were repeated time and time again, abiding in the memory of viewers who were too young to recall their heyday or the ethos that they celebrated. Their heroes would forever be John Steed and Mrs Emma Peel, Jeff Randall and Marty Hopkirk, Lord Brett Sinclair and Danny Wilde, William Bodie and Ray Doyle – and Terry and 'Arfur'.

The Avengers

When ABC Television first aired *The Avengers* on 18 March 1961, it was a crime show akin to the *Edgar Wallace or Scotland Yard* series of cinematic second features. The narratives feature Brylcreemed spivs with horizontally striped ties; 'The Girl on the Trapeze' even guest stars Edwin Richfield, that ever-shifty habitué of Merton Park Studios. The show was a vehicle for Ian Hendry, as Dr David Keen was a GP avenging the murder of his wife with the assistance of an MI5 agent named John Steed. The latter was played by a little-known character performer named Patrick Macnee, who was then considering a move into production, notably with *The Valiant Years* (1961), an American Broadcasting Company documentary on the life of Winston Churchill.

Macnee was an intriguing performer with the voice of an affable club man and the hooded eyes of a bounder who is constantly on the lookout for the main chance. Asides from his jocularly untrustworthy Young Marley in the 1951 film *Scrooge* (Brian Desmond Hurst) British cinema had found little use for Macnee's talents. He could be found as a supporting officer in *The Battle of The River Plate* (The Archers, 1956) or *Three Cases of Murder* (Wendy Toye, George More O'Ferrall and David Eady, 1955), typically displaying a stiff upper lip in the background of a scene while the higher-billed actors emoted. Ironically, one of his earliest screen roles was as a spy in *Dick Barton at Bay* (Geoffrey Grayson, 1950), an early Hammer Films feature that looked as though it has a budget of 3s 6d.

Hendry left *The Avengers* after the first series, making Steed the main protagonist, partnered by judo-throwing anthropologist Cathy Gale, as played by Honor Blackman. Macnee adopted a new wardrobe: 'I use the Edwardian look – it's different. I have a number of peculiar likes and dislikes. They mean a lot but I can't give reasons for them. I've chosen my clothes on my own instinct completely' (quoted in Diana Lancaster, *TV Times*, 1 November 1963: 4–7). Blackman saw Dr Gale as 'a fantasy and not touchable' (quoted in Tony Geraghty, *The Guardian*, 11 January 1964: 5), and her incisive public-school headmistress-like tones were even more threatening to this week's villains than her expertise at judo.

Honor Blackman departed the show in 1964, and Season 4 was to be shot entirely on film. *The Avengers* also gained a new theme tune from Laurie Johnson and a new leading lady: Diana Rigg, a 27-year-old Shakespearean actress who famously auditioned for the show without having seen a single episode. The pairing of John Steed and Mrs Emma Peel was one of the finest duos on British television since Tony Hancock fired Sidney James. The idea of a crime-fighting couple was far from new on either side of the Atlantic. Pre-war cinema featured the upper-class bantering of Jack Hulbert and Cicely Courtneidge while Patrick Macnee saw John Steed as:

> A combination of Leslie Howard's Sir Percy Blakeney in *The Scarlet Pimpernel*, and a performance by Ralph Richardson in a film called *Q Planes*. In developing Steed's character, I considered one of the most important facets was to give him good manners. (Quoted in Rogers, 1983: 29).

Mrs Peel was a character much in the tradition of Joan Greenwood in *Kind Hearts and Coronets* (Robert Hamer, 1949) or Kay Kendall, who remains one of the finest high comediennes to appear in British films. She would have been a perfect *Avengers* leading lady – the juvenile and ebullient Kenneth More in *Genevieve* (Henry Cornelius, 1953) and the petulant West End leading man of Peter Finch in *Simon and Laura* (Muriel Box, 1955) both quailed before her wit and self-determination. Mrs Peel (Steed almost always uses her formal title) is not to be objectified in the manner of so many of her large- and small-screen contemporaries[1] – any luscious gaze or off-colour remark is returned with interest, thereby shattering 'the ideologies of objectification and containment behind it' (Miller, 2000: 204). The PR material for *The Avengers* claimed that 'if Emma represents the future of Britain,

---

1   The mid- to late 1960s did see an awful lot of television in which female character development consisted of screaming and the fluttering of false eyelashes.

Steed stands for the best of the past', both characters entirely at ease with each other and themselves. They were at the centre of an idiosyncratic vision of the 1960s with a blend of Edwardian and Lotus Elan sports cars – and where a spy with the brisk manner of a Mary Poppins would favour Pierre Cardin fashions.

By now Steed was, on the surface at least, the dandy as a middle-aged man who has adopted the manners and mores of his grandfather while enjoying the comforts of the present. When reviewing the notorious 'A Touch of Brimstone' episode (1966), Michael Billington thought that what mattered was that the villains behaved as if they took it all seriously[2] while Steed was able to point out the ludicrousness of the situation (*The Stage and Television Today*, 24 February 1966). If there is one word that summarises Macnee's performance, it is 'insouciance', just as with Rigg it is self-assurance. Gale joined force with Steed partially as a response to the death of her husband at the hands of the Mau Mau in the early 1950s, but with Mrs Peel, it is a spirit of adventure.

The investigations of Steed and Mrs Peel now encompassed upper-class eccentrics, some of whom created their own steam railway in the grounds of their lands as a retreat from the 1960s, and, for those traditionalists who can adapt to the modern world, Ronnie Barker's cat-obsessed Lord of The Manor of 'The Hidden Tiger' (1967) uses a fleet of uber-1960s Mini Mokes. Each story concludes with the reassuring message that in *The Avengers* there is still honey for tea and the duo chiefly encounters eccentrics, mad scientists and bounders who try to maintain the status quo by any means possible. At the end of 1965, *The Stage* reported that:

> As most of our readers will know ABC's series *The Avengers* has been sold to the American Broadcasting Company Inc. for showing on their network. ABC's managing director said last week that the total value of the transaction exceeds five million dollars. (2 December 1965: 11).

---

2   One thinks of Peter Wyngarde's The Honourable John Cleverly Cartney in 'A Touch of Brimstone' (1966); he was an actor born to play a Lord of Misrule who would stage a private Hell Fire Club in his basement.

Season 5 was also to employ colour film, the better to enhance its chances of being aired in the States. Dominic Sandbrook suggests that it was the success of the Bond films that persuaded the ABC in the US to screen the series (2015: 74) although to watch *Thunderball* (Terence Young, 1965) after a Steed/Mrs Peel adventure is rather akin to travelling by Austin A40 immedicably after experiencing an E-Type Jaguar. It is the epitome of the spy thriller as travelogue, with an apparent running time of three weeks and a hero who viewed contemporary Britain with as much contempt as any *Avengers* mastermind; Simon Winder remarks that when in *Goldfinger* (Guy Hamilton, 1964) 'Connery says that drinking un-chilled Dom Perignon is like listening to the Beatles without ear-muffs, the entire swinging sixties collapses' (2006: 2001).

Teaming Macnee with a strong female lead elevated *The Avengers* far beyond the conventions of contemporary Bond films, where various ingenues tended to exist either to conveniently drop dead after two reels or fall prey to the charms of 007's chest hair. It also elevated the programme above the vast bulk of the output of ITC[3], the company that made shows such as *The Saint* (1962–69) or *The Baron* (1965–66), which never managed the verve of *The Avengers*. Steed and Mrs Peel did not travel to an Elstree/Pinewood/Shepperton approximation of 'overseas' where the use of the suffix 'ski' denoted somewhere behind the Iron Curtain ('Hotelski', 'Gargeski', 'Telephonski', et al.).

Nor would the scripts deliberately employ US expressions that ITC deemed essential for a programme's sale to American TV networks (Chapman, 2002: 256) which only served to create a jarring effect when uttered by a stalwart British character actor.[4] Most important was the chemistry between the two leads; Fiddy noted that 'they both would alter the scripts' and regardless of this week's adventure, Emma Peel would often take the lead and Steed providing bantering support.

---

3   The Incorporated Television Company which effectively acted as the export wing of ATV.

4   'He's in a white sedan!' No, it's a Ford Corsair with a Dagenham registration number parked in Elstree Studios.

The standard-issue mini-skirted and mascaraed ingenue of *The Saint* had no place in *The Avengers*.

Crucially, Brian Clemens and his team did not attempt to evoke a Britain that was 'alive with birds and beetles, buzzing with minicars and telly stars, pulsing with half a dozen separate veins of excitement' (Halasz 1966: 30). The fourth season of *The Avengers* went to air a year before the famous Piri Halasz article about Swinging London appeared in *Time*. Fortunately, the viewers were spared the prospect of Steed transforming into a Playboy Club denizen in the style of Peter Lawford in *Salt and Pepper* (Richard Donner, 1968) or any other virtual embodiment of Blossom Dearie's *I'm Hip*. The later Simon Templar adventures would feature that dread moment when Roger Moore paid a visit to the 'All The "Young People" Look About 35' club somewhere near the Kings Road. He would then proceed to dance in the manner of a drunken uncle at a wedding disco with various mini-skirted extras to a 'happening tune' that sounded BBC Light Programme circa 1961.

As Shaun Levy points out in his indispensable *Ready Steady Go! Swinging London and The Invention of Cool*, the mainstream London media moved at a glacial pace, if at all, to embrace youth culture (2002: 127). The process was even slower when conducted by middle-aged film and television producers,[5] so *The Avengers* was wise to follow in the tradition of *Quatermass II* (Val Guest, 1957), *The Damned* (Joseph Losey, 1963) or *Village of the Damned* (Wolf Rilla, 1960), where the seemingly mundane hid a country of infinite menace. The colour episodes encouraged a more surrealist, almost cartoon-like atmosphere. For many devotees of the show, the finest story is 'Who's Who' (1967), with Freddie Jones and Patricia Haines as two decidedly démodé enemy agents. Steed and Mrs Peel often travel to a countryside reminiscent of Angus Calder's ideal village – 'a pleasant Anglican vicar, an affable squire, assorted professionals, tradesmen, many of whom will be "characters"' (1991: 188). But in *The Avengers*, there will probably be an army

---

5   Exhibit B for the prosecution: the 'hippies' in *Carry On Camping* (Gerald Thomas, 1969).

black-suited judo-throwing heavies in the secret control room located in the basement of manor house.

Alas, pay disputes between Diana Rigg and the producers meant that her first colour season was also her swansong on the programme. The final 1968–69 series suffered from a lack of chemistry (that word again) between Macnee and Tara King (Linda Thorson) and scripts that were more self-consciously 'zany'. When re-watching the sixth series, one is put in mind of Steve Martin's description of the end of his stand-up career: 'In 1981 my act was like an overly plumed bird whose next evolutionary step was extinction' (2008: 193). The last episode of *The Avengers*, 'Bizarre', was screened in March 1969 but there was a tired revamp in the form of *The New Avengers* (1976–77), with Steed now supported by the Head Prefect-like Joanna Lumley, and Gareth Hunt (all scowls and flared trousers). There was also a 1998 film version (Jeremiah Chechik) that is best not spoken of, but the real end was with 'The Forget Me Knot' (1968).

Possibly the best description of the Macnee and Rigg dynamic is of a Noel Coward and Gertrude Lawrence for the 1960s. Barry King referred to the latter as 'two people deeply fond of each other but constantly bickering and testing the limits of that friendship in the certain knowledge it is unbreakable' (2014: 182). Exchange 'bantering' for 'bickering' and you could be describing Steed and Mrs Peel, and just as the three plays that Coward and Lawrence appeared in together were enough to secure their legend, those two series of *The Avengers* meant that Macnee and Rigg would forever be Steed and Mrs Peel. When the pair say farewell, the actor's insouciant mask drops for the first and last time. His use of the name Emma conveys far more emotional impact than any number of self-important dramas. Patrick Garland saw a 'close connection between the art of high comedy and a capacity for rage' (1998: 237), but another is the receptiveness to emotional pain. When Emma Peel departs from the series the dream has ended; there would be no more honey for tea.

Randall and Hopkirk (Deceased)

'We were ITC's first real comedy double act', mused Kenneth Cope. The theme of *Randall and Hopkirk (Deceased)* was that the private detective Marty Hopkirk is murdered and returns from the grave to assist his friend and partner Jeff Randall. The latter was to be played by Dave Allen, but Mike Pratt was ultimately assigned the part. The grim-faced actor was a regular ITC 'heavy', glowering his way through several episodes of *Danger Man* or *Gideon's Way* (1965–66). Pratt could also be seen in films wearing a vest and scowling with aplomb – you can see him thus attired in *This Is My Street* (Sydney Hayers, 1964), *Face of A Stranger* (John Llewellyn Moxey, 1964) and *Repulsion* (Roland Polanski, 1965).

In the mid-1960s Pratt reflected that 'it's great to get away from playing the amiable slob characters at last' (quoted in *The Stage*, 21 May 1964: 9) but even when he was cast as a police inspector in *Impact* (Peter Maxwell, 1963), the actor evinced an agreeably louche air. He was also a songwriter and musician – notably in collaboration with Tommy Steele and Lionel Bart – before becoming an actor; in the Free Cinema short *Mama Don't Allow* (Karel Reisz and Tony Richardson, 1956) he can be seen sporting a way-out beard and playing the kazoo. By the early 1960s, Pratt's career encompassed revue and straight drama, and he even appeared in the highly controversial beatnik drama *The Party's Over* (Guy Hamilton, 1965) as a pot-smoking Cuban jazz drummer; a true masterpiece of off-beat casting.

His partner in crime fighting was played by Kenneth Cope, a versatile actor who was the master of nervous apprehension, his characters often looking over their shoulders for any possible retribution. In the 1960s Cope was best known for his comedy roles in the BBC's *That Was The Week That Was* (1962–63) and playing Jed Stone in *Coronation Street*; Joseph Losey used his insecure bluster to good effect in *The Criminal* (1960) and *The Damned* (1963). Cope also made a charmingly a wry and determined hero in the B-feature *Death Trap* (John Llewellyn Moxey, 1962). As Jeff Randall and Marty Hopkirk, the two actors created as memorable a double act as seen on British television – in Kenneth

Cope's words, 'Mike Pratt was a lovely man, and we gelled. We wanted to create characters who people could believe that they really were friends.' The pair bicker, banter, squabble – and are rarely out of each other's sights. Completing the main cast was the Australian-born actress Annette Andre as Marty's widow Jeannie, who managed to create a real character from a very underwritten part.

Pratt and Cope created a double act that was, despite the show's premise, totally believable, one where the characters had a credible past and a mundane present; in Cope's words 'they were always arguing about the car'. Nor, fortunately, were there many attempts at glamour. Across the studio floor, Peter Wyngarde as Jason King presided over *Department S* with an insouciant disregard for his expense account while Jeff Randall is in perpetual need of funds and operates in a London of beige wallpaper and rickety plumbing. His idea of fine dining involves a thermos flask of soup while sitting in the laundry, while Marty will appear at regular intervals to inspire or goad our downbeat hero. Even their character names are believably mundane.

The programmes was not a critical success, but five decades later, the 'TV public' still enjoy the adventures of Jeff and Marty. In 2000 *Randall and Hopkirk (Deceased)* was revived as a vehicle for Reeves and Mortimer, but it could never aspire to the charm of the original programme. There was no Annette Andre, Mike Pratt or Kenneth Cope, missing the two multi-talented performers who had created a relationship that was very real. It was the nearest that ITC ever came to Morecambe and Wise, with Pratt's world-weary straight man gripping the Victor's steering wheel and moaning 'Why can't you stay dead like anyone else?'

The Persuaders!

In 1970 ITC re-tried the double act formula on an enhanced budget with *The Persuaders!* a show which established its theme from the outset. If you are Roger at the wheel of a Bahama Yellow Aston Martin DBS6 women will automatically find you irresistible despite a green shirt-and-cravat combo that can fairly be described as 'interesting'. Indeed, the show's PR claimed that:

> The series has sartorial elegance. Danny Wilde and Brett Sinclair have the money to buy only the (most) expensive clothes. Ultra-modern but not Carnaby Street. Modes for the modern man. And Roger Moore designed his own clothes for the series. (Quoted in Hunt 1998: 66).

The Persuaders! even carried the famous end credit 'Lord Sinclair's clothes designed by Roger Moore'. The show's basic premise was that a British aristocratic playboy (Roger Moore) teams with a self-made US millionaire (Tony Curtis) to fight crime and rescue damsels in distress. Filming in France was blended with studio work in Pinewood and placing the main characters in the real Monte Carlo tended to highlight the fact that *The Persuaders!* was a colour supplement – that 1962 innovation dismissed by Bernard Levin as 'the nadir in the advocacy for conspicuous consumerism' (2003: 185) – writ large.

The message was clear: drink this brand of vodka, consume these after-dinner mints, wear this aftershave, venture out in public in this orange cravat and you too could enjoy the same lifestyle as Brett and Danny – even if you live in Southampton or Yeovil. When *The Persuaders!* entered production, much publicity derived from its budget of £2.5 million or £80,000 per episode but it wholly, and rather charmingly, lacked class. John Steed would have almost certainly dismissed Brett as a parvenu, and you could image a teenaged Alan Partridge sat in from of a rented Rediffusion TV set in the living room of a semi-detached villa in Norwich, frantically scribbling notes about the various brand names. Beneath an exterior that was as glossy as the packaging of a box of After Eight mints was an extremely dated format, a fact that was noticed even at the time:

> It is a thriller based on the theory popular in very old movies that if you tap a man lightly on the point of the chin he will shoot into the

air, fly backwards across a bar breaking a good deal of furniture into the bargain and at least 20 bottles, and then emerge, totally unscathed, to do exactly the same to you. (Mortimer, *The Observer*, 26 September 1971: 31).

Two points. Firstly, John Mortimer's description perfectly describes the standard-issue Roger Moore fighting style, be it as Lord Brett Sinclair, Simon Templar or 007. Secondly, predictability was what the average ITC viewer craved; regardless of budget there had to be that 'white Jaguar off a cliff' footage and at least one villain wearing a fez. In that sense, Danny and Brett did resemble a Variety act in that the audience demanded the same routines on a weekly basis, including the bantering and the vain attempts at disco dancing.

In short, this is the archetypal 'Safari Suit' man series (Hunt, 1998: 66) with our duo acting as vigilante tourists in a succession of Mediterranean resorts. It is a show that celebrates a comic-strip double act; a middle-aged duo who exist merely to banter, dance really badly, wear some quite appalling clothes and leer at women. But it was the dynamic between the two leads that was the main reason for tuning in, even if Roger's gentlemanly memoirs hinted at a not-entirely-smooth shoot (Moore, 2014: 73–74). Brett is the deadpan straight man and Danny is the ad-libbing and kinetic comic, but the stars did have a chemistry that made the programme.

The show ran for twenty-four episodes and enjoyed considerable success in world markets, apart from in the USA. Lew Grade boasted that ITC made £17 million in export sales during 1971 thanks to *The Persuaders!* and *Robinson Crusoe on Ice*[6] (*The Guardian*, 21 December 1971: 14). But by 1972 Roger Moore was shooting *Live and Let Die* (1973), so a second season was never going to be a serious proposition. Brett and Danny were not in the same comic league as Jeff and Marty and every aspect of *The Persuaders!* contains more cheese than a warehouse full of Red Leicester. Still, as, 'The Old, The New, and

---

6   Let us hope this evident masterpiece survives.

The Deadly' (1971) so clearly demonstrates, who could resist a show in which Tony Curtis and Roger Moore arrive by Aston Martin DBS to an evening of far-out grooving?[7]

The Professionals

The next programme in this chapter is one that I debated long and hard about including. British television has a long tradition of serious crime-fighting double acts – one could cite Douglas Wilmer and Nigel Stock as Sherlock Holmes and Doctor Watson, Barlow and Watts of *Z-Cars* and *Softly Softly*, the Flying Squad's Jack Regan and George Carter and even David Callan and Lonely to name but a few. How, therefore, could I devote space to *The Professionals* (1977–83), a series that evolved as a partial response to a grim period in British history? The answer is that after listening to scripts which required actors playing threats to civilisation actually to say 'You vill die. All of you,' it fast became apparent that it would not be fair to exclude it.

The Professionals was made for LWT by Brian Clemens's Mark One Productions and concerned the government department CI5. According to Gordon Jackson's ranted voiceover, it was formed to defeat anarchy, acts of terror, crimes against the public. 'To combat it I've got special men – experts from the army, the police, from every service – these are The Professionals!'. The tone was set from the outset in the opening episode 'Private Madness Public Danger', which aired on 30 December 1977 and boasted opening credits that had Bodie and Doyle skipping around a gym while trying (and failing) to look uber-hard.[8] In the quite brilliant words of Taylor Parkes in *The Quietus*:

---

7 That is, dancing like two drunken uncles at a wedding.
8 All that was required to perfect this sequence would be Yakety Sax from *The Benny Hill Show*. Alas, for the second season, there was a new 'Ford Granada through plate glass' opening credits.

Since they couldn't yet afford to shoot on location in central London, things keep kicking off in leafy corners of the Home Counties: Amersham, Rickmansworth, Burnham Beeches. You can barely move on the mean streets of Marlow for left-wing extremists with fluttering accents, hanging out the side of Cortinas, pumping bullets into startled golfers. (1 April 2014).

In Clemens's *The Avengers*, Steed and Mrs Peel defeated rotters, cads and megalomaniacs within the confines of a fantastical landscape (Sandbrook, 2015: 71) but *The Professionals* attempted to engage with the late 1970s of terrorist gangs and kidnapping. Alas, what they often created was a low-rent British *Starsky and Hutch* filmed in the Home Counties with Austin Allegros in the background, plus, for the later editions, plentiful scenes of Lewis Collins and Martin Shaw running around goods yards, various abandoned factories plus the occasional gasworks.

Some critics were initially very unkind, Clive James pointing out that even the title had been previously used on a Burt Lancaster film and that 'everything else about *The Professionals is* as predictable as industrial action at British Leyland'. This is a world where 'the terrorists take hostages, snipe at politicians, blow people up, park on double yellow lines' although James was of the opinion that the suspects usually caved in to avoid being subjected to any more of Brian Clemens's dialogue (*The Observer*, 29 January 1979: 29). However, elements such as Roger Lloyd Pack in 'Long Shot' (1978) as 'Ramos' – the overdubbed hitman with a George Harrison in *Rubber Soul* hairstyle – or a luckless Ford Cortina Mk I[9] being hurled down an embankment at this week's gang of terrorists in 'Heroes' (1978) – created a comedy equal to any *Monty Python* sketch.

At the time of writing, you still might encounter some truly deluded types who bemoan how the perfidious impact of 'political correctness'

9　Second-hand Ford Cortinas were usually doomed, together with any FD-series Vauxhall. Over the course of fifty-seven editions of *The Professionals* it became increasingly apparent that many anarchist gangs were operating on a very restricted budget.

has not only deprived them *of Love Thy Neighbour* but has also ensured that *The Professionals* could not be made today. Yes, PC is depriving viewers of Martin Shaw scowling from beneath that aforementioned hairstyle, villains with evil moustaches (David Suchet as Krisvas in 1978's 'Where The Jungle Ends' wins the coveted award for 'The Most Menacing Facial Decoration in CI5 History') and international assassins recruiting hitmen from the local greaser café (in 'Look After Annie' (1978)). They are further being deprived of narrative twists that leap the Rubicon from 'implausible' to 'frankly demented' with undercover agents adopting fetching poses so their macho profiles could be silhouetted in warehouse doorways.

To watch the box set today is to learn a lesson that is no less sad for being predictable. There were some ambitious episodes – notably 'Everest Was Also Conquered' (1978), 'In The Public Interest' (1978) and 'The Madness of Mickey Hamilton' (1979) – but in the main what seemed the height of televisual sophistication when you were aged 10[10] and counting down the minutes to nine o' clock on a Friday evening, does have the capacity to date badly. When you are a male of that age, the condemnation by Mary Whitehouse – 'violent, uncouth and thoroughly unsavoury!' – seemed like the ultimate in critical raves, and a further excuse to purchase that Corgi scale model of Bodie's Ford Capri 3.0S Mk III. Four decades later, you tend to marvel at the po-faced nature of the entire enterprise and plots centred on ruthless London gangsters not knowing what the Home Secretary looked like. In 1984 Keith Allen and Peter Richardson famously wrote and starred in the Channel Four spoof *The Bullshitters* but little could have the comedy value of the life and times of CI5.

But for all the many and various faults of *The Professionals* – many of the scripts, most of the storylines and the fact that in 'Stake Out' (1978) Tony Osoba was billed as 'Handsome Negro' – the fact remained that Bodie and Doyle remained inseparable. Clemens may have threatened to replace the boys with other members of CI5, but to any true devotee of

---

10 Parkes makes the most acute observation that 'on the subject of women, Bodie and Doyle, both in their thirties, talk to each other like teenage virgins'.

the series, Bodie and Doyle were the show. They would drive to excess, chase anyone who wore their sunglasses indoors and who spoke with an all-purpose 'Evil Foreigner' accent and receive their shouted orders from Gordon Jackson. Indeed, in 'New Dog With Old Tricks', Cowley announced to the new CI5 recruits that 'You'll be paired off and from then on you're The Bisto Kids!'

Leaving aside the unworthy idea that a Bisto Kid might be more credible in a fight scene than Martin Shaw, it was clear that Bodie and Doyle were both essential to the show's viewing figures. The star of the show was Lewis Collins, whose performance was indicative of an actor loving every moment of being on screen, a man born to smirk in a driving mirror or, at certain moments, coming close to breaking the fourth wall with a broad grin to the camera. Although Jackson's Cowley is Bodie and Doyle's boss – standard lines 'Malt Scotch', 'Aye!' and 'You're off the case!' – the straight man is Shaw's Doyle, a sensitive sort of a CI5 agent whose default facial expression is of one already wearied by the ways of the world and the constant jokes about his perm.

The fifth and final season of *The Professionals* was filmed in 1981, and towards the end of our period, those ITV viewers who craved explosions, Ford PR cars and implausible chases through the docklands were rewarded with *Dempsey and Makepeace* (1985–86). The premise – US detective lieutenant and female London Met detective sergeant – was a throwback to *The Scarlet Web* (1954) and other forgotten 1950s B-features and the result made *Howard's Way*[11] resemble *Titus Andronicus* by comparison. Possibly the most memorable aspects of the series were that (a) it managed to be even worse than *C.A.T.S. Eyes*[12] and (b) it was the inspiration for a brilliant *Spitting Image* parody *Sheep and Anteater*. But it was never on a par with *The Professionals*, and you could even argue that Doyle and Bodie represent the Apollonian and Dionysian

---

11 1985–90. An everyday BBC story of yachting folk that did for the Solent Region what Jess Conrad did for British pop music.

12 A 1985–87 TVS espionage series whose atmosphere of international glamour was fatally undermined by the shots of Southampton and a theme tune that sounded as though it was recorded on a used Casio keyboard.

dichotomy in televisual terms. Except the duo would probably then place you under arrest on the grounds of being a Greek terrorist.

Minder

'Minder is a new type of action/character television series featuring an independent bodyguard who often operates on the fringe of legality but always seems to end up on the side of the angels.' (Leon Griffiths' original proposal, quoted in Alvarado and Stewart, 1985: 87)

Leon Griffiths created *Minder* from an abandoned film project: 'a pretty nasty story – dark, gloomy, black and tough' (quoted in Alvarado and Stewart, 1985: 87). It was the comic relief characters of the spiv and his bodyguard who became the eventual protagonists of the TV series, but their misadventures always took place against a grim background for, as with *The Avengers*, the programme did not begin as a comedy. To watch the first season, which started with 'Gunfight at the OK Laundrette' on 29 October 1979, is to vicariously experience a city of grey-faced extras and cafes serving fried botulism with optional HP sauce. The landscape of 'Come in T-64, Your Time Is Ticking Away' (1979) is dominated by 1960s Le Corbusier-style estates that are already falling into decay and streets littered with dead Ford Zodiacs. In 1979 Nancy Banks-Smith observed that 'George Cole, that fine comic actor, seems oddly subdued as Waterman's greasy governor' (*The Guardian*, 20 November: 11) but as the 1980s progressed the series began to create its own mythology. By the middle of the decade *Minder* was 'an enormous success both in Britain and overseas (particularly in Australia) and Thames keep asking Euston if they can make just one more series' (Alvarado and Stewart, 1985: 96).

In the third season, the focal point became more Daley and less Terry McCann. Once Dennis Waterman and George Cole appeared on *Top of The Pops* 'singing' 'What Are We Gonna Get 'Er Indoors' in 1983 and the spin-off comic books, *Minder* was now more of a comedy show. Had Euston's original casting choice of Denholm Elliot played Daley, the character would probably have lacked any veneer of outward sympathy. It is quite easy to envisage a fake squadron leader type wearing a fake regimental badge on his blazer and giving Waterman's Terry McCann orders in an equally fake RP accent. Waterman's eponymous hero could have been Detective Sergeant George Carter's less intelligent cousin, but the casting of George Cole was a masterstroke.

Griffiths referred to Daley as dressing like a 'well-dressed, dodgy employee of the Citizens' Advice Bureau' and Cole plays him with a combination of patently false bonhomie and wounded pride. Arthur's near contemporary as a small-screen wide-boy was Derek Trotter of *Only Fools and Horses*, but David Jason's initially hard-edged and aggressive little spiv rapidly became 'lovable'.[13] The script editor for *Minder*, Linda Agran, once argued that 'I think the more society is going the way it is, the more people are understanding and identifying with the little men trying to fiddle, or whatever, their own success and somehow get an edge' (quoted in Cooke, 2015: 161). Yet, beneath some of the finest lines to be heard on British television[14] and the faux-matey cross-talk was not a sentimental 'little man' hero but a venal 'businessman' who exploits anyone who comes within his orbit. His modus operandi is to keep stronger forces – be they police or real villains – at bay and Terry from becoming too ambitious. George Cole never lost sight of how there was, behind the constant patter and the catchphrases, a ruthless individual of a deliberately vague background.

When *Minder* began, Terry McCann was aged about 30 but had already served two prison sentences, one for grievous bodily harm and the other for attempted robbery. A promising career as a boxer was destroyed when he took part in a rigged match (Hawkins 2014: 15). The younger Arthur Daley would never have worked directly for the Krays

---

13 Another of the many reasons for enjoying *Minder* is that no one ever utters the phrase 'Lovely Jubbly'.

14 'You make contact with your customer. Understand their needs. And then flog them something they could well do without.'

or the Richardsons, but he might well have provided one of their minor associates with a Vauxhall Cresta – with no questions asked of course. Today he might operate in a London of shod and chipped Formica tables, but he no longer resides there; Arthur delights in his children's private education, his second-hand Jaguars and Daimlers plus a sub-Savile Row wardrobe.

These props also serve to mask a character who was memorably described by Clive James as attaining 'such depths of seediness that a flock of starlings could feed off him ... His past might catch up with him. The future looms' (*The Observer*, 28 February 1982: 48). And so, Daley will use Terry to stave off the negative possibilities of both. *Minder* was not the first ITV show to be centred on a seedy underworld, and when the first episode aired some viewers recalled the 1971 LWT series *Budgie*. But that was shot on videotape, and Adam Faith's eponymous wide boy was terrified by the towering figure of Iain Cuthbertson's Charles Endall, the series' comic-sinister nemesis. Terry and Arthur are not just more of a double act than Bird and Endall; McCann is trying to live honestly in a world that wishes to use only his anti-social skills. He is the tarnished knight of Acton and Hammersmith, whose battered white charger was probably issued with a dodgy MOT certificate.

The show was supposed to have ended with the 1985 Christmas special 'Minder on the Orient Express', which marked the definitive transition into a comedy show; Julian Barnes bemoaned that 'towards the end there even an insulting "comic" fight and the decline into caper was complete' (*The Observer*, 29 December 1985: 24). But it returned for a seventh season in 1989 when Nicolas Davis argued:

> I would have no qualms about describing the first couple of series of *Minder* (way back in the late seventies and early eighties) as perfect adult entertainment. They had everything from witty scripts to gut-wrenching plots: a mixture of black humour and often explicit violence that was beautifully placed in time (the present) and place (London) (*The Stage*, 12 January 1989: 56).

But Davis went on to describe very accurately how the temptation to emphasise the Daley/McCann double act had overbalanced the programme into light entertainment and 1989 Terry now seemed to be totally disillusioned. A further element in the programme's success was that from the outset Terry craved self-improvement and perhaps some form of recognition from Daley. By Series 7 the banter seems to be more forced, the background faces in the Winchester Club look distinctly tired, and Terry was verging on middle age. Arthur had recently stored stolen video recorders in his flat, thereby earning his employee another prison sentence. The ratings were lower than on the previous season, and Cole reflected that this might have reflected how the Terry/Arthur relationship 'had reached a definite low' (Cole and Hawkins, 2013: 200).

Minder, to quote Clive James once more, was a series concerned with 'the life on the verge of criminality, where nothing is nailed down' but now the balance has been tipped. It was also frequently concerned with dreams of seldom realised victories for so many of the principal characters: 'Mr Chisholm' (the great Patrick Malahide) once moans 'I'm up for promotion to Inspector this afternoon … again' – and in 1989 it is as if Terry has finally realised that Arthur is never going to treat him as a surrogate son. When we discover at the beginning of Series 8 that Terry has married and emigrated to Australia, the sadness at the dissolution of the partnership is mixed with a sense of relief for the character. A double act can withstand many blows, but rarely betrayal; it was time for it to end.

With thanks to Kenneth Cope, and Dick Fiddy of The British Film Institute.

Bibliography

Books
Ackroyd, Peter (2001), *London: The Biography*. London: Vantage.
Alvarado, Manuel and Stewart, John (1985), *Made for Television: Euston Films Limited*. London: BFI.

Bray, Christopher (2014), *1965: The Year Modern Britain was Born*. London: Simon & Schuster.

Calder, Angus (1991), *The Myth of The Blitz*. London: Pimlico.

Chapman, James (2002), *Saints and Avengers: British Adventure Series of the 1960s*. London: IB Tauris.

Cole, George and Hawkins, Brian (2013), *The World Was My Lobster: The Autobiography*. London: John Blake.

Cooke, Lez (2015), *British Television Drama: A History*. London: BFI.

Garland, Patrick (1998), *The Incomparable Rex: Rex Harrison*. London: Macmillan.

Hawkins, Brian (2004), *The Complete Minder*. Hong Kong: Inkstone Books.

Hunt, Leon (1998), *British Low Culture: From Safari Suits to Sexploitation*. London: Routledge.

King, Barry (ed.) (2014), *The Letters of Noël Coward*. London: Bloomsbury.

Levin, Bernard (2003), *The Pendulum Years: Britain in The Sixties*. London: Icon Book.

Levy, Shawn (2002), *Ready Steady Go! Swinging London and The Invention of Cool*. London: Harper Collins.

Martin, Steve (2008), *Born Standing Up: A Comic's Life*. London: Simon & Schuster.

Miller, Jeffrey S. (2000), *Something Completely Different: British Television and American Culture*. Minneapolis: University of Minnesota Press.

Moore, Roger (2014), *Last Man Standing: Tales from Tinseltown*. London: Michael O'Mara Books.

Rogers, Dave (1983), *The Avengers*. London: ITV Books in association with Michael Joseph Ltd.

Sandbrook, Dominic (2015), *The Great British Dream Factory: The Strange History of Our Imagination*. London: Allen Lane.

Winder, Simon (2006), *The Man Who Saved Britain: A Personal Journey Into the Disturbing World of James Bond*. London: Picador.

Journals and Periodicals

'Another Big Part for Mike Pratt' (1964), *The Stage*, 21 May, pp. 9.

'ATV to export £17 million' (1971), *The Guardian*, 21 December, pp. 14.

Banks-Smith, Nancy (1979), 'Television Review', *The Guardian*, 20 November, pp. 11

Barnes, Julian (1985), 'Television Review', *The Observer*, 29 December, pp. 24.

Billington, Michael (1966), Report, *The Stage and Television Today*, 24 February.

Davis, Nicolas (1989), 'Television Today', *The Stage*, 12 January, pp. 56.

Geraghty, Tony (1964), 'Avenging Angel', *The Guardian*, 11 January, pp. 5.

Halasz, Piri (1966), 'London: The Swinging City (You Can Walk Across It On The Grass)', *Time*, 15 April.

James, Clive (1979), 'Television Review', *The Observer*, 29 January, pp. 29.

James, Clive (1982), 'Television Review', *The Observer*, 28 February, pp. 48.

Lancaster, Diana (1963), 'The Immaculate Avengers', *TV Times*, 1 November, pp. 4–7.

Mortimer, John (1971), 'Television Review', *The Observer*, 26 September, pp. 31.

'Report' (1966), *The Times*, 25 November, p. 12.

Shulman, Milton (1970), 'Television Review', *Evening Standard*, 18 February.

'The Avengers is ABC's First Series Sold to US Network' (1965), *The Stage*, 2 December, pp. 11.

Online sources

Parkes, Taylor (2014), 'Hunks Punch Lunks: The Fascist Sex Cult Of The Professionals', *The Quietus*. 1 April. http://thequietus.com/articles/14873-the-professionals

6

The Subtle Art of the Straight Man

'Kindly Leave The Stage!'

They can be the authority figure, the bureaucrat or schoolteacher, the smooth almost oily partner to the zany comic, or an example of apparent sanity whose attempt at a straightforward presentation keeps being thwarted. In the words of Syd Little, 'He has to be straight! It is not your job to get the laughs – the straighter you are, the funnier the act!'. In a comic duo, the straight man further re-emphasises the comic's marginal status in addition to diverting the attention or the affection of the audience. Oliver Double argues that 'the joy of the classic double act is seeing idiocy triumphing over soberness, chaos over order, the higher brought down by, the lower. In this sense, the funnyman is usually the most important member of the act and usually the bigger star' (2012: 117). To which one might argue that this might be the case with the audience but seldom if ever within the mechanics of the act.

Regarding the minstrel shows of the nineteenth century, Lawrence E. Mintz notes that US audiences responded to the Dionysian freedom of Tambo and Bones and their 'common-sense victories over the stuffy, pompous, dull Interlocutor' (1985: 76). This would apply to audiences to Victorian England and one common persona for a straight man in British comedies is the equivalent of the American 'stuffed-shirt' – a Malvolio-like character who might be 'perhaps a high-ranking officer who specialises in parade ground manoeuvres but never sees the front' (Klapp, 1962).

By contrast, Chesney Allen reacted with tolerance and amusement towards Bud Flanagan or with stern admonishments as the human embodiment of red tape. A straight man might exploit the comic, as with Ben Warriss with Jimmy Jewel, or react to his antics with the resigned bemusement of Ernie Wise. Mike Winters believed that his role was to create the atmosphere 'pacing it, timing it' adding that it was 'more difficult to be a double act than a single act. You have to have the personal relationship. A lot of acts break up because they don't see eye to eye, and because the stage is such an emotional thing anyway' (*Birmingham Post*, 1 October 1969: 10).

Gary Morecambe points out that with Ernie Wise 'he regarded it as a nine to five – not that it ever was nine to five of course!' – job; Ernie made the decision to switch off once he left the studio. The focal point was the comic, the responsibility of maintaining the rhythm and the tempo was that of the straight man – and to judge which is the most stressful and exacting role is akin to deciding which limb is the most valuable. When the Winters brothers split in 1978, Bernie reflected:

'I relied on Mike. It was his hand I reached for when we went on stage, his presence dispelled the fear of facing an audience. But over the years the excitement went, we got tired, dispirited'. Bernie saw his St Bernard as more than a gimmick but 'my only method of survival. Schnorbitz is the new Mike. I can stroke him, hold his collar, even cuddle the dog when I'm terrified or cannot think of the next line. He is the warm living presence of a mate on stage.' (Quoted in Marriott, *Liverpool Echo*, 22 September 1979: 7).

Bernie's observations are a prime example of how it was not the public but the comics themselves who valued the straight man's role – devoid of Mike he saw himself as 'a half-person; a guy with a silly grin' (Mariott, 1979). One thinks once more of the musical routines of Flanagan and Allen, Chesney always standing a half-step behind Bud, always supportive, never attempting to take the limelight for himself. Some acts were fluid with the positions of comic and straight man, such as *The Two Ronnies*. It was Corbett who proved to be particularly adept in the role, whether his character displays a menacingly blank insouciance, the qualities of a suburban innocent who finds himself adrift in a world of genteel confusion or irate managers confronted by the eccentric or the plain stupid portrayed by Ronnie Barker.

On *The Goon Show* (BBC, 1951–60) Harry Secombe as Neddie Seagoon was the essential conduit between the world of post-imperial wasteland that was *The Goon Show* and the listener: 'Catalyst chorus, figure and scapegoat in his relations with the inspired defectives voiced by Milligan and Sellers ... He represented the Odysseus on the madcap expedition who, however moonstruck himself, encountered its ordeals as the audience would have done' (Fisher, 2013: 365). When Milligan was away from the show, Sellers could play his roles; during his one absence from *The Goon Show*, four actors were required to take his place. But Secombe's rare breaks from the programme could be filled by neither Graham Stark nor Dick Emery; he was the heart of the Goons, the eternal hero who was undefeated by the mad, the useless and the second-rate.

A straight man is not to be confused with the stooge who was 'not a partner to the comic and never gets co-billing; sometimes the stooge is unnamed on the bill'. As with US comedy, 'the stooge is only part of the act, an assistant to the star' (Cullen et al., 2006: 257). In Vaudeville, such a performer might play the part of the drunk or the heckler from the audience, while some stooges would remain absolutely silent. From the 1940s to the 1970s Hylda Baker worked with a succession of tall male partners whose job was to don the wig and frock of the star's silent companion 'Cynthia': 'She knows, y'know. She just won't let on, that's what!' Maureen Lipman pointed out that in the 1980s, television sketch comedies frequently employed actresses as the stooge, and they were typically cast for either their 'glamour' or 'old bagness' (quoted in Banks and Swift, 1988: 252). After the Second World War, one of Arthur Askey's most famous partners was Sabrina, a.k.a. Norma Sykes, a model who was cast to add publicity to the comic's 1955 BBC TV series *Before Your Very Eyes*. In the comic's own, rather dispiriting words:

> I felt I wanted to give the show a gimmick of some sort. So I hit on the idea of having a dumb blonde around the set ... We held auditions for a suitable dumb-cluck and found one in Norma Sykes. She had a lovely face and figure, but could not act, sing, dance, or even walk properly, although she had come to London to try her luck as a model. (Askey, 1975: 164)

The name 'Sabrina' was selected as a reference to the stage show *Sabrina Fair,* and within weeks she was attracting headlines that made the worst Talbot Rothwell script appear Proustian by comparison. The lady herself once wryly reflected of her publicity, 'even clergymen ask me to open their garden parties and bazaars. They don't do that because I sing in the choir or because they think I'm Dame Edith Evans' (Sykes, *Lancashire Evening Post*, 28 October 1957: 4). But Sabrina was never an equal part of the act, Askey writing in his memoirs that 'she eventually became bigger than me (in every sense) in the show ... The tail had begun to wag the dog, so she had to go' (1975: 165).

After the break-up with his double act with Joe Baker, Jack Douglas appeared with Des O'Connor as Alf Ippititimus, a far more active character than either Cynthia or Sabrina, but remaining a stooge to the star. By 1968 Benny Hill had established what was to be the abiding template of *The Benny Hill Show* with two main stooges. Jackie Wright was an ex-jazz musician turned film and TV extra who was almost born to have his bald head slapped by the star. Bob Todd was given more lines (he was a splendid 'Major Johnnie' to Hill's 'Fanny Craddock'), and according to Half Man, Half Biscuit, his tall dissipated appearance helped him to resemble 99 per cent of all gargoyles. A bankrupt farmer who became an actor in middle age, Todd had already stooged for Dick Emery and appeared in the West End production of the Spike Milligan/ John Antrobus comedy *The Bedsitting Room* before he joined Hill's cast. Milligan's habit of referring to 'Borrowing Bob Todd!' or 'Bob "Hide The Silver" Todd!' at the curtain call inferred a performer with considerable personal problems and in 1975 he vanished before he was due to appear in *Hans Christian Anderson* at the Palladium (Hall, *Daily Mirror*, 20 May 1975: 8). Todd was discovered in a Dublin hospital several days later and was suspended from *The Benny Hill Show* for the next five years. A stooge is an employee of the principal comedian, and his or her services may be dispensed with if and when required.

For comics who specialised in sketch work or film vehicles, there was the often-adroit option to work with a straight actor. Midwinter points out that Will Hay never failed 'to surround himself with fine character actors, and, without doubt, his own high standards were most frequently attained when he was working with such talented confreres' (1979: 58). *The Ghost of St Michael's* (Marcel Varnel, 1941) benefits immeasurably from Raymond Huntley, the master of scandalised disdain. Such was Huntley's screen persona that the audiences would hardly have been surprised at the revelation that the headmaster was, in fact, a Nazi spy. Garry Marsh – tall, imposing, and with a smoothness that was usually on the wrong side of 'shifty' – was always a welcome part of any George Formby picture even if he initially agreed to appear in *I See Ice* (Anthony Kimmins, 1938) after a producer informed him that his receding hairline would preclude leading roles (Bret, 2014: 68).

After the Second World War Terry-Thomas used Peter Butterworth[1] to play his chauffeur in his BBC television series, *How Do You View?* and even in the most unwieldy of films, a straight actor could anchor the narrative. Elspeth Grant wrote a notably unenthusiastic review of *Carry On Constable* (Gerald Thomas, 1960) – 'a fairly daunting little piece of British vulgarity' – but contrasted the 'admirably human' sergeants of

---

1 An actor with the ability to unobtrusively steal virtually any scene, even from Margaret Rutherford in *Murder She Said* (George Pollard 1961).

Hattie Jacques and Sidney James with PCs Kenneth Connor, Charles Hawtrey, Leslie Phillips and Kenneth Williams: 'They are not characters; they are not even caricatures – they are simply incredible' (*The Tatler*, 9 March 1960: 45).

Benny Hill's most notable straight men – Jeremy Hawk, Nicholas Parsons and Henry McGee – were all skilful and elegant actors.[2] The last-named reflected that while few performers had a burning desire to adopt the role, it was an extremely exacting one, with Shakespeare's 'Say no more than is set down for them' applying more to the straight man than the clown. 'Concentration and an acute sense of timing are essential, for the success and failure of the comic's material depend on the placing of the straight man's lines. Too fast or too slow and the impact vanishes' (quoted in Selway, *Aberdeen Evening Express*, 6 June 1975: 10). This was the case with the character actors who worked with Norman Wisdom. The Yorkshire-born Edward Chapman specialised in Alderman-like pomposity that could occasionally descend into viciousness or even psychopathy[3], which translated into 'Mr Grimsdale' – self-righteous, generally po-faced, and forever standing on a dignity that the Gump was forever poised to undermine.

Another indefeasible member of the Wisdom retinue was David Lodge, one of the best supporting actors of post-war British cinema, his Superintendent Hobson proving a lynchpin of *On the Beat* (Asher, 1962). Lodge often appeared as uniformed authority in film dramas, and his senior police officer is a wholly plausible creation – the clipped moustache, the almost permanent look of suspicion and the way in which he adjusts his gloves when emerging from his Humber Hawk to survey the chaos caused by Wisdom. His bellow to the assembled rank and file PCs of 'Who sounded the alarm!' is funny precisely because Hobson is a rational man attempting to deal with the irrational.

---

2   In my view, McGee was even better value as the straight man to the Honey Monster, explaining to the camera in wearily precisely diction 'I am not his Mummy'.

3   One thinks of the murderer in *The October Man* (Roy Baker, 1947), fulminating about 'middle-class filth' or the brutal sanctimonious father-figure in *The Intruder* (Guy Hamilton, 1953).

The combination of two master character actors often provided to be equally joyous, as demonstrated by the acerbic pairing of Lionel Jeffries as the desperate comic hiding behind his uniformed authority and the mockingly sardonic straight man of Peter Sellers. The service/uniform comedy has a long tradition in British cinema. Andy Medhurst characterises the service films of Frank Randall as 'an ideal canvas in that it placed a bunch of disrespectful clowns in a rigid hierarchical environment which they could gleefully subvert and trash' (2007: 76). Many male cinemagoers would also have been all too familiar with the rigours of wartime or post-war National Service, with an array of petty, almost self-obsessed, rules, but in *The Two-Way Stretch* (Robert Day, 1960) Jeffries's chief prison officer Crout is confronted not by an anarchic clown but Sellers's cynical, calculating wide-boy.

The slashed peak of the regulation hat, the neat moustache and Jeffries' robotic body language all hide the fact that his characters were often beset by doubts and almost constantly bedevilled by the thought that they had achieved their current rank via a blend of luck, front and grovelling. 'Most of the people I played were caught in desperation. In their hearts, they knew that they were failures – but they would never admit it, even to themselves' (*The Telegraph*, 19 February 2010).

Worse, Sellers' somnolently insolent crook knows Crout's Achilles Heel only too well, and this applies even more to Inspector 'Nosey' Parker of *The Wrong Arm of The Law* (Cliff Owen, 1962). If Scotland Yard and the London underworld need to join forces to defeat a gang of Australian interlopers, this means Parker working with one 'Pearly' Gates, whose front is the French courtier M. Jules. Gates, who is as touchy about his status as any self-made businessman who now drives an Aston Martin DB4 GT; the epitome of the 1940s spiv turned ostensible pillar of the Establishment. He also knows Parker almost certainly became an inspector via a fluke: 'When thieves whip a bag of jewels from under his nose, the thoughtful way he (Parker) taps his fingers on the place where it is stood is indelibly funny' (Gilliatt, *The Observer*, 17 March 1963: 29). Gates is equally aware that no constable bothers to salute Parker and that his sergeant calls him 'Nosey'. As an entrepreneur of vision,

Gates despairs of the inspector's rigid mindset and the Establishment's shoddiness – the decoy van provided by the Yard is falling to pieces – just as Parker rails against fate: 'Why me', he moans, after the IPO mob have stolen his 6/99 squad car.

As a black and white fantasy England just before the myth of 'the Swinging Sixties', *The Wrong Arm of the Law* contains virtually all the ingredients for sublime entertainment – Wolseley police cars, the hoardings outside of corner shops advertising Tizer – and two character actors who merited an Academy Award apiece. It was one of the last black and white British comedies to feature Sellers, whose professional aspirations were now increasingly focusing on the 'international' market. Mention should be made of *A Shot in The Dark* (Blake Edwards, 1964), by far the finest of the Clouseau films and the title that established two memorable screen partnerships with Sellers. Cato Fong (Burt Kwouk) is aggressive, cunning and the perfect manservant – some of the best moments of the series are when Fong switches from quasi-homicidal frenzy to the formal Inspector Clouseau's residence.

Back at the headquarters of the Sûreté Herbert Lom's Commissioner Charles Dreyfus is reduced to maniacal insanity in the face of Clouseau's innocent stupidity. With *The Ladykillers* (Alexander Mackendrick, 1955) Lom portrayed 'Mr Harvey' in the manner of one of his many cinematic Soho mobsters now confronted by the repressive gentility that is Edwardian England, responding to the escaped parrot 'General Gordon' with an exasperated 'I don't care if he is a Field Marshal!' As the commissioner, Lom subtly charts the officer's descent from calm authority to mental collapse in the face of dignified stupidity:

Clouseau: It is possible that his intended victim was a man and that he made a mistake.
Dreyfus: A mistake? ... in a nudist camp?
Clouseau: Nobody's perfect.
Dreyfus: Idiot! Nincompoop! Lunatic!

There were also those acts where the straight man was vital to the success of the comic without being equally billed; when Morecambe and Wise were teenage entertainers, Ernie's template was Jerry Desmonde. In 1942 the 34-year-old actor and comedian was invited to become the straight man to Sid Field. Wilmut argues that Field was 'not really a Variety comedian in the strict sense ... he spent most of his time in revues where he could appear in a number of different sketches written by various different people – as opposed to touring the same one or two for a lifetime' (1985: 201). One common adage of that era was that the 'Variety artist' was one whose act never varied but, as with his fellow Brummagem Tony Hancock, Field was both comedian and comedy actor and thus required a straight man of equal thespian weight.

The pair appeared in three stage shows, with the reviews noting how the star was 'ably assisted throughout by that Prince of Feeds, Jerry Desmonde and Mr Field would be the first to admit, it is certain, the invaluable help he receives from Mr Desmonde (*The Stage*, 7 December 1944: 1). There were also appearances together in pantomime and the film musical *London Town* (Wesley Ruggles, 1946). It was one of the Rank Organisation's vain attempts at a production made along Hollywood lines for the US market, but the picture was a commercial and a critical disaster – it set the career of its ingenue, Kay Kendall, back several years. *The Monthly Film Bulletin* complained that 'around the laborious narration of this story is built the most costly British musical to date. Presumably if it had cost less it could have been cut by a further half-hour. An editor with authority and intelligence could still turn it into a musical of the average Hollywood standard' (October 1946: 134).

London Town certainly does suffer from the lack of an audience, with the elephantine pace and the laborious direction it does manage to capture the interplay between Field and Desmonde – 'The traditional double act of the unctuous intolerant straight man and daft distraught clown at its most brilliant' (Fisher, 2013. 199). Whatever role the comic adopts – the world's worst golfer or a society photographer – Desmonde responded without ever breaking character. After the death of Sid Field in 1950, he worked with several comedians and one occasion he was even considered to have outshone Bob Hope when the US comic was appearing in London. 'Mr Jerry Desmonde, once the aide-de-campe to the late Sid Field, who appeared briefly with him, administered a sharp lesson in the current standards of cross-talk technique' (*The Talter*, 23 May 1951: 15).

Jerry Desmonde's most famous latter-day role was as the straight man to Norman Wisdom in *Trouble in Store* (John Paddy Carstairs, 1953); the Rank Organisation understandably wished to reinforce a comedian with barely any cinematic experience with the best available supporting cast. Wisdom described Desmonde as 'one of the world's great straight men, someone who could keep his dignity' (Wisdom with Hall, 1992: 145) and his Sir Hector, the new MD of 'Burridge's Department Store' is a wholly believable business executive. He is pompous and vain but extremely good at his job and filled with wholly understandable wrath at the short annoying twit who threatens to ruin his enterprise. It was a role he repeated with Wisdom for six successive films, notably *A Stitch in Time* (Robert Asher, 1963), in which he, quite understandably, wishes to ban the Gump from his hospital. The pair also appeared on stage and in his review of the London Palladium review *Painting The Town*. Youngman Carter cited that in addition to Wisdom's talents:

> He has one other paramount advantage, in the shape of Jerry Desmonde. This actor, called a stooge or feed in the profession, is the greatest ambassador a comic ever enjoyed. He is suave, handsome, and utterly at home. A prank may shake him, but we are confident that he can never really be out of countenance. Some men are designed by nature to have well-creased trousers and to underline with one raised eyebrow the absurdities of lesser beings. Without his aid Mr Wisdom would be as indifferent as his detractors find him; with it he can make superior criticism fatuous, because Mr Desmonde with infinite grace has implied it already. (*The Tatler*, 31 August 1955: 19).

One doubts if Mr Wisdom responded positively to such a critique, or to the same publication's review of his film *Follow a Star*:

'Mr Jerry Desmonde is impeccable as the singer who pinches Mr Wisdom's voice. Why anyone should want it, I'll never know' (Grant, 1959: 36). Aside from the fact that the comic was rarely a favourite of British film critics during the 1950s and 1960s, the review of *Painting the Town* is a near perfect depiction of how a great straight man makes his comic funny. The Gump rarely, if ever, understood social hierarchy; Desmonde's characters were both aware of their status and determined that others should appreciate it too.

Jerry Desmonde last appeared with Wisdom in *The Early Bird* (Asher, 1965), the comic's first picture in colour, but the managerial class into which the Gump fought to be accepted was beginning to dissipate. Penelope Gilliatt, who was empathically not a fan of Norman Wisdom, wrote 'he tugs desperately at strings of social pathos that aren't connected any longer to a context' (1973: 165). He also undertook dramatic roles such as an appearance as a pub landlord in the Granada TV play *Three To A Cell*: 'We are inclined to forget how well he can act' (Edmund, 1965: 14). It is almost infinitely sad to him in the likes of *Gonks Go Beat* (Robert Hartford-Davis, 1965), a pop musical not so bad it was good but so bad that it was not released but escaped into the community. Desmonde committed suicide in 1967; he had been suffering bouts of depression since the death of his wife. His legacy to comedy is priceless; to watch this tall, elegant Krakatoa in the verge of erupting as a misfit is on the verge of destroying his professional world is to witness the masterclass in the art of the straight man.

For post-war radio comedians who specialised in sketch comedy, there was, as with on screen, the option to use straight actors as the voice of authority against which to react. We have previously encountered the retinue of tutors for Archie Andrews, while Laidman Browne played Ted Ray's employer on *Ray's A Laugh* (1949–61) while other shows employed their announcer as a straight man. Ronald Fletcher of *Bedtime With Braden* (1950–51) was one of the voices that back then defined the BBC's identity: impeccable breeding, good school, absolute authority but, in Fletcher's case, just enough raffishness 'to make a distinction between the BBC and the Institute of Chartered Accountants' (Stafford and Stafford, 2013). The cast members and the writers Muir and Norden sensed this faint decadence, and so Fletcher would deliver the announcements in a way suggestive of a Jeeves with nothing left to lose: 'The programme you have just heard will be reprinted in *The Listener* over the editor's dead body.' On other occasions he might conclude the half-hour with a warning: 'It is an offence to have a wireless on too loud these still summer evenings. It can annoy your neighbour. An even better way is to throw a dead cat on the lawn' (quoted in Braden, 1990: 141).

By the 1960s the unctuous Douglas Smith in *Round The Horne* (1965–68) would attempt to sell various products between being berated by the star, Barry Took and Marty Feldman allowing themselves the treat of creating 'odd roles for him to play ... I don't think the Announcers' Common Room prepared him for the raucous response of the *Round The Horne* audience, but he stuck to it manfully and was a great asset to the programme' (Took, 1990: 109). On *The Goon Show* the announcers became subverted figures of authority in a programme dominated by dissolute members of the Establishment – notably Major Bloodnok and Hercules Grytpype-Thynne. Andrew Timothy and especially Wallace 'Bill' Greenslade entered the atmosphere of a post-imperial wasteland with aplomb. Greenslade was an ex-P&O purser who joined the BBC in 1945, replacing Timothy seven years later. Before long he had a fan club – 'The Greensladers: Two – four – six – eight – Who do we appreciate? GREENSLADE!' (Gifford, 1985: 101) – and in 1955 he achieved the honour of having an episode written around him, 'The Greenslade Story'.

Rick Cousins makes the fascinating point that as Milligan, Secombe and Sellers[4] occupied a world that was firmly fixed in its own reality, *The Goon Show* required 'that its announcer act as an associate Lord of Misrule far more than a voice of reason' (2016: 55). Ronald Fletcher commented sarcastically on the antics of Braden and Co. Douglas Smith became a Uriah Heap figure, and, of course, his 'employer' Kenneth Horne remained entirely unphased by the disparate mob in his midst.

---

4   Note for pedants: Greenslade joined *The Goon Show* in 1952 after the departure of Michael Bentine from the regular cast.

Stephen Fry and Hugh Laurie in *Jeeves and Wooster*. (Author's collection)

Jennifer Saunders
and Dawn French.
(Author's collection)

Tommy Cannon and Bobby Ball. (Author's collection)

Julie Walters and Victoria Wood. (Author's collection)

Ben Miller and Alexander Armstrong. (Author's collection)

Prunella Scales and John Cleese in *Fawlty Towers*. (Author's collection)

Adrian Edmondson and Rik Mayall. (Alamy)

Sid James and Tony Hancock in *Hancock's Half Hour*. (Alamy)

Hattie Jacques and Eric Sykes in *Sykes and a Suspicion*. (Alamy)

ELSIE AND DORIS WATERS

A cigarette card depicting Elsie and Doris Waters. (Alamy)

The incomparable Eric Morecambe and Ernie Wise. (Alamy)

Dudley Moore
and Peter Cook in
Bedazzled. (Alamy)

Chesney Allen and Bud Flanagan. (Alamy)

The Two Ronnies: Barker and Corbett. (Alamy)

Michael Flanders and Donald Swann. (Alamy)

But Wallace Greenslade's stentorian tones would be used to give fake warnings about UFOs – 'Will listeners seeing any strange light please phone the Defence Board at Millthorpe 0203' – and many people did (Davis, *Daily Mirror*, 5 December 1953: 9).

In time Greenslade came to be played as a voice of authority who was almost as desperate as Major Bloodnok, accepting tips in a metal cup for another successful announcement or concluding a show with 'For all you cretins who want a happy ending – here it is.' On one memorable occasion, Peter Sellers ended the actual recording with the order 'Stop the show – it's time to auction Greenslade's bum!' (Lewis, 1994: 220) while the great man himself once halted in the middle of the *One O'Clock News* with a line that could have been written by Spike Milligan or Eric Sykes. 'I'm sorry for the delay but I've run out of news and no-one seems to be here to give me any' (quoted in *The Daily Herald*, 22 April 1961: 3). This tradition was continued by Kenny Everett, who employed the urbane character actor Brian Colville to play his radio butler Crisp and, after our period, the magnificence that was Humphrey Littleton of *I'm Sorry I Haven't A Clue* (1972–present), who took the voice of BBC authority to new heights of sardonic displeasure. Everything to 'Chairman Humph' – the game, the contestant, the studio – all were unbearably tedious, but there was little point in complaining as that would be such bad form. At times when listening to *Clue*, it was akin to hearing a Roman emperor with the benefits of an Etonian education debating whether to give the thumbs down this week or next week.

And one of the great straight women in the history of the wireless, or any other broadcast medium, was June Whitfield. As we saw in Chapter 4, without her talents, *Terry and June* would have probably consisted of Scott roaming around the set, shouting 'Cor' at random passers-by and sitting on a chocolate cake for no well-defined reason.[5] The actress once observed of her post-RADA career that 'when I started, women weren't supposed to be particularly funny. Women were supposed just

---

5   Admittedly, this might have proved amusing as the premise for a one-off episode.

to be the foil' (quoted in Banks and Swift, 1988: 62). Neither Beryl Reid nor Hattie Jacques, two of her contemporaries as character actress/ comediennes, fulfilled the template of 1950s conventional female good looks but when Anthony Carthew interviewed Whitfield for *The Daily Herald*, the article was headlined with 'I met Eth – and what a shock I got!' (1 July 1955: 6). He followed this not-overly-chivalrous banner with 'June Whitefield is slim, vivacious and blonde and her public fame is based on two words: "Oh Ron!"'

The impact of Eth of the radio comedy *Take It From Here* (1948–60) is but one example of how Whitfield created not foils but characters. Barry Took claimed that Whitfield had 'been a support to more actors than the Department of Health and Social Security' (*The Stage*, 10 January 2002: 12), but her characters were far more than mere feeds. The way in which her Sister in *The Blood Donor* is reacts to Hancock's claim to have been at least a major during the Second World War is one of the highlights of the episode. Shortly after Whitfield joined the cast of *Take It From Here* in 1953, the writers Frank Muir and Denis Norden introduced the Glum family as an antidote to the many incredibly nice families who populated the BBC Home Service. Moreover, as Muir subsequently recalled, the engagement of Eth to Ron Glum (Dick Bentley) was akin to being in:

An unnatural state of suspended animation, a social arrangement not found in nature which had its own rules of semi-permissive behaviour. To the boy, it was like driving with one foot on the accelerator and one on the brake. (Muir 1997: 153)

To Eth, it means entrapment in an almost perpetual state of frustration, expressed in the shabby-genteel wail of 'Oh Ron!' Everything she has read in *Peg's Paper* or *Woman's Realm* has reinforced the social code of behaving 'nicely', except that her almost supernaturally dense fiancé is incapable of finally asking the question and relieving her frustrations. Nor does it help that Ron appears to have the romantic instincts of a Hillman Minx – when asked by Eth if she has the slightest of defects, his eventual response was 'you're a bit ugly'. As an actress, June Whitfield could an evoke a plethora of suppressed passion with her opening line alone, an entirely memorable character, and moreover one who helped to distract from why Ron Glum had an Australian accent.

For a time, as the Variety tradition gradually disappeared from British television in the 1980s, and as the old-style double acts began their retreat to Butlins, it seemed as though the classic straight man was doomed. Chris Ryan's role as 'Mike the Cool Person' in *The Young Ones* (BBC, 1982–84) must be one of the most thankless parts in British sitcom history. However, as we saw in the introduction, it is a format that abides, just as forms of comedy can re-invent themselves. Stewart Lee's indispensable book *How I Escaped My Certain Fate* describes how his partnership with Richard Herring was based on the fact that:

> I was thinner than Richard at the time, and as some kind of contrast between the two players is all that is required in a double act really, we were able to elaborate our minimal weight difference into a full-formed comic relationship and take the act to BBC2 with the series *Fist of Fun*. (2010: 20)[6]

In their television series, (1995–96), Lee was the voice of mildly bored authority, trying to convince the almost permanently excitable Herring that a very bad Rod Hull impersonator (Kevin Eldon) was not the genuine article, and that Ice T did not really pen the introduction to the *Fist of Fun* book. A 1995 interview quoted Stewart as saying 'The other night in Chiswick there were loads of drunk people there, just shouting, and I said, "I hate the public, and I'm glad I'm not a member of it". I really felt that. What a disgusting lot they are sometimes" (Taylor, *The Observer*, 6 August 1995: 71). This is the member of the double act who makes no effort at ingratiating, eyeing the audience and Herring with an expression of

---

6   Another of the many reasons why *How I Escaped My Certain Fate* is essential reading, is its reminders of the hype that was 'Comedy is The New Rock & Roll' era of the 1990s. 'We usually played to largely empty rooms in unloved council-run theatres, where disillusioned programmers booked whatever was pushed at them, regardless' (2010: 20–21).

jaundice of the only sane man in a nation of Cornish-faced curmudgeons. If only someone at the BBC had the insight to revive *Crackerjack* with Lee and Herring as the resident comics; children's television would have been revolutionised. In the twenty-first century, David Mitchell of Mitchell and Webb is a straight man of subtly and quiet genius, adapting to the requirements of the sketch with the fluency of a young Jerry Desmonde from the desperately enthusiastic MC of the post-nuclear-holocaust *Quiz Programme* to the director of a '1970s bawdy hospital'. And, providing memories of the days when the comic would be asked 'Well, my boy, what did you do today?', is Julian Barratt of *The Mighty Boosh* (BBC, 2004–07), who deserves to be ranked among the great British straight men. Your attention is constantly drawn towards self-regarding, inept and cowardly Howard Moon; part Ernie Wise, part Desmond Olivier Dingle of the National Theatre of Brent and part every wine-bar jazz-guitarist you have tried to avoid. Moon always regrets his questions to Vince Noir (Noel Fielding), discovering that the programme's budget has been largely used on hair products for his partner. Barratt is a master of wounded dignity and who could not warm to the tall, woebegone character with the wilting moustache who believes 'Yorkshire is a state of mind'?

On the wireless, Steven Punt your genial narrator to the grotesque characters played by Hugh Dennis on *The Now Show* (BBC, 1998–present) and *Just A Minute* (BBC, 1967–present) is still hosted by the firm but fair Nicholas Parsons, guiding the show in the great tradition of Wallace Greenslade. Parsons's name has featured a few times in this book, largely because of his seemingly effortless versatility. In addition to working with Benny Hill, he appeared with Kenneth Horne and Richard Murdoch, and faced Rik Mayall and Adrian Edmondson at their most menacing. He was also an essential part of *The Arthur Haynes Show* (ATV, 1956–66) as one of the highlights of the programme was the interplay between the comedian – simultaneously impish and blankly menacing – and Parsons, his impeccable straight man.

'Mr Nicklarse' – be he a doctor or a civil servant – was constantly faced with Haynes's blank-eyed malcontent whose row of medal ribbons may have demonstrated that he was once 'up to his neck in muck and bullets'

– or he may have acquired them from a market stall in the Caledonian Road. Fisher refers to the character, which was created for the show by Johnny Speight, as one of 'almost Pinteresque menace' (2013: 465). If Davies of *The Caretaker* had finally made it to Sidcup, he might have found Arthur Haynes had arrived there before him. Parsons and Haynes would subsequently appear together in summer season, and by 1965 the prospect of the straight man leaving the show was the subject of newspaper headlines. The actor's agent explained that the two had separate careers, 'but Nicholas has held himself available to work with Arthur on television' (*The Stage*, 5 May: 13), even including a condition to that effect in a theatrical contract. Haynes passed away in 1966, the prospect of a sitcom starring himself and Parsons never coming to pass.

The straight man's most fervent fan was often the comedian. Spike Milligan, not always one to bestow compliments, referred to Harry Secombe's 'sheet metal voice, coming through with perfect timing, and saying exactly what I wrote – you never had to correct him … He was the greatest straight man in comedy' (quoted in Carpenter, 2003: 124). And Eddie Braden, Morecambe and Wise's scriptwriter during their glory years, pointed out that 'everyone loves the funny man', but Wise was a 'genius in the way that he could literally read Eric's face and anticipate every ad-lib'. Oliver Double referred to the art of the comedy duo as 'collusion in both directions – dividing attention between partner and audience' (2012: 131), and it was the role of the straight man to ensure this balance could be achieved.

Bibliography

Books

Askey, Arthur (1975), *Before Your Very Eyes: An Autobiography*. London: Woburn Press.

Banks, Morwenna and Swift, Amanda (1988), *The Joke's On Us: Women in Comedy from Music Hall to the Present*. London: Pandora.

Braden, Bernard (1990), *The Kindness of Strangers.* London: Hodder and Stoughton.

Bret, David (2014), *George Formby: An Intimate Biography of The Troubled Genius.* Morrisville: Lulu Press.

Carpenter, Humphrey (2003), *Spike Milligan: The Biography.* London: Hodder and Stoughton.

Cousins, Rick (2016), *Spike Milligan's Accordion: The Distortion of Time and Space in 'The Goon Show'.* Leiden: Brill.

Cullen, Frank with Hackman, Florence and McNeilly, Donald (2006), *Vaudeville Old & New: An Encyclopaedia of Performers in America Vol. 1.* Abingdon: Routledge.

Double, Oliver (2012), *Britain Had Talent: A History of Variety Theatre.* London: Palgrave.

Fisher, John (2013), *Funny Way To Be A Hero.* London: Preface Publishing.

Gifford, Denis (1985), *The Golden Age of Radio: An Illustrated Companion.* London: Batsford Press.

Gilliatt, Penelope (1973), *Unholy Fools; Wits, Comics, Disturbers of the Peace: Film and Theatre.* London: Viking Press.

Herring, Richard and Lee, Stewart (1995), *Lee and Herring's Fist of Fun.* London: BBC Books.

Jewel, Jimmy (1982), *Three Times Lucky: An Autobiography.* London: Enigma Books.

Klapp, Orrin E. (1962), *Heroes, Villains, and Fools: The Changing American Character.* New Jersey: Prentice-Hall.

Lee, Stewart (2010), *How I Escaped My Certain Fate: The Life and Deaths of a Stand-Up Comedian.* London: Faber & Faber.

Lewis, Roger (1994), *The Life and Death of Peter Sellers.* London: Century.

Medhurst, Andy (2007), *A National Joke: Popular Comedy and English Cultural Identities.* Abingdon: Routledge.

Midwinter, Eric (1979), *Make 'em Laugh: Famous Comedians and Their Worlds.* London: Allen & Unwin.

Muir, Frank (1997), *A Kentish Lad: An Autobiography of Frank Muir.* London: Bantam Press.

Stafford, David and Caroline (2013), *Cupid Stunts: The Life and Radio Times of Kenny Everett*. London: Omnibus Press.

Took, Barry (1990), *A Point of View*. London: Gerald Duckworth and Co.

Wilmut, Roger (1985), *Kindly Leave the Stage: Story of Variety 1919–60*. London: Methuen.

Wisdom, Norman with Hall, William (1992), *Don't Laugh at Me: An Autobiography*. London: Century.

Journals and Periodicals

'A Straight Man Has His Ups and Downs Too' (1969), *Birmingham Post*, 1 October, pp. 10.

Carter, Youngman (1955), 'London Limelight: A Prize for Everybody', *The Tatler*, 31 August, pp. 19.

Carthew, Anthony (1955), 'I met Eth – and what a shock I got', *The Daily Herald*, 1 July, pp. 6.

Davis, Clifford (1953), 'Goon Show's Flying Saucer Shook The Listeners … It Was Meant To Be A Joke', *Daily Mirror*, 5 December, pp. 8.

Edmund, Bill (1965), 'Television Today', *The Stage*, 21 January, pp. 14.

Gilliatt, Penelope (1963), 'Films', *The Observer*, 17 March, pp. 29.

Grant, Elspeth (1939), 'Cinema: Cameras Invade The Congo', *The Tatler*, 23 December, pp. 36.

Grant, Elspeth (1960), 'Cinema: A Flashback to Real Fun', *The Tatler*, 9 March, pp. 45.

'Greenslade of The Goons is Dead' (1961), *The Daily Herald*, 22 April, pp. 3.

Hall, Margaret (1975), 'Tommy Steele in Plea to "Lost" Actor', *Daily Mirror*, 20 May, pp. 8.

'London Limelight' (1951), *The Tatler*, 23 May, pp. 15.

Marriott, Val (1979), 'Bernie Enjoys It Going Alone', *Liverpool Echo*, 22 September, pp. 7.

Mintz, Lawrence E. (1985), 'Stand Up As Social and Cultural Mediation', *American Quarterly* 37(1).

'No Row With Arthur, Says Nicholas' (1965), *The Stage*, 6 May, pp. 13.

Obituary: Lionel Jeffries (2010), *The Telegraph*, 19 February.

Pattinson, Iain (2008), 'The Joke's On Me', *The Guardian*, 20 October.

Review: London Town (1946), *The Monthly Film Bulletin* 13(154), pp. 134.

Review: Strike It Again (1944), *The Stage*, 7 December, pp. 1

Selway, Alastair (1975), 'On Stage – A Play Adding To Henry's Success', *Aberdeen Evening Express*, 6 June, pp. 10.

Sykes, Norma (1957), 'Prudes Who Make Me See Red Says Sabrina!', *Lancashire Evening Post*, 28 October, pp. 4.

Taylor, Sam (1995), 'The Customer Is Always Wrong', *The Observer*, 6 August, pp. 71.

'The Wonder of Whitfield' (2002), *The Stage*, 10 January, pp. 12.

7

Double Acts That Weren't

'Didn't Bob Monkhouse used to be in a double act?'

In the 1980s, the last decade before the internet, even recent history was comparatively inaccessible. *Dentist on the Job* (C.M. Pennington-Richards, 1961) might occasionally be aired on Saturday morning television revealing a be-quiffed and bushy-tailed Monkhouse, but none of his TV shows from the black and white era were ever re-screened. But a few older viewers sometimes had vague memories of a dapper young man who looked like a slightly smaller clone of Monkhouse. In the middle of *Family Fortunes* (ITV, 1980–2003) just as a team from Gosport were failing to win this week's star prize, a parent might casually remark in that the perma-tanned host once had a partner whose life ended in tragedy.

The gentleman's name was Denis Goodwin, and we will encounter him later in this chapter as one of the saddest examples of a double act that failed to gel. The reasons are many – a divergence of ambitions, short-sightedness on the part of the management at Pinewood or Elstree or a lack of chemistry resulting in apathy on the part of the public.

The first phenomenon is illustrated by Norman Wisdom and Benny Hill, for after the former turned professional in 1945, one of Wisdom's earliest incarnations was in the form of a double act with the magician-comedian David Nixon. The two were appearing at Scarborough for the summer season in 1948 when Nixon devised the idea of Wisdom as a planted 'volunteer from the audience', Wisdom acquiring a 30s second-hand suit to differentiate this character from his regular routines (Dacre, 2012: 128).

The routine was extremely well received and repeated across the country – 'a clever turn ... in which he is a somewhat demented youth who goes up on the stage to secure an artiste's autograph' (*Eastbourne Gazette*, 13 October 1948: 4). However, the Gump came to be the mainstay of Wisdom's career and a reconstruction of his act with Nixon for the television cameras in the 1970s revealed not so much an equal partnership but the future template for his solo career. The tall, elegant Nixon, increasingly frustrated by this short, aggressive audience member, anticipated his cinematic routines with Jerry Desmonde, Edward Chapman or David Lodge and his later stage work with Tony Fayne: essential to the comedy but definitely billed below the star. There was a tantalising glimpse into how Wisdom appeared with a partner of equal status when only he and Bruce Forsyth appeared on *Sunday Night at the London Palladium* on 3 December 1961 during the Equity strike. The ensuing fifty minutes were more than enough to make the audience realise that there was a great double act; Forsyth's genial bumptiousness and askance look at anyone who did not appreciate that he was in charge perfectly matched Wisdom's aggressive need to please, but the show was never to repeat the experiment.[1]

The double act of Benny Hill and Reg Varney was longer lasting, being formed in Cliftonville in 1948 for the summer season revue *Gaytime*. Hill served as the second spot comic and acted as Varney's

---

1   This teaming was echoed in Wisdom's one stellar role in a Hollywood film, *The Night They Raided Minsky's* (William Friedkin, 1968); the narrative was dominated by his expat English comic Chick Williams, with Jason Robards as his straight man Raymond Paine.

straight man (Lewisohn, 2002: 144). This led to further appearances together on stage and radio: 'Reg Varney and Benny Hill provide an abundance of laughs in the Beta Productions review *Sky High*' (*The Stage*, 22 March 1951: 13). But when appearing at the Sunderland Empire in 1951 Hill's solo spot was so poorly received – he was slow hand-clapped – that the management decreed that he could only continue as Varney's partner. It was an unacceptable proposal to the Southampton comic and the act dissolved, but it would be too simple to suggest that this was ego on the part of Hill, of a burning desire to be lauded and seen by the public as more than a foil. As with Norman Wisdom, Benny Hill had a single-minded and idiosyncratic view of comedy that did not allow for a double act, let alone being billed 'and Benny Hill'.

Sunderland also intensified Hill's ambitions for success on television (he gave up stage appearances entirely by 1961), and on the small screen, *The Benny Hill Show* (BBC, 1954–68/Thames, 1969–89) would feature straight men and women but never an equal partner. The skills he showed as a straight man were subsequently expanded upon as an actor in his own show, the review of *The Stage* on 1 May 1958 praising how 'it was impossible to say whether this show was his best or only one of the best. At a rough count the morning after I can recall *eleven* different characters he mimicked (not counting one in which he played a man taking *four* parts in the parish hall play' (Darton, 1958: 5).

The 1960s saw one of Hill's finest pieces of work, a spoof documentary *The Lonely One* for the BBC's 1964 *Christmas Night With The Stars* and a starring role as Bottom in *A Midsummer Night's Dream* (Joan Kemp-Welch, Associated-Rediffusion, 1964). On film he played the Toymaker in *Chitty Chitty Bang Bang* (Ken Hughes, 1968) and Professor Simon Peach in *The Italian Job* (Peter Collinson 1969)[2] – dramatic talents that were seen in embryonic form when appearing in summer season with Reg Varney. 'From the very first go I could see he had potential. He did the verbal stuff on stage, and I did all the "business". Once we got used to one another we were good together, and we knew it' (quoted in

2   It is wholly possible to envisage Hill playing Bob Rusk in *Frenzy* (Alfred Hitchcock, 1972).

Lewisohn, 2002: 145). The apotheosis of Hill's comic viewpoint, a fusion of Jacques Tati, Pierre Etaix and just about every principal comedian he saw on the Bournemouth Pier during the 1930s, came in the melancholic semi-silent short film *Eddie in August* (Hill/John Robins, 1970) and by then Varney was also a national figure as Britain's worst bus driver, their partnership long forgotten.

Equally lost to time were Bob Monkhouse and Denis Goodwin, although when asked about them Barry Cryer shook his head and merely remarked that 'they were not really a double act'. Both had attended Dulwich College, and by the mid-1950s they wrote scripts together and appeared in pantomime, on stage and the wireless. They also performed the PR stunts that were de rigueur for the era. In May 1958 the citizens of Birmingham were advised that 'Bob Monkhouse and Denis Goodwin will be waiting to see you at the opening of S&U stores' and, moreover, you should 'be at the store in good time to see their arrival by a most unusual method'.

But as the decade progressed, it was the name of Bob Monkhouse that was almost always to the fore, with the 1957–58 BBC sitcom *My Pal Bob* having his partner in a starburst in the corner of the screen as the announcer-narrator. The show did receive a measure of praise: 'Bob Monkhouse and Denis Goodwin came close last night to equalling American programmes in the Lucille Ball and Jack Benny bracket' (Bowkers, 1957: 15) but Denis was now literally isolated from the comedy. *Carry On Sergeant* (Gerald Thomas, 1958) had one half of the pair receiving the special billing 'and Bob Monkhouse', but there was no role for Goodwin. A profile in the *TV Times* entitled *My Life/Laugh Story* by Bob Monkhouse had 'occasional interruptions … from his pal Denis Goodwin (Monkhouse, 1960: 16–17). The feature was dominated by photos of the star looking pensively handsome in the manner of one auditioning for the role of a dashing young inspector in a crime film while Goodwin was not so much a partner but a Greek chorus, providing narrative interjections.

Monkhouse wrote extensively about Denis Goodwin, in his memoir *Crying With Laughter: My Life Story*, which remains one of the most beautifully written and self-lacerating autobiographies ever published. He recalled that they originally performed as a duo where 'the laughs were evenly distributed; neither was the straight man' (1993). It was Monkhouse who was the more confident stage and screen performer and by the end of the 1950s 'disloyal or not … I knew I had to break free of our restrictive partnership' (Monkhouse, 1993: 136–37).

In the event, it was Goodwin who left Monkhouse in 1961, and two years later he joined Bob Hope's scriptwriting team: 'He will be the first British gag writer to work for a top American comedian' proclaimed the *Daily Mirror* (14 August 1963: 2). By the late 1960s, the headlines were considerably more dispiriting; 'Shoplift a "Film Plot" says writer' (*Daily Mirror*, 1 November 1968: 5). Goodwin committed suicide on 26 February 1975, the coroner's report referring to years of 'mental difficulties' (*The Guardian*, 8 March 1975: 6). Eighteen years later Monkhouse wrote, 'Lastly you might ask me, "Do you feel guilty about what became of Denis?" My answer is "Are you kidding?" Just go back over the last page and count the cop-outs and excuses I've offered to accommodate my conscience' (Monkhouse, 1993: 136–37).

Denis Goodwin was not to be Monkhouse's sole partner, as he was teamed with other comedy actors for a handful of comedy films made during the late 1950s and early 1960s that, in later life, he referred to with mild disparagement. There were two *Dentist* films – *In The Chair* (C.M. Pennington-Richards, 1959) and *On The Job* (C.M. Pennington-Richards, 1961) – and aside from the central premise a further problem is Monkhouse's obvious desperation to be liked. He had all the attributes of a light comedy leading man – photogenic looks, pleasant speaking voice – but his eagerness to please is in marked contrast to the laconic approach of his screen partner, the highly experienced revue light comedian Ronnie Stevens. *A Weekend with Lulu* (John Paddy Carstairs, 1961), one of Hammer's last comedy outings before the horror that was *On The Buses* (1971), paired Monkhouse with Leslie Phillips, thereby emphasising the problem. The latter was relaxed and assured while the former was visibly nervous, as well as labouring under a strange attempt at a cockney accent. It was with the upper-class farce *She'll Have to Go*

(Robert Asher, 1962) that the comic found his ideal cinema partner with the saturnine Alfred Marks. For all the picture's truly bizarre casting – the ingénue, and one performs a classic double-take at this moment, was Anna Karina[3] – you do believe that Monkhouse and Marks are siblings.

Brian Rix, the unofficial king of Whitehall, is also not a figure who is automatically associated with the double act. Before the Second World War he had been a member of Donald Wolfit's troupe and after serving with the RAF founded his own production company. In 1949 Rix saw the potential in a Colin Morris National Service farce entitled *Reluctant Heroes*. The play transferred to London on 11 September 1950 and when the play was adapted for cinema by Bryon Productions he and Ronald Shiner repeated their stage roles as Private Horace Gregory and Sergeant Bell. These roles set the template for a handful of joint cinematic appetence. Rix was the good-hearted North Country naïve oaf while Shiner, for years a reliable character actor, appeared to be the very personification of Cockney guile.

Reluctant Heroes (Henry Halstead, 1952) was a vast commercial success[4] while Shiner, by 1952, had come first in the Cinema Trade Poll, having never previously appeared among the top ten commercial attractions. The two teamed up for a further three films. Shiner was now a star, but Leslie Halliwell was essentially correct, albeit curmudgeonly when he argues that the performer was essentially a 'cockney supporting actor, and that is exactly what he remained even when billed above the title' (1987: 195). The films that Shiner made with Rix, *Dry Rot* (Maurice Elvey, 1956), which was based on the Whitehall Farce of the same name, and *Not Wanted On Voyage* (Maclean Rogers, 1957) revealed that while he almost always gave a loud, theatrical performance, it was Rix who was the far more naturalistic film actor. There could be no sense of development or

---

3   Where else but an Anglo-Amalgamated comedy of the early 1960s would you have
    a character played by the star of *Vivre sa vie: film en douze tableaux* (Jean-Luc Godard,
    1962) falling for the 1950s crooner Denis Lotis?
4   It took ten times its budget of £45,000 at the box office (Harper and Porter,
    2003: 254)

progression in their screen relationship and Rix's very effective dual role as a senior RAF officer with the Victoria Cross and his Aircraftman Second Class doppelganger in *The Night We Dropped a Clanger* (Darcy Conyers, 1959) inferred a range beyond trouser-dropping and being berated by an aggressive spiv. It is not insulting to suggest that most effective Rix/Shiner filmic partnership was *The Night We Got The Bird* (Darcy Conyers, 1961), in which Shiner played a wide boy reincarnated as a parrot named Cecil. I'll repeat that: this is a farce which involves Brian Rix chasing a wide-boy parrot named Cecil (moreover, one that squawks in the voice of Ronald Shiner) around Brighton.

The formula of *The Night We Got the Bird* was never repeated – although it is a concept that might well appeal to Guillermo del Toro – and to watch much of the output of British cinema is also to be aware of a myriad of lost opportunities. Maggie Smith and Kenneth Williams did not transfer their stage partnership in Peter Shaffer's *The Private Eye and The Public Ear* to the cinema, a matter of great regret, while the Smith/Peter Ustinov double act of *Hot Millions* (Eric Till, 1968) remains one of the many lost opportunities for British cinema. The confidence trickster Marcus Pendleton and the secretary Patty Terwilliger Smith are both lonely, highly intelligent and semi-resigned to being overlooked and their eventual romance is so touchingly delineated that you wished for a sequel.[5] In *Genevieve* (Henry Cornelius, 1953) the double acts of John Gregson and Diana Sheridan and Kenneth More and Kay Kendall were the equals of any Golden Age Hollywood couple as well as being that rarity in British cinema: sophisticated adult comedy in the true sense of the term. But there was little chance of their going on to star in a *Thin Man*-style comedy film centred around the sardonic female lead and her brash, almost schoolboy-like male partner. In the 1950s Rank was so devoted to the formula of 'family entertainment' that they created one of the worst romantic comedies of this, or any other, decade. *An Alligator*

---

5   *Hot Millions* is so charming that it even compensates for the interminable *Death on the Nile* (John Guillermin, 1978), a film which seemed to haunt Bank Holiday television.

Named Daisy (J. Lee Thompson, 1955) teamed Donald Sinden with a reptilian co-star for much of the running time as the female lead Jeannie Carson dances on dustbins for no good reason whatsoever.[6]

Finally, we arrive at two double acts, one which did not endure for reasons of personal ambition/terrifying ego (the jury remains out on this issue) and the other which ended due to public apathy. The first double act created for ITV was Jack Edwardes and Charlie Drake as 'Mick and Montmorency' for Associated-Rediffusuon. The two had originally met in the RAF during the Second World War, the dignified Edwardes, who was over a foot taller than his partner, contrasting with Drake's 'heavy, troubled head and kewpie-doll limbs' (Gilliatt, 1973: 158). Between 1955 and 1958 Mick and Montmorency starred in ninety-one television shows, pantomime and a strip in *Radio Fun* magazine but their partnership was never going to last long. The shorter half of the team was ever eager to move towards adult comedy, and there was the further issue of 'a supreme ego that put himself first in everything he did' (Gifford, 2006). There was a dispiriting postscript to Mick and Montmorency, with Drake's first *This Is Your Life*, transmitted on the 11 December 1961. Midway through the show, there was a guest appearance from Edwardes, who gives a not-so-veiled plea to Drake to resume their act, a moment of painful desperation that echoes throughout the decades.

The second duo is an example of how a successful act may be formed of professional expediency, as demonstrated by so many of the sitcom pairings within this book. The audience so often has the innate ability to discern a contrived comedy duo. In 1977 Lennie Bennett, the Blackpool journalist turned stand-up, was teamed with comedian and singer Jerry Stevens to host *International Cabaret* on BBC2. The former observed, 'We're not a double act. In fact we'd never worked together before … but the producer Ernest Maxim said he saw something original in both

---

6 It is small wonder that in the great *Devil Girl From Mars* (David MacDonald, 1954), Patricia Laffan's eponymous villainess spends most of the running time zapping male cast members with her 3s 6d ray gun. Nyah, the leather-clad Maritain warrior, clearly stands for all actresses that were contractually obliged to play 'comic' scenes opposite tweedy actors who were prone to saying 'gosh' at inopportune moments.

of us, and wanted to put us together to share the compere's job' (quoted in Irwin, 1978: 16).

The act lasted for three more series, with a review of their 1979 BBC1 series strongly inferring that Bennett and Stevens were not going to become the new Morecambe and Wise: 'They are two pleasant unremarkable young men Lennie Bennett and their show Lennie and Jerry ... is, likewise, pleasant and unremarkable – the Rosencranz and Guildstern Show' (*The Stage*, 5 April 1979: 26). The act ended in 1980 with a report in the same journal that inferred divergent ambitions: 'The decision was made by Bennett who believed that it was time to call it a day – "I honestly thought that we had done as well as we were ever going to do"' (15 May 1980: 3).

The two parties were highly experienced show business professionals and individually talented – but that was never a guarantee of a successful double act. Of all the elements that decide why a double act fails to gel, the most damning is because the audience discerns a lack of chemistry, or senses that the duo could never be regarded as an indivisible entity. The viewing public who decided that Hancock and James were a partnership or that Eric Morecambe would forever be suffixed with 'and Ernie Wise' could also decree if an act did not meet with their favour.

Bibliography

Books

Dacre, Richard (2012), 'Norman Wisdom: Rank Studios and the Rise of the Super Chump', in Hunter, I.Q. and Porter, Larraine (eds.), *British Comedy Cinema: British Popular Cinema*. Abingdon: Routledge.

Harper, Sue and Porter, Vincent (2003), *British Cinema of the 1950s: The Decline of Deference*. Oxford: Oxford University Press.

Lewisohn, Mark (2002), *Funny, Peculiar: The True Story of Benny Hill*. London: Sidgwick & Jackson.

Monkhouse, Bob (1993), *Crying With Laughter: My Life Story*. London: Century.

Rix, Brian (1995), *Life In The Farce Lane – Or Tragedy with its Trousers Down*. London: Andre Deutsch.

Journals and Periodicals

Anonymous, In The Provinces (1951), 'Sky High' review, *The Stage,* 22 March, pp. 13.

Bowkers, Raymond (1957), '"My Pal Bob" is Almost A Wow', *Daily Mirror*, 18 January, pp.15.

Darton, Harold (1958), 'Our View: The Benny Hill Show', *The Stage*, 1 May, pp. 5.

Ebert, Roger (1969), Review: Staircase, *Chicago Sun-Times*, 4 November.

Gifford, Denis (2006), 'Obituary: Charlie Drake', *The Independent*, 26 December.

Irwin, Ken (1978), 'Star Spotlight; Doubled With Laughter', *Daily Mirror*, 16 January, pp. 16.

'Light Entertainment News: Lennie without Jerry; That's Final!' (1980), *The Stage,* 15 May.

Monkhouse, Bob (1960), 'My Life/Laugh Story', *TV Times*, 7–13 August, pp. 16–17.

'Review' (1948), *Eastbourne Gazette*, 13 October. p.4.

'Scriptwriter Goodwin Joins The Bob Hope Team' (1963), *Daily Mirror*, 14 August, pp. 2.

'Shoplift a "Film Plot" says Writer' (1968), *Daily Mirror*, 1 November, pp. 5.

'Television Today: Alas, it Ended in Disaster' (1979), *The Stage*, 5 April, pp. 26.

'Writer Took His Own Life' (1975), *The Guardian*, 8 March, pp. 6.

8

Two Chaps
(With or Without a Piano)

I would go so far to say that British people have a love affair with two-man stage duos; they adore the form. (Donald Swann, 1991: 183)

Flanders and Swann

The smoking concert, where 'the social goblet … with its cheerful companions, the soothing weed and the winsome song' (*Sporting Life*, 23 January 1885: 2) were originally staged in the nineteenth century by professional bodies and university societies in an all-male setting. It was entertainment of licensed informality, without risk of the participants sacrificing their dignity or social status. Griff Rhys Jones once observed that 'a double act thrives on the intimate drama of a miniature relationship' (*The Telegraph*, 9 October 2005) and this is so with Michael Flanders and Donald Swann. It is the bond that unites the bearded, wheelchair-using master-of-ceremonies with the bespectacled and ever-jolly pianist that is at the heart of their act as much as songs about railway stations.

The first collaboration of Flanders and Swann was the Westminster School revue *Go To It* in 1940 and after the Second World War they contributed to the revues *Penny Plain* (1951) and *Airs on A Shoestring* (1953). The two presented a lecture on their craft at the Dartlington International Summer School where, in the tradition of Victorian music hall patter numbers, Flanders realised that his introductions were as popular as the songs. *At The Drop of A Hat* was staged on 31 December 1956 at the New Lindsey Theatre before a transfer to the West End. Kenneth Tynan praised the show as 'a witty and educated diversion' with Donald Swann 'bent over his piano like a small mad scientist agog over some wild experiment' and Michael Flanders exuding from his wheelchair 'the robust authority of him who came to dinner' *(The Observer,* 6 January 1957: 9).

To a few steely-eyed critics of the day, often those fond of reciting Jimmy Porter's more self-pitying rants at full volume, the songs of Flanders (lyrics) and Swann (music) were those that encapsulated all that was wrong with British revue and theatre in general.[1] As the 1950s progressed the fact that they appeared on Broadway with *At the Drop of a Hat* and achieved critical acclaim on both sides of the Atlantic was a demonstration of all that was decadent in the West. How could anyone present numbers about bus routes, trains and gnus when the bomb could be dropped at any moment?

The response to such a diatribe, variations which may still be heard at the time of writing concerning whimsy in comedy, is that the art of Flanders and Swann was to conceal their art. Every aspect of the songs and the stage presentation had the ease and fluidity to which only the most sublime of double acts could aspire. The first *Hat* show was produced when London revues were criticised for their 'parish-pump twitter, most of which would be double-dutch to a visitor from, say, St Albans or Woking' (Trewin, 1953: 22). Flanders saw himself as an actor – 'I suppose the writing was basically to give myself something to perform. It was a period when I was rather miserable and depressed, and my writing helped

---

1   'Edgy'. 'In your face'. 'In someone else's face'. 'So groundbreaking the series on ITV2 was cancelled after five minutes'.

a bit' (quoted in Fiddick, 1970: 9). His stagecraft empathised that this was a true double act, rather than an entertainer with his piano player:

> There is something of a Belch and Aguecheek in the relationship they choose to present – Flanders affectionately hectoring, Swann primarily foolish ... two faces of comedy here – the one rich gusty and irrelevant, the other pinched, wry and regretfully foolish. (Lloyd Evans, *The Guardian*, 11 September 1963: 7)

The show was revamped in 1963 with fresh numbers as *At the Drop of Another Hat* and the act finally dissolved in 1967 – Donald Swann had wearied of the constant touring and wished to diversify his songwriting. A report in *The Stage* stated that 'they said they will remain in touch with each other on the development of another revue' (27 April 1967: 1). The first part of the statement was true, but there was never to be another formal collaboration. There is limited filmed material of the act, but a colour recording of their last New York performance in 1967 exists, with Flanders addressing the audience with an authority to which even James Robertson Justice would have deferred.

The legacy of Michael Flanders and Donald Swann lies in work and the realisation of pain that was so often behind the lyrics; physical, mental and inflicted by the British authorities when they removed a mask of self-serving eccentricity. Swann had served with the Quaker Friends' Ambulance Unit during the Second World War, and Flanders had contracted polio when he was a sub-lieutenant in the navy. On his discharge, he decided to resume his studies in Oxford and informed the authorities he would now need ground-floor rooms. Their reply was brutal: that this was a university and not an almshouse. Flanders was never to forgive his alma mater. The sense that the genial bombast could flare into anger was present in Flanders; it infuses a rare dramatic acting role as the long-term resident of a home in *The Raging Moon* (Bryan Forbes, 1971). With the *Hat* shows the tone is one of gracious wit, with Swann as the butt of his ebullient colleague. It is only after re-experiencing the albums that the listener realises that so many of the songs concerned the mundane pleasures that were now beyond the reach of their lyricist – 'the bus he couldn't get on, the train where he could only travel in the luggage compartment' (Swann, 1991: 147). If their beautifully crafted songs – J.C.T. Trewin compared their work with W.S. Gilbert (*Illustrated London News*, 9 February 1957: 34) – were sometimes flippant, who could possess the arrogance to say that they were the work of artists who did not understand human nature? Their elegies for the soon-to-be Beechingised railway stations of *Slow Trains* mourned the passing of a civilised world: 'No churns, no porter, no cat on seat.' These small pleasures were not an adjunct to gracious living but of its very fabric.

Cook and Moore

The second of our double acts has been celebrated in a tribute film *Not Only But Always* (Terry Johnson, 2004), the subject of biographies and articles innumerable plus variously learned and ranted debates online. When *Not Only ... But Also* first aired in 1965 its format would not have been entirely unfamiliar to the average viewer. Your two hosts were as neat and well groomed as young barristers staging an after-hours smoker in their chambers and there were musical interludes. Peter Cook and Dudley Moore had the traditionally contrasting appearance of the classic double act: 'there is an obvious advantage in my being tall and his being short; him being cuddly and me being stone-faced' (quoted in Wilmut, 1980: 106). Where the programme differed from the morass of light entertainment of that era was its freewheeling air[2] and the fact that one of its stars did not court the favours of either the camera or the viewing public

Peter Cook was a former president of Cambridge Footlights which, by the 1950s, had undergone something of a metamorphosis. When it was founded in 1883 as an all-male club, the emphasis was on music and

---

2   Thereby causing Dudley to corpse during the Dagenham Dialogues.

chaps wearing dresses. The Footlights temporarily admitted women in 1932, but the revue of the following year may indicate the success of this radical move with the bold fellows. It was entitled *No More Women,* and one number contained these delightful lyrics 'There are no *women* in the *Footlights* show. There are no *women* here. They were awfully pleasant little girls to know ...' (Hewison, 1983: 71). By 1959 *The Last Laugh,* written by Cook and John Bird, took place in a nuclear bunker and marked a move away from self-conscious and self-regarding whimsy. Alistair Cooke thought:

> The Footlights have put on what is simply the most inventive, the best directed and the most brilliantly scored Footlights show there has been since the fancy of our grandfathers ran to Gaiety Girls, 'Jolly good tunes' and all that jazz. (*The Guardian*, 10 June 1959: 7).

He further observed that 'In bringing in Miss Eleanor Bron, the club has passed up the easy guffaws available in all public demonstrations of transvestism'. In that same year, Cook co-wrote the West End revue *Pieces of Eight* with Harold Pinter with music from Sandy Wilson and a cast led by Kenneth Williams and Fenella Fielding; it was a West End revue with a distinct sense of various eras colliding in amazement.

Dudley Moore graduated from Magdalene College and was a member of the Oxford Theatre Group; the review of *Just Lately* referred to a fascinating cast: 'Dudley Moore is an amusing little comedian, and Ken Loach, Nicholas Salaman and Denis Moriarty also display versatility' (*The Stage*, 4 September 1958: 18). He joined the band of John Dankworth and even appeared in a 1961 B-feature *The Third Alibi* (Montgomery Tully), to provide a momentary distraction from Laurence Payne's overacting.

As the world knows, the postgraduate revue *Beyond The Fringe* starring Cook, Moore, Jonathan Miller and Alan Bennett was to premiere in the August of 1960. By 1963 the term 'satire boom' had entered the lexicon of popular terminology to the extent that an ITV *This Week* documentary report commented on its various manifestations – the

Establishment Club, *That Was The Week That Was*[3] on the BBC and *Private Eye*. Satire had become fashionable with the 'Top People', as noted by Malcolm Muggeridge: '*Private Eye*, too, I should suppose, has a largely Top People clientele … its contributors, if they are not careful, will find themselves before long carving their initials on the Punch table' (1966: 323). The likes of Tony (James Fox) in *The Servant* (Joseph Losey, 1963) would have been delighted to attend the Establishment as befitting a fashionable young man about town without realising that he was being mocked. However, by 1964 all four members the original cast had left *Beyond the Fringe* (it would run for two more years), the club had fallen prey to Soho racketeers, and *TW3* went off the air in December 1963. Henry Fairlie contented in *The Spectator*:

> It is not the chosen causes which are at fault so much as the assumption that any list of causes can be used as a test of 'dissent' or 'radicalism.' One might as well feed a punched card into a computer. The effect of this categorising is to petrify what ought to be an alert, free, constantly questioning and, above all, constantly self-questioning attitude of mind. There is no doubt that this petrification was one of the weaknesses of TW3: in the end, it substituted reflexes for responses. (27 December: 7)

Just as *Look Back In Anger* did not lead to an immediate assigning of all French windows to a municipal tip after 1956, *Beyond the Fringe* did not cause in the demise of all previous forms of comedy. Their legacies came with their vocalisation of what was previously largely unsaid in public and the presentation of innovative ideas. Cook's writing and performances defined easy categorisation; his E.L.Wisty, the park-bench philosopher of *On The Braden Beat* (ATV, 1962–67) was less concerned with social reform than with world domination or, failing that, an army of nude ladies. It was this sense of melancholic ennui that he brought to the BBC's *Not Only … But Also*, which the BBC originally

---

3   Cook famously referred to its MC David Frost as 'The Bubonic Plagiarist'.

envisaged as a vehicle for Moore. The programme made its bow in the death throes of the 'satire boom' with the critic Mary Crozier referring to *Not So Much Of A Programme, More a Way of Life*[4] as 'slow and heavy', unlike the new show. She was especially taken with the 'versatility, mischief and lightning wit of Dudley Moore … the scriptwriter, music writer and chief performer, with Peter Cook' (*The Guardian*, 22 March 1965: 7).

Tom Sloan, the then head of BBC Light Entertainment, was not impressed with the show's lack of Tiller Girls, traditional showbusiness trappings or glamour in general (Thompson, 1997). The dominant host was a tall, elegant young bounder while Moore was the human conduit to the audience; the straight man who made Cook likeable. He was the half of the double act who would duet with Cilla Black or Marian Montgomery and clown with the band. The Moore/Black duet of 'If I Fell' is truly delightful, with Dudley at the piano making asides to the camera and causing the guest star to burst out laughing while Cook was always at his least convincing – and most patrician – when he was performing the closing announcements.

The show ran for two years on the BBC before transferring to ATV in 1968 and returning to the Corporation for one final series. Cook – and especially Moore – were polished sketch actors and superb judges of their material. *Not Only* contained the definitive Gerry Anderson parody, 'SuperThunderStingCar', and acute depictions of the changing social landscape in several father/son routines. 'We're not prudes, are we Squire?', asks Moore's car salesman like Reg as he requests to move in with the daughter of Cook's middle-aged bastion of respectability, to receive the gentle reply 'Yes, we are prudes Reg'. One routine concerned an army sergeant (Moore) being interviewed by a journalist (Cook) in the last days of the Aden Emergency, a reminder that *Not Only* was produced in the twilight of the British Empire. Cook himself was once destined for the Colonial Office, until, as he was informed, the country was running short of colonies.

---

4   The successor to BBC3 (1964), which had in turn replaced *TW3*.

The most famous characters of *Not Only* were the cloth-capped sages of the Dagenham Dialogues, named for Moore's birthplace. His contribution to the writing gradually increased, and in one exchange he recalled a failed attempt at a grand romantic gesture. 'I used to get the 62B up to Chadwell Heath Merry Fiddlers; then I used to go down the hill and get the 514 trolley down to Rainham Crescent. Then I used to go over by the railway bridge and go across those fields by the dye works'. The result of these efforts is that Dud is too exhausted to approach his would-be girlfriend Joan – 'I used to lay panting on the platform for about ten minutes.' His characters in sketches are often enthusiastic when they are not driven to distraction by Cook, whereas his partner, as Harry Thompson writes extensively in the definitive biography of the comic, was often driven by boredom.

A dominant theme of *Not Only* is of time hanging heavy, be it in a visit to an art gallery or the zoo. The asp routine of *Pieces of Eight* had originally been inspired by the fact that Cook seemed to have 'the sort of face that inspires confidence in a railway carriage and on that account, I have had to listen to many an unutterably boring conversation from people who delight in wittering on and on' (quoted in Johns, 1959: 19). Even when 'Pete' makes an effort to escape the torpor that was life in Essex and engage with occult he discovers that the local black magic session is combined with bingo (Wilmut, 1980: 113).

Not Only further explored the unloveableness of the British upper-class eccentric. *Beyond the Fringe* was said to have shattered the culture of deference and Sir Arthur Strebe-Greebling is a museum piece who, in his younger days, possibly led insane battles and mismanaged any number of colonies via his obsession with utterly futile purists. 'Oh yes, I've learned from my mistakes, and I'm sure I could repeat them entirely'. He is emphatically not the jovial upper-class eccentric of MGM-British films of the early 1960s and the gulf between Sir Arthur and the judge of *The Secret Policeman's Ball* (1979), advising the jury that a key witness is 'a loathsome spotted reptile and a self-confessed chicken strangler' is a narrow one. Cook was seldom cast in a dramatic acting role, but it is certainly possible to envisage him as a district officer in

Graham Greeneland. Flanders and Swann, and Ustinov and Jones, had an ultimately benign view of the world but Cook and Moore are less trusting. The Pinteresque menace of 'Taxi Driver'[5] in the 1971 revue *Behind The Fridge* was not yet present in *Not Only … But Also*, but nor was it far from the glassy-eyed stare of Peter's clubmen.

The 1970 series of *Not Only* was to be last Cook/Moore formal collaboration for television, and by the end of the decade, Dudley had relocated on the USA. Their last work together was Derek and Clive, the vision of the Dagenham Dialogues as relocated to a circle of Hell. Some enthusiasts like to defend the albums as targeting bourgeois sensibilities, but the work has the taint, not so much of Rabelaisian free spirits, but a middle-aged couple in the penultimate stage before their break-up. Griff Rhys Jones later recalled that in the 1980s Cook was:

> Performing an E.L. Wisty sketch and had drafted in a famous actor-comedian as a volunteer stand in for Dudley Moore. Peter was funny. The actor-comedian was funny. But the sketch never really took off. Peter got cross afterwards. You could tell that if he felt any resentment for Dudley it was because he had marooned him. (*The Telegraph*, 9 October 2005, pp. 23)

The Peter Cook and Dudley Moore stories have already been told and re-told at length, and if one were forced to select just two sketches as their legacy, they would be 'The Glidd of Glood' and 'Some Incidents in the Life of my Uncle Arly'. Cook was open about the artistic influences of Lewis Carroll[6] and Edward Lear (Cook, 2004: 121) on his work, and he wrote 'The Glidd' for a book of children's verses. That project never came to fruition, but at least it was filmed for the 1970 series Cook wandering through Bodiham Castle as a medieval king wearing an expression of self-satisfaction at odds with his regal outfit of a brown paper parcel. Naturally,

---

5   A member of the House of Lords (Moore) becomes slowly convinced that his minicab driver (Cook) is a contract killer.

6   Cook appeared as the Mad Hatter in Jonathan Miller's unsurpassable adaption of *Alice in Wonderland* (BBC, 1966).

the cruel monarch is robbed of his wealth by his aged court jester, played by Moore as a pier-end comic who is growing positively homicidal at the prospect of reciting the same banter night after night.

Little of Cook and Moore's 1970 series now exists, but 'The Glidd of Glood' is everything that Spike Milligan's Q... (BBC, 1969–82) was frequently not. 'Uncle Arly' was filmed in 1965, and it is a vignette that embodies just how different Cook and Moore were to the average comic duo of the mid-1960s.[7] Peter Cook was Lear's hero with shoes that were far too tight, meandering through autumnal parkland to a plangent musical accompaniment. There is no sense of ennui here, just freedom from the poet's 'They'; 'The realists, the practical men, the sober citizens in bowler hats who are always anxious to stop you doing anything worth doing' (Orwell, 1950: 182). Dudley, the narrator, recounts from a distance but always with sympathy how 'on a little heap of barley / Died my aged uncle Arly'. Flanders and Swann might have performed the poem as a comic number, but the sense of melancholy in the Cook/ Moore interpretation is palpable. One can understand Sloane's sense of confusion – this was certainly not 'proper' light entertainment – especially for the 'They' among the viewing public.

The Two Ronnies

Our next set of decent chaps were not a classic duo. Their disparity was firmly within the tradition of British comedy, and Nancy Banks-Smith once memorably referred to Corbett as having the appearance of 'one of those small shopkeepers who are being smitten, little hip and tiny thigh, by big business. Ronnie Barker fits around him squarely like a corner shop, cosy and overflowing' (*The Guardian*, 26 May 1978: 12). When *The Two Ronnies* was first aired in 1971 Barker and Corbett were always careful never to appear as a formal double act per se – the 'and

---

7   Try to imagine a Mike and Bernie Winters interpretation of Edward Lear. Better still, try not to.

it's a goodnight from him' close to their show was famously born of an openly expressed difficulty of appearing as a comic duo. The image of two jovial fellows at a smoker was a well-crafted illusion:

> We knew we were not, strictly speaking, a double act; we weren't joined at the hip the way Eric Morecambe and Ernie Wise were and this meant we had no way of talking to each other in front of an audience. That kind of relationship did not exist for us; it only comes from being a double act from a very young age. If you try to create it, the effect is false and the audience recognises there is something artificial about it. (Corbett with Nobbs, 2001: 201)[8]

Throughout the sixteen-year run of *The Two Ronnies*, Corbett and Barker maintained high-profile individual projects and their 'Newsreader' characters, who hosted the show, made a virtue of their lack of a traditional bond. There were also solo turns – Barker's often self-penned address in the guise of a government spokesman, Corbett's monologue written by Spike Mullins or John Renwick – that would have been unthinkable for Eric and Ernie. A further double act of the same period that was formed of two actors was Ryan and Ronnie. Ryan Davies was a songwriter with the face of a devious Osric; Ronnie Williams had worked as a television presenter for BBC Wales, and the two were teamed in *Ryan and Ronnie*. The English-language version premiered in 1971 and was well received: 'BBC Wales have come up with their own bright mini *Laugh-in*, which if not original in concept, was presented with such style and professionalism that it put many a spectacular to shame' (Towler, 1971: 11). Both Davies and Williams

---

8   The most accurate demolition of a contrived double act is from Stewart Lee and Richard Herring: 'Chalk and Cheese. Ian Chalk and Ian Cheese are two men. They are very different. As different as chalk and cheese. Do you see? ... Chalk and Cheese are forced to live with each other against their will for some reason. Perhaps terrorists are holding their families. But occasionally they might do something which makes them realise they are more similar than they think and then they look into the camera a meaningfully. Then, Ian Cheese falls over to break the seriousness of the moment' (1995: 58).

wrote the material, including the songs, but the partnership ended at the behest of the straight man in 1975. Ryan died of an asthma attack in 1977, Williams twenty years later of depression. Their closing song had the pair harmonising in a way that Corbett and Barker would never attempt – music in *The Two Ronnies* was for parody, not bonding.

Corbett and Barker had first worked together on *The Frost Report* in 1966; the latter also wrote material under the pseudonym Gerald Wiley. Ronnie Barker was also a noted scene stealer within British films, as adept as unobtrusively grasping a moment from the ostensible star as Richard Wattis or Colin Gordon. Corbett was a light comedian with a gift for character acting that British cinema seldom exploited; his fisherman 'Drooby' was one of the few enjoyable elements of *Rockets Galore!* (Michael Relph, 1957), the Rank semi-sequel to *Whisky Galore!* (Alexander Mackendrick, 1948) with Eastmancolor cinematography and Donald Sinden saying 'gosh!'.

By the early 1980s *The Two Ronnies* had become formulaic, a fate that had befallen many a show of a lesser calibre. The infamous *Not the Nine O'Clock News* (1979–82) parody 'The Two Ninnies' with Mel Smith and Griff Rhys Jones was especially painful to Barker, who claimed that he was annoyed because 'it was a bit inaccurate. It was saying all we did was swear and say rude words, which was absolutely untrue' (quoted in McCabe, 2005: 205). In fact, 'The Two Ninnies' accused the older show's formula of being tired, of Corbett having the worst lines because his partner wrote much of the material, of featuring contrived musical numbers and of indulging in relentless innuendo. Gerald Wiley was indeed over-fond of the last-named at times and the feature-length semi-silent specials *The Picnic* (1976) and *By The Sea* (1982) were akin to being submerged in a stack of postcards.

A further reason for the impact of 'The Two Ninnies' was because, as John Fisher notes, Barker and Corbett were rarely exposed to the critical disdain that was the lot of Southampton's most famous son (2013: 441). One probable reason was that Benny Hill consciously aimed at a music-hall atmosphere while *The Two Ronnies* had an air of golf-club respectability. The world they inhabited in their sketches, and in Corbett's monologues, was that of 1970s *Punch* magazines with its advertisements for sports jackets. Hill, as with Corbett and Barker, was of a lower-middle-class background[9] but his screen persona was one who had strayed from an end-of-the-pier show at Bournemouth. There was also the problem that by 1980, and abetted by his producer Dennis Kirkland, the dance routines in *The Benny Hill Show* became overtly ghastly. Hill's clever and sometimes beautiful devised and written earlier sketches – especially those created in BBC days – were forgotten. His ability as an actor was now equally overlooked, and his image as an overgrown schoolboy was at increasingly at odds with his physical appearance.

An audience often has *idée fixe* about their favourite double acts or solo comics – when Morecambe and Wise moved to ITV in 1978 Eric changed his style of glasses, and Ernie's hair was now whitening, thereby marking the end of their 'classic look'. J.B. Priestley thought that the British 'did not like a comedian to be different, but to be forever himself, or, if you will, to be more himself each time they see him' (1929: 38). After 1985 Hill looked too old to be 'himself' while *The Two Ronnies* always seemed to be hovering around the age of 49, even when the series commenced.

When *The Two Ronnies* was seven years into its run, Banks-Smith already regarded it as a survivor of an older tradition: 'Like a small grocer's shop absorbed into a tower block, a disco on its left and a sauna on its right, the old firm of Corbett and Barker (Telegrams: Corker) survives defenced but defiant' (*The Guardian*, 26 May 1978: 12). The outfits that were often favoured by the Ronnies – striped blazers (Barker) and the Pringles pullovers (Corbett) – lent them an air of two genial managing directors presiding over the staff's annual cricket match. Despite this imaage of genteel respectability the best of *The Two Ronnies* was not the puns but an acute sense of observation. Barker's finest hour as a writer may well be the 'Four Candles' sketch, which is as much about two not overly bright men to whom every transaction is a struggle as it is concerned with wordplay. Even better, in the humble opinion of

---

9   In 1932 Hill's father purchased outright a three-bedroom semi-detached villa in a pleasant suburb; that is not 'working class'.

this writer, is 'Hello', written by Terry Jones and Michael Palin, where Corbett is the apparently innocent party who remains sanguine in the face of Barker's increasingly paranoid guest:

> Barker: Oh! I don't mean those exact words ... I was only using them as an excuse ... It might have been more on the lines of 'Hello, you fat ugly, mealy-mouthed sadist, I wish you were dead!'
> Corbett: No, I didn't say anything but 'hello'.

And in 'Nothing is Too Much Trouble', the polite veneer of Barker's sweet-shop owner finally cracks beneath the demands of Corbett's new customer, a curiously menacing figure with his polite tones and trilby hat. It was in such moments that *The Two Ronnies* displayed a sense of anarchy that was the equal, dare we say it, of Cook and Moore or even Monty Python, beneath the gracious smiles and 'Ladies and Gentlemen – Barbara Dickinson'.

Smith and Jones

There is a certain irony in 'The Two Ninnies' being played by Mel Smith and Griff Rhys Jones, the double act that emerged from the ashes of *Not The Nine O Clock News*. *Alas Smith and Jones* ran for fourteen years – billed as *Smith and Jones* from 1989 onwards – and the tone of its sketches followed the theme established by the earlier show. The producer John Lloyd explained that while in *The Two Ronnies*, characters still played shove ha'penny in pubs and encountered working telephone boxes, 'None of us had ever seen a shove ha'penny board. Phone boxes were swilling with wee, and the phone was hanging off the receiver[10] (quoted in *The Guardian*, Wroe, 10 April 2009). Even when Smith and Jones were addressing the audience as 'themselves' the impression was less two elegant chaps introducing a programme of whimsical diversions and more two executives trapped in the sales conference somewhere near Basingstoke.

A prevalent element in the sketches in *Alas Smith and Jones*, aside from the consistently high quality of the acting and the writing[11] it was a sense of cynicism. When *The Two Ronnies* were not in a party sketch or a filmed spoof, their blue-collar characters were largely amicable, prone to asking 'goin down the pub?' – where there might indeed be shove ha'penny and a barmaid from the Barbara Windsor/Dora Bryan Academy of Inn-Keeping. Smith and Jones functioned in a 1980s that would have been very familiar to anyone who recalls that decade; the shopping precincts that would look semi-derelict within just five years, sub-par eateries and shops populated by the apathetic and the desperate. It would be impossible to think of Barker and Corbett in a 1985 sketch about police brutality, with a journalist asking Smith's senior officer, 'Is it true that the police beat up blacks and homosexuals indiscriminately?' only to receive the considered response, 'It depends how many men are available.' *The Two Ronnies* almost always had a musical guest, but the end credits of Smith and Jones would be accompanied by an apathetic cabaret duo who are visibly desperate for the evening to end.

Neither Smith nor Jones was the straight man. The former's expression of a disgruntled potato made him ideally suited to prison inmates, oafish middle-managers and NCOs; he was the bomb-disposal sergeant doing his utmost to cope with Smith's recruit character who arrives wearing the grin of vacuous inanity, or the long-term prison inmate marvelling at the world's worst prison visitor. When the roles were reversed, Jones delivers his line in measured but uneasy tones that have the quality of one plotting the best route out of a nightmare created by Smith's oafs

---

10 One of the minor fascinations with the 1950s comedy films that was often aired on BBC2 at that time was not so much the telephone boxes with their 'A/B' button mechanism but that they were unvandalised and actually worked.

11 The script team included Clive Anderson, Colin Bostock-Smith and Paul Merton.

or fanatics. A chief inspector tries to investigate a complaint from a Londoner who can only communicate in sub-Euston film clichés, or a minister conducts a burial where one of the mourners drops his teeth in the open grave.

The most high-profile creations of *Alas* was the 'Head To Head' characters – Mel Smith as the idiot who thinks he possesses insight and wisdom, Griff Rhys Jones as the idiot who knows they are both entirely devoid of such laudable qualities. Cook's bores are the creations of a master parodist, but *Alas Smith and Jones* present their duologues as horrendously plausible, and a highlight of the complete series was the *Homemade Xmas Video* of 1987. Jones (dense but reasonably good-natured) is the paterfamilias and cameraman, Smith (thick but with a measure of bovine cunning) is his friend and lodger and the entire special is largely devoid of geniality. Flanders and Swann celebrated the idiosyncrasies of English life, but three decades later this is seen to be a mask for crassness and total self-indulgence. If there was an underlying theme of *Alas Smith and Jones,* it was a faint but palpable disdain for lack of intelligence in every aspect of society, including – a moment that stands high in the annals of television comedy – the raid on a forest for a Christmas tree, with an Austin Maxi as the getaway car.

Fry and Laurie

Our next pair of gentlemen emerged, with grace and good manners, during the 1980s, for Stephen Fry and Hugh Laurie would never seek to impose themselves. Roger Wilmut and Peter Rosengard claimed that alternative comedy sought to reject 'the erudite middle-class approach of university wits'[12] as much as racist and sexist elements of 'traditional comedy' (1989: iv). In reality, Fry and Laurie cameoed on *The Young Ones* (BBC, 1982–84) and they were often the sole watchable element of an

---

12 Leaving aside the fact that many alternative comedians were not exactly from a working-class background.

average *Saturday Night Live* (C4, 1985–88) with cross-talk routines that were seemingly effortless. Both parties were tall and positively elegant, but Fry often portrayed figures with the patronising good humour of a don who knows his position in life is secure, presenting advice to Hugh Laurie as his bemused acolyte. Just follow these simple rules, old chap, and success and respect will be yours; you might even succeed in being like me.

Fry and Laurie were part of the Cambridge Footlights revue *Cellar Tapes* that won the Perrier Award in 1981; the other cast members included Tony Slattery and Emma Thompson. It was the first award for individual comedy in the thirty-four-year history of the Edinburgh Festival Fringe. By the late 1950s, the Fringe had organised its own society and was becoming regarded by those affiliated with the 'official' Festival as a threat rather a complementary attraction. Even the title of *Beyond the Fringe* came about because, according to Jonathan Miller:

> The Fringe had become a competitive irritant to the organisers of the official Festival and … *Beyond the Fringe* was an attempt to outbid the presumptuous outsiders who opportunistically pitched their tents on the edges of the REAL festival. (quoted in Bartie, 2014: 81).

There remains an impression in some quarters that winning the Edinburgh Comedy Award is the automatic path to conquering world comedy at best or, at worst, dominating the output of light entertainment in a Hydra-headed cartel of 'Footlights graduates'. The truth is most likely that those victors would have succeeded without the Fringe and this would certainly apply to Fry and Laurie, the first real double act in the history of the Cambridge University Footlights Dramatic Club. By 1987 they had appeared on the Royal Variety Show, and the reviewer of *The Guardian* sniffed that Fry and Laurie had thereby sacrificed their 'alternative' credentials (Rubnikowicz, 1987: 11.), but in the late 1980s such divisions were starting to blur.[13] The pilot of *A Bit of Fry and Laurie*

---

13 By 1989 Ben Elton was standing in as the host of *Wogan* (BBC, 1982–92).

was screened on Boxing Day of 1987, leading to eight utterly glorious years of erudition, wit and parodies of television shows.[14] Their faux vox-pops were as glorious as the non-sequiteurs uttered by the Greek Chorus in *The Knack – and How to Get It* (Richard Lester, 1965), one gem being 'these tumble-dryers are useless'. In 1990 they created the perfect Jeeves and Wooster for television, although it is a thousand pities that no-one thought to re-make *School for Scoundrels* with Laurie as Henry Palfrey and Fry as Stephen Potter. And 'Please Mr Music Man' was much in the spirit of Flanders and Swann, with Fry requesting Laurie at the piano create 'a dizzying jazz pattern of sound'. One feels that the creators of *Slow Train* would have approved.

Armstrong and Miller

Our final set of splendid chaps are Alexander Armstrong and Ben Miller. Armstrong and Miller formed a double act in 1994 and they were nominated for a Perrier Award two years later. Their television programme (Paramount and C4/BBC, 1997–2001/2007) was one of the finest sketch shows in the history of the medium, starring two light comedy actors who, had they been born fifty years earlier, would have almost undoubtedly been stars of Ealing Studio[15] or the satires of the Boulting Brothers.[16] As with Stephen Fry and Hugh Laurie, their images were not dated but deliberately archaic, but while Fry and Laurie have the faint manner of Bright Young Things, Armstrong and Miller seem more of the Macmillan era.

Neither member of the act was the straight man, and both were expert at the fine art of cliché demolition. Miller's teacher switches from

---

14 After the Fry and Laurie spoof of *Countdown* (C4, 1982–present), it almost seemed that Richard Whiteley was parodying Stephen Fry's impersonation of himself.

15 As in the films of Alexander Mackendrick or Robert Hamer, as opposed to the glib 'warm beer and cricket on the village green' mythology.

16 Armstrong as Major Hitchcock and Ben Miller as Stanley Windrush?

cod-Robin Williams inspirational tones to bored South London the moment the school bell rings – 'Fuck off – this is my time now.' Armstrong is jovial and booming in the manner of chaps who were either named 'Roger', or who really should have been. The show was at its finest when it explored past cinematic and televisual tropes through the eyes of the late twenty-first century. The RAF officers from a 1950s Second World War feature – the look of the luminous back and white film stock is archetypal post-war Elstree – who can only communicate in teen slang were their most famous creations. An even more accomplished routine in the opinion of some observers (i.e., me) was 'How Many Hats?', a lovingly observed evocation *What's My Line?* (BBC, 1951–63) and any number of mind-numbingly boring 1950s BBC parlour games. The panel consists of a Katie Boyle-style Lady of the Shires, a pop singer of the Larry Parnes stable of artists, an understudy for Gilbert Harding and Ben Miller as a comedy scriptwriter with a bohemian beard and the cynicism of the late twentieth century. Armstrong played the glacial host who knows the show is reliant upon a sense of decorum that surpasses any desire to point out that the central theme is totally futile. Manners are the fabric of decent society, regardless of the fact that every contestant arrives very visibly wearing a number of hats. But to openly state this – and thereby shatter the illusion – is a solecism that cannot be tolerated, as Miller's character is soon to learn.

The sheer attention to detail in 'How Many Hats?' is typical of a double act that, unlike so many programmes, did not assume their viewers had the attention span of a distracted mayfly. The musical numbers for *Armstrong and Miller* are from Donald Brabbins and Teddy Fyffe, a parody of Flanders and Swann; every aspect of the sketch is a homage to *At The Drop of a Hat*. The joy of the routine is in the homage to Michael Flanders and Donald Swann – Armstrong rolling his wheelchair towards the footlights, Miller giggling at the keyboards – and although Brabbins and Fyffe engage in modern smut in a 1950s manner, the older double act had anticipated the lyrics to their numbers. It is a short journey from 'Pee, po, belly, bum, drawers …' to 'I'd still do Mrs. Palmer'.

Bibliography

Books

Bartie, Angela (2014), *The Edinburgh Festivals: Culture and Society in Postwar Britain.* Edinburgh: Edinburgh University Press.

Cook, Peter and Cook, William (ed.) (2004), *Goodbye Again: The Definitive Peter Cook and Dudley Moore.* London: Arrow Books.

Corbett, Ronnie with Nobbs, David (2001), *High Hopes.* London: Ebury Press.

Fisher, John (2013), *Funny Way To Be A Hero.* London: Preface Publishing.

Herring, Richard and Lee, Stewart (1995), *Lee and Herring's Fist of Fun.* London: BBC Books.

Hewison, Robert (1983), *Footlights!: A Hundred Years of Cambridge Comedy.* London: Methuen.

Hunt, Leon (2013), *Cult British TV Comedy: From Reeves and Mortimer to 'Psychoville'* . Manchester. Manchester University Press.

McCabe, Bob (2005), *Ronnie Barker: The Authorised Biography.* London: BBC Books.

Muggeridge, Malcolm (1966), *The Most of Malcolm Muggeridge.* New York: Simon and Shuster.

Orwell, George (1950), *Shooting an Elephant: And Other Essays.* London: Secker and Warburg.

Priestley, J.B. (1929), *English Humour.* London: Longmans.

Swann, Donald with Smith, Lyn (1991), *Swann's Way: A life in Song.* London: William Heinemann Ltd.

Thompson, Harry (1997), *The Biography of Peter Cook.* London: Hodder and Stoughton.

Wilmut, Roger (1980), *From Fringe to Flying Circus: Celebrating a Unique Generation of Comedy 1960–1980.* London: Methuen.

Wilmut, Roger and Rosengard, Peter (1989) *Didn't You Kill My Mother-in-law?: The Story of Alternative Comedy in Britain from the Comedy Store to 'Saturday Live'.* London: Methuen Drama.

Journals and Periodicals

Banks-Smith, Nancy (1978), Review: Palladium, *The Guardian*, 26 May, pp. 12.

Cooke, Alistair (1959), 'Revue in Best Jazz Groove', *The Guardian*, 10 June, pp. 7.

Crozier, Mary (1965), Review: Not Only ... But Also, *The Guardian*, 22 March, pp. 7.

Fairlie, Henry (1963), 'That Was A Year That Was', *The Spectator*, 27 December, pp. 7.

Fiddick, Peter (1970), 'The Complete Michael Flanders', *The Guardian*, 3 July, pp. 9.

Johns, Eric (1959), 'Peter Cook Is A Humourist Inspired By Conversation', *The Stage*, 10 December, pp. 19.

Lloyd Evans, Gareth (1963), Review: At the Drop of Another Hat, *The Guardian*, 11 September, pp. 7.

Review: The Edinburgh Festival (1958), *The Stage*, 4 September, pp. 18.

Rhys Jones, Griff (2005), 'It's like being in a marriage – except that you always end up in bed together', *The Telegraph*, 9 October.

Rubnikowicz, Renata (1987), 'Déjà Vu', *The Guardian*, 24 December, pp. 11.

'Smoking Concerts' (1885), *Sporting Life*, 23 January, pp. 2.

'Temporary Parting for "Hat" Men' (1967), *The Stage*, 27 April, pp. 1.

Trewin, J.C.T. (1957), Review: At The Drop of a Hat, *Illustrated London News*, 9 February, pp. 34.

Trewin, J.C.T. (1953), Review: Airs on a Shoestring, *The Sketch*, 6 May 1953: pp. 22.

Tynan, Kenneth (1957), Review: At The Drop of a Hat, *The Observer*, 6 January, pp. 9.

Wroe, Nicholas (2009), 'A Life in Comedy: John Lloyd', *The Guardian*, 10 April.

9

The Double Act and Children's Entertainment

'That's the way to do it!'

Introduction

Britons who were raised during the 1970s were often exposed to forms of entertainment with roots dating back centuries, and often taking a form that was even more disturbing than watching *The Changes* on BBC1.[1] In December there might be a visit to the pantomime, accompanied by paternal grumblings to the effect that this year's current pop sensation as 'no good without his backing group' and how £1.35 for a box of Maltesers was 'naked profiteering'. But if the show in question was Cinderella, the real stars of the show were the Ugly Sisters.

---

1 A 1973 adaption of John Dickinson's novel; think of a *Quatermass and The Pit* (Roy Ward Baker, 1967) for children and you will have an idea of how frightening it really was.

On 26 December 1860 H.J. Byron staged *Cinderella: or The Lover, The Lacky, and the Little Glass Slipper* at the Royal Strand Theatre and it was 'in this burlesque version of the story that the sisters came to full ugliness' (Frow, 1985: 111). Clorinda was played by an actor named Jimmy Rogers as an arch-villainess, and 120 years later, members of the audience were watching template established by Henry Byron in an atmosphere of excitement, Toffo wrappers and warm bottles of Cresta cherryade, enjoying 'business' that had passed through generations of performers via oral tradition (Taylor, 2007: 71). Furthermore:

> A young actor might start as a broker's man or Chinese policeman with simple chases and knockabout comedy and observe the comic and the Dame in action and learn the routines they performed. The youngster would then graduate to comic roles before arriving at the pinnacle as Dame or Ugly Sister. (2007: 39)

The broker's men who come to seize the Baron's furniture or the 'Chinese policemen' (in *Aladdin*) are incidental to the pantomime, whereas the Ugly Sisters were, and are, a stellar attraction: loud, wicked but always vibrant. You might have briefly considered the same when on holiday in Weymouth or Blackpool when encountering an even more ancient – and alarming – form of double act during a seaside holiday. The shops selling faded picture postcards, plastic windmills and sticks of almost luminously pink rock plus the posters advertising a pier-end performance for a beat combo which was now ten years beyond their last chart hit all provided a suitably surreal background to the Punch and Judy Show. Little can be stranger than the juxtaposing of eras, not least viewing a puppet show harking back to Pulcinella, the Lord of Misrule of seventeenth-century *Commedia dell'arte* staged in a booth surrounded by a Greek chorus of morose donkeys attended by an equally despondent middle-aged Teddy Boy.[2]

---

2 Or such was my experience.

Mr Punch, Pulcinella's anglicised counterpart, was originally the star of marionette theatre; Samuel Pepys famously went to 'see an Italian puppet play that is within the rayles there, which is very pretty, the best that ever I saw, and a great resort of gallants' in his diaries of 9 May 1662 (Latham, Matthews et al., 1995: 80). The move to a puppet show was a development of the next century and the historian Rosalind Crone argues that it was during this period that Mr Punch acquired a spouse and that this was an English development: 'She was commonly called Joan, an appellation that was also a colloquialism that described country women' (2013: 51). By the early 1800s, the first name of Mrs Punch was now Judy, and her husband wore a jester's motley in place of the sugarloaf 'coppolone' hat of his Italian ancestor.

The Victorian era saw two major developments to the show: the acceptance of Punch and Judy as entertainment for the middle-class home and the rise of the seaside resort. The couple may still be seen in some resorts long after the disappearance of the Sandman and other entertainers; in the twenty-first century, some puppeteers began to include a health and safety official among their cast of villains. But the core is still the dysfunctional marital relationship in a show described by Charles Dickens in 1849 as 'one of those extravagant reliefs from the realities of life' (quoted in Andrews, 2013: 44) the nature of its anti-heroic male protagonist never quite contained by staging his antics in a gaudily a striped booth. As with the pantomime, the Punch and Judy Show gives the youthful audience the very faintest sense, among the discarded Zoom and Space 1999 wrappers, that you are watching the proof that your world is not immutable.

These are but two examples of the double acts who permeate children's entertainment and the youthful members of the audience were often most discerning as to the key elements. *Roobarb and Custard* (BBC, 1974), the first fully-animated television series to be made entirely in the UK, were akin to Hancock and Sid in animated canine and feline forms, the former teeming with enthusiasm, the latter a one-cat cynical Greek chorus. The essence of the double act is also present in Eric Thompson's version of *Le Manège enchanté* (ORTF 1964–74).

The BBC's *Magic Roundabout* with entirely new scripts and narration from Thompson was, in essence, a programme in its own right. Margotte became Florence; the other children were eventually dropped from the line-up,[3] while Pollux became the decidedly East Cheam-like Dougal, forever sparring with optimistic Brian the Snail. Thompson believed the programme succeeded because his scripts used 'long words, intricate phrases, and everything funny anyone had ever told me, regardless of how sophisticated (quoted in Stott, 1972: 9).

This lack of patronage was the essence of any double act of quality aimed at the younger audience, such as *Danger Mouse* (ITV, 1981–92). No adventure of an eye-patch-wearing rodent hero voiced by David Jason would be complete without Penfold, and it is no insult to the memory of Terry Scott to suggest that he was born to play a be-spectacled hamster as much as to say 'Cor!' every week in *Terry and June*.[4] Southern Television's *Worzel Gummidge* (1979–81), adapted by Keith Waterhouse and Willis Hall, features one of the most endearing villainesses in the history of the medium. The Aunt Sally of Una Stubbs created an enduring screen partnership with Jon Pertwee. Over the many indelible moments over the four series two stand tall: Worzel and Sally performing 'The Scarecrow Hop' and 'The Return of Dolly Clothespeg' (Lorraine Chase); the latter remains a prime example of how a show could transcend its remit. The moment when the Crowman (Geoffrey Blaydon) orders Worzel to employ his sense of free will and choose between the future partner who represents happiness and the wooden narcissist with who represents 'total misery' makes one wonder if this is a programme for the Sunday teatime slot. Worzel is trapped with Aunt Sally, forever the satellite of a wooden doll with a faux-genteel accent whose main loves are (a) herself and (b) cream cakes.

---

3   Resulting in generations of British television viewers wondering who the children on the roundabout were, as only seemed to appear in the opening credits.

4   It is also no insult to Sir David Jason to suggest that there are those of us who would infinitely prefer to hear him say 'Penfold, shush' to an over-enthusiastic hamster than to see that 'Batman and Robin' clip ever again. Beware a sitcom that decides it is 'lovable'…

Nor did a double act have to appear on a comedy show to make an impact on the youthful audience; aside from the wonderful Roger Delgado aiming the Master's beard of evil at the third Doctor Who, there were John Noakes, Peter Purves and their apparently limitless supply of sticky-backed plastic. Noakes had joined *Blue Peter* in late 1965 and Purves replaced Christopher Trace in 1967, forming the double act who were to take the programme into the colour era in 1970. For almost nine years their contribution to the programme often seemed to fall into the classic funny man/straight man mode.[5] Valerie Singleton and later Leslie Judd were the anchors of the programme. Purves was tall, groovily dressed (by early 1970s standards, at any rate) and with the demeanour of a firm but approachable geography teacher. John Noakes was shorter, sported a pudding basin haircut, drove a Marcos and had an accent that became progressively more northern during his tenure on the show.

And of course, one long-running post-war double act contained only one human and was a show that ranks alongside the Austin J40 pedal car, hula hoops and Shirley Abicair 78 rpm records as emblematic of a 1950s British childhood. If one poses the question 'What was the name of the ventriloquist's show that ran on BBC radio for eight years and whose cast, at one time or another, included Julie Andrews, Tony Hancock, Benny Hill, Sidney James, Hattie Jacques, Max Bygraves, Bruce Forsyth, Bernard Miles, Beryl Reid, Gilbert Harding and James Robertson Justice?', the answer, of course, would be *Educating Archie*. According to Wilmut, ventriloquists first began using a doll around 1750, and in the early days of music hall, it was not uncommon for acts to use a life-size partner (1985: 178). Peter Brough worked for the family textile business and performed ventriloquism as a sideline. During his time with Entertainments National Service Association (ENSA) in the Second World War, he encountered the music publisher Wally Ridley who pointed out his less-than-perfect technique and that his dummy lacked finesse. On the advice of comedy scriptwriter Ted Kavanagh a new doll was commissioned to be Archie Andrews.

---

5   This was wonderfully celebrated by Ben Miller in his 1992 tribute *Gone With Noakes* which was awarded the Pick of the Fringe Award at the Edinburgh Festival.

Educating Archie went on the air on 6 June 1950 as a summer replacement for *Take It From Here* (1948–60) and at its peak the show attained listening figures of 15 million. Archie was insured for £10,000, and when he went missing from the London to Leeds train in October 1951, this made front page headlines.[6] By the end of the year he was presiding over *The Archie Andrews Christmas Party* at the Prince of Wales Theatre and throughout the decade there were Archie-branded lollipops, board games, jigsaw puzzles and road safety campaigns.

The idea of a ventriloquist show on the radio was hardly a new one – in the USA Edgar Bergan and his dummy Charlie McCarthy had been broadcasting since 1936 – but the character as created by Brough and his writers was so strong that the show did work on the wireless. An attempted transfer to television in 1958 ultimately failed as it highlighted Brough's technical limitations – Wilmut noted that 'years of working on radio eventually eroded his ability to hide his lip movements' (1985: 180). More importantly, the ITV series destroyed the fantasy world that had been so carefully created by the cast and scriptwriters. This was a problem that was not restricted to *Educating Archie* – from 1957 to 1972 Jimmy Clitheroe in *The Clitheroe Kid* was partnered by Danny Ross as Alf Hall but when Clitheroe made a series for ABC, *Just Jimmy* (1964–68) he was already aged 43 when the first programme aired. As more than one critic pointed out, the schoolboy costume meant that his wrinkled knees could not be successfully disguised.

The other challenge with transferring Archie to television was that although Brough would perform with the dummy for the benefit of the studio audience *Educating Archie* was essentially the double act as a domestic comedy show. Publicity photos display of the 1950 display Archie's master looking like the ideal patriarch from a Ladybird book of the period. Brough was dapper but genial and approachable. By contrast Archie looked mildly terrifying; it is wholly understandable that Tony Hancock suffered from nightmares after seeing the dummy hung on a peg in a dressing room.

---

6   A letter was subsequently delivered to Brough stating that 'You will find Archie at the King's Cross lost property office – sorry chum.'

Another amiably harassed father figure of the decade was Harry Corbett, but while Sooty was mischievous he was very much his own bear rather than a wooden Sybil who spoke in the voice of another. *Muffin The Mule* (BBC, 1946–52) and Shari's Lewis's Lambchop, who frequently guested on British television shows during the 1960s and 1970s,[7] were more appealing characters although Rod Hull and Emu were rather more disturbing. The ITV programmes *Emu's World* (Central, 1982–84) and *Emu's All Live Pink Windmill Show* (1984–88) never quite conveyed the same sense of anarchic menace of the BBC's *Emu's Broadcasting Company*. At some moments it appears that Hull's arm was possessed, à la Peter Sellers as Dr Strangelove, but, for all his destruction, and Michael Parkinson-related shenanigans, Emu still looked docile in comparison with the terrifying blank visage of Archie. Peter Brough's father Arthur had devised Hugo, who tormented Michael Redgrave in *Dead of Night* (Alberto Cavalcanti, Charles Crichton, Robert Hamer and Basil Dearden, 1945). While I am not saying that Archie would ever have emulated such behaviour – with Peter Maddern announcing 'a quiet Sunday afternoon, as Archie lays waste to all of suburbia' – he did have the countenance of one who might think about it from time to time.

But despite such occasionally nightmarish qualities, and although Peter Brough may not have been an artist who was on a par with Ray Allan or Saveen (Albert Langford),[8] his partnership with Andrews was so strong that some listeners were convinced that Archie was real. Eric Midwinter was not a fan – 'I once summoned up the stamina, over three or four Sunday afternoons, to listen and note the thirty-minute programme. I reckoned there were fifty-two sayings, situations, characteristics and so forth which cropped up every week' (1979: 134). But in *Educating Archie* the key to the success of the act on the wireless was the premise of a single parent and his wayward charge rather than a 'vent act'. Brough retired from broadcasting in 1962 to return to the family business, but nine years later he gave a memorable insight into

---

7   Neither were Nookie Bear or Orville the Duck; now we do not have to speak of
     either again.
8   Who predated Brough as a British ventriloquist act appearing on the wireless.

the dynamics of the act. When giving evidence to the High Court in a case to determine the compensation to be awarded to the widow of his friend and fellow ventriloquist Dennis Spicer, who had been killed in a road accident in 1964, Brough stated that Andrews could earn him £240,000 per annum. When counsel asked if was the dummy rather than himself that the public was paying to see, his reply was 'I don't mind if they were. It was a double act' (quoted in *The Birmingham Post*, 10 October 1969: 13).

Crackerjack

'It's Friday! It's five to five!'

It is a matter of history that the first edition of *Crackerjack* did not air on a Friday, as 14 September 1955 fell on a Wednesday. The 'Telebriefs' column in *The Stage* of the following day referred to how the team of Joe Baker and Jack Douglas had commenced a ten-week run of the show (15 September 1955: 11), but very few would have guessed that the last edition would be broadcast in 1984. Ronnie Corbett and Michael Darbyshire succeeded Baker and Douglas[9] as resident double act, and throughout the series, it was the role of the host to act as genial traffic officer – i.e. keep the show moving – and to bring order to the main sketch before the closing credits. Don Maclean, the show's resident comic of much the 1970s, saw *Crackerjack* as 'being effectively two separate shows in one. You'd have the host, who'd announce the musical act and compere the quiz section "Double or Drop"[10] and the two comics.'

---

9 The act broke up in 1961, Baker going solo and Douglas subsequently becoming the stooge for Des O'Connor and a late member of the *Carry On* team. His best outing as an actor was probably *The Shillingbury Tales*.

10 Which was devised by Andrews.

By 1960 Leslie Crowther, a 27-year-old light comedy actor and a fixture with the 'Fols-de-Rols' concert party, was appointed as the principal comedian. His partner was Peter Glaze, a comic of vast experience who had understudied every member of The Crazy Gang between 1949 and 1959. He had also performed similar duties for Arthur Askey, Arthur Riscoe and Lupino Lane. On television Glaze had been threatened by Tony Hancock in *The Bowmans* and in later life he appeared in *The Sweeney*; in 1978 he even starred in a one-man show at the Edinburgh Fringe. But it was as the perpetually affronted straight man of *Crackerjack*, a man born to say 'doh', that he would achieve lasting fame.

Crowther eventually took over from Andrews as host after 1964, and it was during his tenure that the show moved from its Thursday slot. The programme did not meet with universal critical acclaim; Judith Cook ranted in *The Guardian* that 'those jolly adults in the depths of the planning department who think that children fold up and hoot with laughter week after week at *Crackerjack* and *Tich* must be simple-minded to a degree' (30 March 1964: 4). *The Stage*, somewhat predictably, was more sanguine, Ann Purser believing that 'one of the secrets of *Crackerjack*'s success is that it is unashamedly aimed at the lower social levels' (20 December 1967: 12), even if this conjures images of studio guests comprised of urchin extras from *Oliver!* (Carol Reed, 1968).

Danny Baker wisely noted in his wonderful BBC *Heroes of Comedy* tribute to Peter Glaze (BBC, 1994) that this was not a 'knowing pastiche'. *Crackerjack* first aired in the last days of the Variety era, when at least some members of the audience might have seen Jimmy Jewel and Ben Warriss topping the bill at the local theatre. Even when the show was in its final season, there were still countless seaside shows and an annual visit to the pantomime was still a part of the December holidays. After Crowther left *Crackerjack* in 1968, there was a serious prospect that the show would be mothballed. But on Friday (at five to five) on 11 February 1973 Don Maclean joined the show as the principal comedian; 'I pointed out to the producers that I was young enough to have seen the programme when I was still at school'. Glaze once more had a partner to truly deflate his air of pomposity and with 'Don and Peter' the viewers were witnessing a tradition that harked back to the days of Murray and Mooney, whose 'The Stake' routine could have graced any *Crackerjack* of the 1970s:

> Murray: Ladies and Gentlemen – a monologue entitled 'The Stake'.
> There's a job to be done
> We must cut out the fun
> And stick to our task, one and all ...'
> Mooney: Pardon me, what is the title of this junk?
> Murray: 'The Stake'.
> Mooney: Have an onion?
> Murray: What for?
> Mooney: To eat with the steak.

Replace 'Ladies and Gentlemen' with 'Boys and Girls' – and throw in a few 'dohs!' and you have a typical Glaze/Maclean opening.

When the show celebrated its 200th edition, Leslie Crowther remarked that 'we regard it as a junior variety show with an audience of people who just happen to be a little younger than other people'. Glaze was more succinct, noting 'we'd be out on our ears' (quoted in *The Stage*, 12 January 1967: 12) if the duo ever patronised the show's devotees. Maclean echoes these views, observing that 'light entertainment made the show rather than the children's division, and it was made to exactly the same standards as an adult Variety show'. He describes the extensive rehearsals, how he and Glaze would polish the scripts. Nor was such a programme suited to all double acts or vice versa; Little and Large appeared on the show for one season but, in the words of Syd Little, 'we didn't want to be typecast as "children's Entertainers"'. Towards the end of his time with the show, Crowther thought that '*Crackerjack* has helped me to be myself in front of the camera – especially after I took over as compere from Eamonn Andrews'. However, he also believed that 'it could be bad for a comedian to be appearing continuously in children's shows and nothing else because children like familiar things and there is always the temptation to keep doing the same sort of things you know are sure to make them laugh' (quoted in Bilbow, 1967: 10).

In the late 1950s the audience was composed of 'children aged from ten to sixteen recruited from schools and other institutions' but in the 1970s they tended to be of primary school age, as they were more attuned to the show's humour (Maclean: 'When we had a party of secondary school students, they were swearing at the microphones in the ceiling'). The classic *Crackerjack* format was now firmly established – 'Double or Drop' was now hosted by the deadpan Michael Aspel who would, not in the time-honoured tradition of *Crackerjack*, bring the final sketch to a close. There were also the pop acts which in the late 1950s meant Pearl Carr and Teddie Johnson, although by 1961 the original line-up of The Shadows was performing 'FBI' and Peter and Gordon sang of 'A World Without Love' in 1964. Three years later Purser noted appearances of The Herd, Cat Stevens and Christine Holmes – acts not automatically associated with light entertainment – on the programme but nothing could equate for sheer charming incongruity the moments when the resident double act parodied a chart hit of the week. Don and Peter not only covered Sparks's 'Something for the Girl With Everything', but they also sang 'Bohemian Rhapsody' – 'live, as well, which Queen never managed,' points out Maclean.

Maclean left the show in 1976 – 'I'm still approached today by people who ask me why I stopped appearing on the programme' – and his replacement was Bernie Clifton. The moment when Peter and Bernie presented their own very special version of XTC's 'We're Only Making Plans For Nigel' fortunately remains in the archive,[11] but in 1980 the series was revamped with a new resident double act. The producer Michael Hurll aimed for 'a funnier and faster-moving show, more in keeping with what kids and families want today. I chose the Krankies because Janette's anarchic schoolboy is in the tradition of Just William and The Clitheroe Kid, both of whom appeal to the whole family' (quoted in *The Stage*, 7 August 1980: 21).

---

11 Comparatively few editions of the show survive.

Janette Tough and her husband – and straight man – Ian had worked in cabaret since 1966 and were 'discovered' by Lord Delfont when they won the Club Act of the Year in 1979. They subsequently appeared on the Royal Variety Performance and with a compere along the lines of Andrews (genial, firm but fair) or Michael Aspel (sardonic and deadpan) their act might have served *Crackerjack* well.[12] Unfortunately, Stu Francis brought an atmosphere of manic over-enthusiasm to the show that was to become a hallmark of 1980s children's TV while the format was starting to look fundamentally dated. On 30 September 1983, the guest stars were the never-to-be-repeated combination of Gary Numan and Basil Brush (who duetted with 'On Broadway') but by now the show was akin to a long-running model of car that can be facelifted no more.

Crackerjack ended in 1984, and the heirs to Don Maclean and Peter Glaze are probably Vic Reeves and Bob Mortimer. *Big Night Out* first aired slightly outside of our period and was not a double act per se – Les (Fred Aylward) has as much screen time as Bob Mortimer – but the acts showcased on 'Novelty Island', or Judge Lionel Nutmeg inviting defendants to swear an oath on the *Daktari Annual 1969* is not so far removed from *Crackerjack*. In 1967 Procul Harum appeared to promote their single 'Homburg', where they were joined on stage by Leslie and Peter. As Gary Brooker sang 'You'd better take off your homburg, 'cause your overcoat is too long' to an audience of probably bemused Scouts and Brownies, Crowther whipped off Glaze's hat (Scott-Irvine, 2012) – a moment that anticipated the world of *Action, Image, Exchange* by more than twenty-five years.

The year after the final *Crackerjack* was aired, *Chucklehounds* (BBC, 1985–86) made its debut. The stars were the siblings Barry and Paul Elliott, better known as the Chuckle Brothers, and their next series *Chucklevision* (BBC) ran for 292 episodes from 1987 to 2009. Their viewing public was experiencing a Variety tradition that dates back literally centuries: 'The Chuckle Brothers are zany with the kind of tight well-structured act that

---

12 Let the record show that their single 'Fan-Dabi-Dozi' reached number 46 in the hit parade in 1981.

would have worked in the halls for years in an era long gone' (Moore, 1980: 10). At that point, the Elliotts had been a double act for almost fifteen years and in 1979 they decided to team with their older siblings Jimmy and Brian Patton ('the Patton Brothers'). Ernest Maxim, the producer of the Lennie Bennett/Jerry Stevens television show, featured the four brothers in a five-minute slot and Paul believed that this would differentiate their act from their rivals. 'The competition is fierce. Think of all the pairs … Morecambe and Wise, Little and Large, Lennie Bennett and Jerry Stevens, just for starters. But can you think of a comedy quartet … all brothers?' (quoted in McGarry, 1979: 41).

It was Paul, the tall straight man, and Barry, the comic, who would become automatically associated with the name 'Chuckle Brothers', who could be relied upon to wreck any given task. *Chucklevision* was made with immense professionalism; Russell T. Davies, who wrote three editions, recalled 'the producer of that show, Martin Hughes, had the highest standards of any man I have ever worked for … He would never permit a blow to the head of any sort, in any context. Not even the smallest comedy frying pan' (*The Guardian*, 31 March 2003).

Barry Elliott died in 2018 but their shows, and their iconic cry of 'To you – To me!', will still echo down the ages. Two inseparable Rotherham-accented *Commedia dell'arte* clowns who brought decades of show business experience to a TV programme that lasted for over 20 years. There are far worse legacies for a double act.

With thanks to Don Maclean.

Bibliography

Books

Andrews, Malcolm (2013), *Dickensian Laughter: Essays on Dickens and Humour*. Oxford: Oxford University Press.

Crone, Rosalind (2013), *Violent Victorians: Popular Entertainment in Nineteenth-Century London*. Manchester: Manchester University Press.

Frow, Gerald (1985), *'Oh Yes It Is': The Story of Pantomime*. London: BBC.

Midwinter, Eric (1979), *Make 'em Laugh: Famous Comedians and Their Worlds*. London: Allen & Unwin.

Pepys, Samuel (1662), *The Diaries of Samuel Pepys: A New And Complete Translation by Robert Latham and William Matthews with Contributing Editors William A Armstrong, Macdonald Emslie, Sir Oliver Millar and T.F. Millar*. London: Harper Collins.

Scott-Irvine, Henry (2012), *Procol Harum: The Ghosts Of A Whiter Shade of Pale*. London: Omnibus Press.

Sykes, Eric (2006), *If I Don't Write It Nobody Else Will*. London. Harper Perennial.

Taylor, Millie (2007), *British Pantomime Performance*. Bristol: Intellect Books.

Wilmut, Roger (1985), *Kindly Leave The Stage: The Story of Variety 1919–1960*. London: Methuen.

Journals and Periodicals

'£240,000 Earnings of Archie Andrews' (1969), *Birmingham Post*, 10 October, pp. 13.

Bilbow, Marjorie (1967), 'Likes to be Thought of as a Friend of the Family', *The Stage*, 8 June, pp. 10.

Cook, Judith (1964), 'Women Talking', *The Guardian*, 30 March, pp. 4.

'*Crackerjack* Reaches 200' (1967), *The Stage*, 12 January, pp. 12.

Davies, Russell T. (2003), 'Boom, Boom and Bust', *The Guardian*, 31 March.

'Hurll Taking Over Two' (1980), *The Stage*, 7 August, pp. 21.

McGarry, Peter (1979), 'Two into Four ...', *Coventry Evening Telegraph*, 31 January, pp. 16.

Moore, John (1980), Review: Ayr Gaiety, *The Stage*, 20 November, pp. 10.

Purser, Ann (1967), 'The Children Laugh and Laugh', *The Stage*, 20 December, pp. 12.

Stott, Catherine (1972), 'Doggone', *The Guardian*, 2 August, pp. 9.

'Telebriefs' (1955)' *The Stage*, 15 September, pp. 11.

10

Alternative Comedy

Sir Richard Dangerous (Rik Mayall): Look, there are a lot of people out there who paid a lot of money to see a lot of crocodile snogging. Now, will you please just grow up! Disguise yourself as a crocodile and make it snappy!

The standard narrative about the history of alternative comedy in the UK sometimes runs thus: with the opening of the Comedy Store in 1979, followed by the Comic Strip in 1980, all traditional forms of humour were completely dead by 1 January 1981 and a post-punk sensibility infused each and every sitcom after that. And, most importantly of all, every right-thinking person who was old enough to recall life in the 1980s had the obligatory anecdote of evenings spent in a comedy club that was so edgy as to be positively rhomboid.

Except that to a sizeable proportion of the population, this was as much as myth as every Briton under 30 living in Carnaby Street in 1966, as opposed to being trapped in the provinces and desperately waiting for the 1950s to formally end. To glance at TV light entertainment of the 1980s is to be reminded just how resistant much of the old guard was to change. Just one example: *The Grumbleweeds* television show haunted Saturday night television for an astounding five (!) seasons from 1983. There were those who believed that its purpose in the schedules was to dishearten the viewing public so that they would seriously welcome *3-2-1* (Yorkshire, 1978–88).[1]

Alternative comedy first came to public attention in 1982 with the transmission of *The Comic Strip Presents...* (C4, 1982–present) on the opening night of Channel 4. A frequently heard question during the 1980s was 'What are they "alternative" to?' and the answer was best expressed by the producer Paul Jackson's reference to 'Tarby and His Golfing Pals Live From Whichever London Theatre is Empty This Autumn'. These were the entertainers of 'the dinner jacket and the velvet bow tie, the frilly dickie and the golden bracelet' whose template appeared to be a Las Vegas MC, with a vaguely mid-Atlantic/ Canadian/Croydon accent in some cases. Their celebration was one of affluence – a Lincoln Town Cars and Country Club membership across the Pond and a Granada Ghia, a Sony C7 VCR and a Soda Stream at the very least back in the UK while their stock in trade was 'telling jokes':

> We all know a man (rarely, revealingly 'the woman') at the local who 'tells jokes'. He may be amusing for half an hour over a Saturday evening pint but the chance of him being truly funny, let alone that engaging, thought-provoking thing we properly call a comedian is remote. (*The Guardian*, 17 November 1988: 27)

Such pre-packaged comics were accused of lacking personality and relying on the same array of tired sexist and racist jokes told to audiences dining off scampi in a basket. Three years earlier Bob Monkhouse, whose 1981–86 BBC2 series often surprised viewers who primarily associated him with game shows,[2] did not mourn the decline of clubland:

---

1 Ted Rogers and Dusty Bin do NOT constitute a double act.
2 Jim Carrey and Steven Wright were among his guests.

Performers in clubs play to audiences relatively low on intelligence and expectation of comedy centred very much around the groin. Youngsters would learn how to deliver comedy the wrong way in such a situation, going for the bluest and most shocking stuff to hold the unstable attentions of customers slurred with drink. (Quoted in Barrow, 1985: 8)

The long-term effects of the Gaming Act were impacting on many establishments, which no longer had the funds to pay for major names, while some venues had been established as a get-rich-quick venture by local entrepreneurs with little or no expertise in entertainment.

The new generation of comics wrote their own material instead of using script-writing teams or standardised jokes, and they hailed from diverse professional backgrounds. Alexei Sayle was a former art lecturer, Rik Mayall and Adrian Edmondson were actors, Dawn French and Jennifer Saunders trained as drama teachers, but none were steeped in what appeared to be a moribund tradition. Their relationship with show business past was frequently ambivalent, both parodying the formulaic material about what went before and paying homage to the best of it. Sayle's diatribe about 'great time for variety acts, though, the fifties, and er, actually people are always going on about, erm, the British music hall, you know, and how and why it died out. I'll tell you why it died out, 'cos it was *shite!*' (Double, 2012: 209), as an assessment of the latter days of live Variety entertainment, was caustic but probably not inaccurate. But even this approach, with allowance for the language and caustic approach, was not so far removed from the music hall chairman; or even the permanently doleful Colin Crompton of *The Wheeltappers.*

Of the trio of double acts within this chapter, Norman Hale and Gareth Pace seemed less comic and straight man than two halves of the same entity. They were former teachers who gained their first starring vehicle for television in 1986. Gareth Hale was big, moustachioed and seemingly jolly, while Norman Pace had a quiet voice and pale eyes of someone of might surface in an episode of *The Bill* (ITV, 1984–2012). The effect was often disquieting and their bouncers 'the Two Rons' was one of the most effective routines – to the extent that hearing the speaking voices of the Kray Twins on a 1965 *Panorama* came as quite a shock. Rather less homogenous an act was Rik Mayall and Adrian Edmondson, who met while studying drama at Manchester University and their first incarnation as a double act was as '20th Century Coyote'. This developed into the Dangerous Brothers: 'Slapstick was central to Mayall and Edmondson's comedy, while innuendo was perfectly acceptable if accompanied by a self-conscious "Oo-er, sounds a bit rude!"' (Hunt, 2013: 34).

Much of the humour with Mayall and Edmondson's creations, as with Pete and Dud, Tommy Cooper's routines or even *The Two Ronnies* battling with 'Four Candles' was not in the written material but how two figures of utter ineptitude managed to carve a pathway through life. Where the siblings differed from Corbett and Barker's many struggles to place an order in a hardware shop was the sense of cartoon violence. Richard Dangerous (Mayall) has the balding, slicked back hair of a 1960s gangster's lackey and the manic overly ingratiating manner of a failed holiday camp comic. At the Comic Strip, Mayall would often appear on stage in the form of a poet who even William McGonagall would look down upon, delivering the material with such a degree of sincerity that the audience would laugh behind their hands. His approach was that of a character actor: 'I don't want people to see me as I really am because the work loses half its power' (quoted in Januszczak, 1985: 8).

Richard Dangerous is as keen to involve the audience – 'ladies and gentlemen!' just as for our entertainment (but primarily his own) he is all too eager to inflict grievous bodily harm on Sir Adrian. His stooge wears the sideburns of a Mud roadie circa 1975, has the IQ of Sooty without Harry Corbett and he cannot imagine life without his ever-manipulative brother.

Needless to say, their stunts manage the rare achievement of being simultaneously pathetic and life-threating as the duo engage in the sort of cross-talk that would have closed any number of traditional clubs. The Dangerous Brothers cannot be trusted to successfully deliver a 'knock knock' joke, let alone one concerning anyone's mother-in-law, for all

Richard's eagerness to convince his public that they were a double act of the highest calibre. As a parody of the worst forms of traditional comedy act that was still much in evidence and a tribute to a Tex Avery animated short, the Dangerous Brothers were without parallel. The shades of The Two Mikes and other music hall duos of the late nineteenth century may well have approved, although the language would not have passed muster with a Victorian impresario. There is also a tremendous sense of catharsis when watching their appearances on *Saturday Live*; a subversion of every sub-par comedy act who haunted the remote corners of regional television.

Mayall and Edmondson were less of a double act on *The Young Ones* – some of the best moments are between Rik and Neil (Nigel Planer) – although in both the student house and the Comic Strip's *Bad News On Tour* (Sandy Johnson, 1983) Vyvyan Basterd and Vim Fuego are the dominant figures. It is Mayall's suburban, and often snivelling, would-be anarchists that are the more submissive figures and in 1987's *Filthy Rich and Catflap*, the failed TV compere Gertrude Richard 'Richie' Richard is treated with a resigned cynicism by his minder Edward Didgeridoo Catflap. If the chain-smoking agent Ralph Filthy (Planer) embodies all that was dismal about mainstream entertainment, then Richie and Edward are verging towards the absolute hell that was *Bottom* (BBC, 1991–95). For the moment, they reside in a comfortable apartment, and Richie has the persistent delusion of a showbusiness career.

It was *Mr Jolly Lives Next Door* (Stephen Frears, 1987) a part of the fourth season of *The Comic Strip Presents*, that provided the finest showcase for Mayall and Edmondson in Dangerous Brothers mode, in the form of the owners of 'Dreamytime Escorts'. It was not a production that met with the approval of Mr Derek Malcolm, who described it as 'way below' Frears's usual standards and compared the experience to 'a drinking spree with a group of West Ham's less salubrious supporters' (*The Guardian*, 5 November 1987: 24). Our heroes would probably not have been able to find their way to the football ground unaided, and the production was probably the only time that Mayall and Edmondson received cinematic direction that was worthy of their talents. With Frears at the helm and a script by the two stars and Rowland Rivron, this is a late 1980s re-imagining of a 'Swinging London' scenario – two male escorts, a mysterious next-door neighbour, nightclubs and a gangster in a big black car (a Citroën DS in this case). There is even groovy pop music from Tom Jones.

But here our heroes are two middle-aged alcoholic psychopaths, the 'nightclubs' are illegal drinking dens, their eponymous next-door neighbour is a hitman with a 1950s quiff, and in place of Judy Geeson, Susan George, Judy Huxtable et al., Rich and Eddie tend to meet confused Japanese businessmen. As a depiction of the sheer tattiness that underpinned much of the so-called 'Yuppie' social revolution, *Mr Jolly* is on a par with Smith and Jones's bovine video-cam family. Both are, in the great tradition of the British male double act, quite incredibly immature, with illegal alcohol replacing bottles of pop and bags of sweets as the ultimate imaginable treat. The conclusion of *Mr Jolly* has Rik pushing Ade into a canal, only for the latter to swim after his best friend and tormentor – the two are inextricably linked. They also possess an innate sense of D.C. Thomson cartoon-style innocence, as if Dennis the Menace and Gnasher had escaped from *The Beano* into a 1987 London. Rik and Ade temporarily remember their manners before running over an OAP at a zebra crossing, and they are almost overwhelmed at seeing television quizmasters in the flesh. Better thirty seconds of Rik excitedly telling all of Shepherd's Bush 'It's Nicholas bloody Parsons! Look, everybody – it's Nicholas bloody Parsons!' than ninety minutes of *Guest House Paradiso* (Adrian Edmondson, 1999).

The same sense of deliberate seediness permeates the first series of French and Saunders in 1987, which used the format of a tatty Variety show in which the guest star would be ill-treated and an exceptionally cheap cabaret act would provide the musical interludes. The template for the programme would have been all too familiar to television viewers of 1987; this was the twilight of *New Faces,* and the Miss World broadcasts Raw Sex style acts could be found performing in many a provincial wine bar on a Wednesday evening. Saunders explained that 'we've tried to create the look of a very low budget television variety show – we knew what we wanted, but it was very important to get the feel of the show just right'. *The Stage* critic grumbled that 'you get the impression that it's a case of everyone trying to out-alternative each other. Sometimes it might be better to be safe than unfunny' (12 March 1987: 20). At times, the murmurings of reproach from the old guard could be heard, often accompanied by the phrase 'alternative to comedy!'. How dare these young upstarts mock the traditions of the silver curtain and the brave evocations of a Broadway-style show on a budget of £45.37 in an obscure ITV station.

But at the heart of the series, with its references to failed sitcoms of the 1970s, was a genuine affection for show business traditions in a vehicle for a double act that broke with so many of them. John Fisher argued that on the halls the female stars 'tended to reveal a masculine attitude to their work, side-stepping any element of femininity, of sexual attractiveness that might obtrude into their stage characterisations' (2013: 245) but Dawn French and Jennifer Saunders did not adopt any pose, the former once pointing out 'We were never "women in comedy"' (quoted in Wilmut and Rosengard, 1989: 274). Nor were they the character actress appearing as supporting 'sex-pot' or 'character-bag' to a top-billed male comic but:

> Britain's most promising double act since Morecambe and Wise. For sheer creativity and professionalism, French and Saunders make Cannon and Ball look like an opening act on a Ralph Reader show. They couldn't have been taught their special skills at the Central School of Speech and Drama. Such artistry comes instinctively or not at all. (Barrow, 1989: 5)

Barrow went on to observe how their partnership relied on 'personal chemistry, a union of souls and you don't get precious extras handed out along with your first Equity Card'. Dawn French and Jennifer Saunders had indeed met at the Central School of Speech and Drama and appeared on stage at the Comic Strip. They also were George and Anne in the original *Comic Strip Presents… Five Go Mad in Dorset* (1982), one of the original programmes that launched Channel 4. French played Blyton's heroine with a winningly toxic blend of Girl Scout style enthusiasm and 1950s-vintage snobbery: 'What a horrid common voice that man has!' and Saunders with the air of faintly superior boredom.

Their sitcom *Girls on Top*, which co-starred Tracey Ullman and Ruby Wax (Central, 1985–86) did not quite work; as with many ITV sitcoms of the decade, it seemed leaden-paced. But for an idea of just how different *French and Saunders* seemed when it first aired, *The Stage* reported in that same year how the reigning Miss World, Giselle Laronda, fled from a performance of a snake-dancing act in Ealing 'like a latter-day Miss Muffet pursued by the show organiser Michael Morley' (Attwood, 1987: 4).

Many brilliant actresses and comediennes of previous generations – Peggy Mount, Hylda Baker, Hattie Jacques and Yootha Joyce to name but a few – were too frequently cast as 'dragons', while Barbara Windsor's increasingly dispirited performances in the *Carry On* films stand for too many stereotyped roles throughout British cinema. In the late 1980s, Victoria Wood and Julie Walters were already the antitheses of such hackneyed casting while a few older viewers were put in mind of Hermione Gingold and Hermione Baddley, the actresses whose London cabarets were a sensation in the 1940s. They also subverted a revival of Noel Coward's *Affairs of The Heart* to the extent that 'it was rather as if these two witty people were parodying the performance of an early Coward play. They revel in the sugared malice, the purring watchfulness, the powdered glass in syrup' (Trewin, 1949: 30).

It could have been a *French and Saunders* sketch – they had a merciless eye for cliché – and their interplay dominated the show. Dawn French was dark and with the overt jolliness that can turn in an instant to anger while Jennifer Saunders was blonde, languid and almost Deb-like. And it would have been impossible to envisage such a female comedy double act being given a television vehicle even twenty years earlier. Alternative comedy understood, appreciated and respected the legacy of earlier generations – but it was not enthralled by it.

Bibliography

Books

Banks, Morwenna and Swift, Amanda (1988), *The Joke's On Us: Women in Comedy from Music Hall to The Present*. London: Pandora.

Double, Oliver (2012), *Britain Had Talent: A History of Variety Theatre*. London: Palgrave.

Fisher, John (2013), *Funny Way To Be A Hero*. London: Preface Publishing.

Hunt, Leon (2013), *Cult British TV Comedy: From Reeves and Mortimer to 'Psychoville'*. Manchester. Manchester University Press.

Wilmut, Roger and Rosengard, Peter (1989), *Didn't You Kill My Mother-in-Law?: The Story of Alternative Comedy in Britain from the Comedy Store to 'Saturday Live'*. London: Methuen Drama.

Journals and Periodicals

Attwood, Brian (1987), 'Beauty Queen's "Reptile Phobia" is An Insult', *The Stage*, 19 March, pp. 4.

Barrow, Tony (1985), 'Do You Know The One About The Mother in Law?' *The Stage*, 29 August, pp. 8.

Barrow, Tony (1989), Review: French and Saunders in Manchester, *The Stage*, 23 February, pp. 5.

Jackson, Paul (1988), 'Did You Hear The One About The …', *The Guardian*, 17 November, pp. 27.

Januszczak, Waldemar (1985), 'Gogol and Me? Just a Pair of Prats', *The Guardian*, 24 January, pp. 8.

Malcolm, Derek (1987), Review: Mr Jolly Lives Next Door, *The Guardian*, 5 November, pp. 24.

Television Diary (1987), 'Alternative Naffness', *The Stage*, 12 March, pp. 20.

Trewin, J.C.T. (1949), Review: *Affairs of The Heart*, *Illustrated London News*, 17 December, pp. 30.

11

Dreamers and Escapists

Candice Marie: Just imagine, Keith, if all the people who lived here could come back … to all these crisp bags and sweet papers, they'd be horrified wouldn't they?
Keith: They'd find it difficult to comprehend all the changes that have taken place in the world.

Escape from Suburbia

A Morris Minor 1000 Convertible disembarks from the Sandbanks Ferry to the strains of a folk duet that would have barely passed muster on *Play School*. The female voice is childlike and hesitant, the male voice nasally self-assured. They are, of course, Candice-Marie and Keith Pratt, played by Alison Steadman and Roger Sloman, and their dream is to return to nature. There are, within the history of the British double act, a number of figures who believe that by following a set of clearly defined rules and guidelines, their dreams will become true. The reality is often that their fantasies either descend into a nightmare or become a reality without them understanding why. As the Morris heads for Corfe, all bodes very badly.

Nuts in May was directed and written by Mike Leigh for the BBC *Play for Today* series and broadcast on 13 January 1976. Keith is a local government official who, beneath the vaguely bohemian beard and sweaters, belonged to the form of English officialdom that expressed itself primarily via joyless officialdom. He is aged only about 30 but he has clearly absorbed the values of the 1950s, and now he wishes to apply such codes to rural Dorset 'for your own good'. After all, if everyone who visited the beach took a pebble, there would soon be none left. 'You're standing on sedimentary limestone,' Keith informs Candice-Marie in a voice that has been honed by years of uttering homilies at his presumably grateful clients.

We never see the Pratts' home life, but a neatly ill-planned suburban villa comes to mind, with their free time filled with the hobbies described by C.F.G. Masterman in *The Condition of England*. 'Busy activity, with interest in cricket and football results, "book talk", lovemaking, croquet and tennis parties for young men and women' (2012). Keith almost certainly organises the last-named, for the good of the wider community, but 'lovemaking' is in some doubt. As with many sitcom characters, the Pratts appear to be childless and celibate;[1] Candice-Marie collects pebbles and defers to her husband's regulations about the correct amount of times to chew her food.

If the Pratts were supporting characters in a situation comedy of quality – as they reasonably might be[2] – the audience would only gain a mercifully brief insight into their world. The narrative would only contain vignettes of their encounter with the farmer (Matthew Guinness), the quarryman (Eric Richards) or, most notably, the unfortunate PE student teacher Ray (Anthony O'Donnell). In such a sitcom scenario the camera would cut away after the first verse of their

---

1 Keith's bedtime reading is *The Guinness Book of Records*.
2 It is very easy to envisage Keith tormenting Basil Fawlty; as it is, he might even have a relative who specialises in spoons.

zoo song but in *Nuts in May*, he – and the audience – are treated to several excruciating minutes. Candice-Marie warns their audience of one about his smoking: 'If I could take out one of your lungs right now and put it on the table in front of you and cut it in half, I think you would be horrified'. Compared with another stanza from the Pratts, this might be the easier option.

The holiday meanders into gloom, for beneath moments that would not have been out of place in a Whitehall farce (notably the scene in which Keith spies on Ray with binoculars), the rules by which Mr Pratt needs to control the unruly elements of society can only function within a self-controlled framework. Even Candice-Marie is in danger of becoming attracted to Ray (the reverse does not seem to apply, as O'Donnell gives a wonderful performance of a man trapped in a nightmare of good manners) while the efforts to return to nature are doomed from the outset. Life in suburbia, contended Masterman, had lost 'that zest and sparkle and inner glow of accepted adventure which alone would seem to give human life significance' (2012) but the Dorset surroundings cannot transform the Pratts. Instead, it just makes them even more themselves without the comforting relief of a daily routine. For Keith, this is especially the case with the biker couple Honky and Finger (Stephen Bill and Shelia Kelley). The straight man as the thwarted voice of authority was familiar throughout the history of the double act but with *Nuts in May*, the unruly elements simply will not leave the stage and 'get back to your tenements!'

Keith and Candice-Marie will probably never make another bid to 'return to nature' while at the same time Tom and Barbara Good (Richard Briers and Felicity Kendal) were reverting to self-sufficiency. *The Good Life* (BBC, 1975–78), beneath an apparent tribute to British middle-class eccentricity, was a considered look at a marriage as much as the Goods' rejection of the corporate life. The scripts by Bob Larbey and John Esmonde establish that Tom and Barbara do go to bed together,[3] with Richard Briers's performance inferring the selfishness beneath

---

3   Cue Terry Scott uttering the word 'cor!' prior to fainting.

the East Cheam vowels and the genial manner. The mannerisms of Tom Good are not always far removed from Keith Pratt, but unlike Candice-Marie, Barbara is acerbic and frustrated with Tom's complete single-mindedness and she occasionally yearns for the lifestyle enjoyed by their next-door neighbours the Leadbetters.

If there is one defining image of the suburban BBC sitcom of this decade, it is Margo Leadbetter emerging from a yellow Volvo 145 with the regal air of one who is about to graciously declare this power station open. With the performance of Penelope Keith, we have the epitome of the insecure lower-middle-class social climber. Everything about Margo – the imperious manner, the mystification at the Goods returning to a life that her own family may have been proud to escape, and the over-enunciated vowels – infer a worry at the mask slipping. 'As quintessentially suburban as Margaret Thatcher' was the view of one critic, and Margo almost certainly celebrated the news on 11 February 1975. Her husband Jerry (Paul Eddington) has the relaxed mannerisms of one brought up with money and the innate intelligence to let others do the work as he rises to the top. He seeks refuge in witty aphorisms, but Jerry is the most perceptive character of the quartet, and the most nuanced, enjoying his material possessions for their own sake and because of consideration for Margo.

Unlike Keith and Candice-Marie, Tom and Barbara never attempt to leave suburbia as they – or, rather, he – wish to reform the neighbourhood from within. *The Good Life* depicts the suburbia that is so frequently shown as a place of entrapment in British sitcoms, as a place where freedom is possible once a mental adjustment has taken place. Andy Medhurst argues that this was a victory denied to the likes of Tony Hancock and that the Goods are the sort of eccentrics John Betjeman would have eulogised (1997: 257). But the 'Surbiton' of *The Good Life* was an Eden constantly under threat from vandals and recalcitrant local traders.

The lesson of attaining freedom within a mental attitude that had been learned years previously by Eric Sykes and Hattie Jacques, for every day in Sebastopol Terrace brings forth adventure. They appeared on 1963 Royal Variety Performance, Eric interrupted in his attempts to play the guitar[4] by Hattie not following his intricate stage directions. 'But where Hancock and James were actively kicking against the pricks, Eric and Hattie have the sublime innocence of children' (*The Stage*, 19 March 1964: 12). What might have been cloying in the hands of lesser performers – and a lesser writer than Sykes – manages the difficult achievement of whimsy in a situation comedy.

Eric Sykes was an amateur dance band musician before the Second World War, and in the late 1940s he was a repertory actor before gaining first break on the BBC writing for Frankie Howerd. On screen, his facial expression described an arc from apprehension to furtiveness and 1964 he was perfectly cast as Mr Kirby in Woodfall's adaptation of N.F. Simpson's *One Way Pendulum* (Peter Yates). Sykes had the air of one with a secret project in his shed – a home-brew kit, a semi-derelict car or indeed a fully-equipped court – so he could put himself on trial for masochism. Hattie Jacques was a former wartime Red Cross Nurse, factory welder and actress-director at the Players' Theatre. Footage exists of a 1955 colour travelogue *Tonight in Britain* of Jacques singing 'My Old Man' to an audience recreating an era that even their parents were starting to forget. But it was the final days of *It's That Man Again*, a.k.a. *ITMA* (BBC, 1939–49) that made her into a national figure as the over-eating schoolgirl Sophie Tuckshop:

> It wasn't until one show where Tommy was supposed to be passing through a department store and knocked a speaking doll (me) that the audience reacted favourably. A large body with a very little voice seemed to hit the spot, so 'Sophie Tuckshop' was born – the terrible child who never stopped eating, with sickening results. (Quoted in Kavanagh, 1974).

Banks and Swift concluded that Jacques had 'no qualms about her weight being an object of fun' (1988: 54), but the truth was far

---

4   Which he did rather well.

sadder – 'I hate the size I am with all my soul' – and there was one film, the art-house project *The Pleasure Garden* (James Broughton, 1953), which provides a rare occasion when Jacques was cast as a mischievously erotic character. A review of the comedy *The Bells of St Martin* simultaneously opined that:

> Miss Hattie Jacques, always on hand throw her weight into any joke going. It turns out usually that her weight is a part, and the best part, of the joke. But though mountainous, she is also agile. She dances lightly. She dances lightly, she has a pleasant singing voice, dark expressive eyes and the effective trick of passing from the demure into sudden, formidable truculence. (Cookman, 1952: 16)

You could argue that, as with many character actresses such as Margaret Rutherford, Jacques was judged on her appearance far more than a contemporary male character performer; one thinks of Raymond Huntley or Colin Gordon. Jacques's appearance was never the 'best part' of the joke; in fact, it was the least, for it is her vocal dexterity that one often thinks of, rather than her size. There was the high-pitched faux innocent voice she employed for Sophie and as the menacingly amorous spinster in the television *Hancock's Half Hour* story 'The Cruise'. Her more formidable characters employed the voice used by the characters described by Nicholas de Jongh: 'A woman of decided gentility and comic pretensions to dignity and even grandeur who was subject to the whims, tantrums and madnesses of her leading men' (*The Guardian*, 7 October 1980: 2). That was Miss Grizelda Pugh, whose bell-like stentorian tones struck fear into Tony Hancock, or Matron in command of her ward in *Carry On Nurse* (Gerald Thomas, 1959).

With *Sykes and a* which ran in its original form from 1960 to 1965, the difference in appearance between Hattie and her thin, almost cadaverous-looking, twin brother was a part of the joke, but it was not the dominant theme of the programme. One is large, the other is almost cadaverous, but they are forever siblings. Eric and 'Hat' are an acolyte and follower, except the sister knows her brother's foibles too well. Much of the programme's comedy depended on the contrast between Jacques's light voice and formidable personality when roused. Her name was never in the title, but she was never reduced to the role of a punchline. The show was revived in 1972 as *Sykes,* and it ran for a further seven years. Dick Fiddy argues that these later colour shows were slower than the black and white episodes, and one factor could have been that Jacques was now looking ill, her TV appearances augmented by films and television adverts that were entirely beneath her talents. Hattie Jacques died in 1980 and although Eric Sykes continued to act for another three decades, he never returned to Sebastopol Terrace.

The ultimate example of suburbia as a trap is *The Fall and Rise of Reginald Perrin* (BBC, 1976–79), in which Leonard Rossiter's performance never fell prey to the curse of many a long-running sitcom performance; the path to being 'lovable'. Reginald Iolanthe Perrin makes bids to simply 'escape', only to learn that 'We can never escape our destiny ... because whatever happens to us becomes our destiny. It had all been a terrible mistake' (Nobbs 1999: 217). The television adaptation of *The Fall and Rise of Reginald Perrin* had originally been intended to star Ronnie Barker before the casting of Leonard Rossiter, whose middle-manager was a kinetic individual whose springs are on the verge of imploding.

Perrin's creator David Nobbs was influenced by the Theatre of The Absurd of Eugene Ionesco and N.F. Simpson – 'I might not be where I am today if they had not existed' (2009: 102). It is possible to perceive elements of Eugene Berenger in Reggie, except that his *Rhinoceros* takes the form of the mass-produced world that he has devoted his working life to create. Perrin is a marketing manager for Sunshine Desserts, his role to create synthetic fun and enjoyment – '"This ice-cream is no good", says the photographer as he slaves to complete his picture of the ice cream. "The ice cream doesn't look like ice cream. It's not got that *feeling*"' (Sandford and Law, 1967: 13). Boxes of chocolates containing lime creams so highly coloured that they virtually glow in the dark, intense debates about the sales prospects of raspberry and lychee ripple. At home, the community offers 'aimless activities'; 'random and meaningless sociabilities' (Masterman, 2012) that 'neither hearten, stimulate, nor inspire' and in the office Perrin knows rhubarb crumble sales figures for Schleswig-Holstein.

It is an existence that Perrin can no longer believe in – if he ever really did – and if the phrases he starts to adopt sound bizarre with insertions of 'earwig' and 'parsnip', they are no more meaningless than the words employed by his colleagues. Reggie can probably quote from N.F. Simpson's first play *A Resounding Tinkle* (1958): 'The retreat from reason means precious little to anyone who has not caught up with reason in the first place; it takes a trained mind to relish a non-sequitur.' Perrin, as with Simpson, focuses on a quest to escape from what appears meaningless existence in the midst of an uber-English suburban environment. The inmates of the villa in *One Way Pendulum* (1959) have descended into their own past-times. John Russell Taylor notes how in Simpson's works his characters could not communicate with each other on even the most elementary level (2013: 68). Reggie can no longer function within a professional environment, and his heartfelt speech at a conference appears to his peers as consisting of little but ranted non-sequiturs.

The one person in the audience who does understand how disturbing Reggie is becoming is his wife, Elizabeth. In a comedy, the ability to portray the voice of sanity is so often overlooked and Nobbs pointed out that 'Few people singled out Pauline Yates for praise when *The Fall and Rise of Reginald Perrin* hit our screens and this in itself showed how perfectly she played the part of Reggie's conventional suburban middle-class wife' (*The Guardian*, 26 January 2015). Outside of the home, Perrin does have a certain degree of liberty to indulge in his behavioural traits and – an extremely 1970s moment – the urge to seduce his secretary Joan (Sue Nicholls).[5] It is Elizabeth who bears the brunt of his mental decline, as demonstrated by the safari park scene of the first series.

---

5   The BBC series omits the book's revelation that Joan cares for a husband who is in a vegetative state, leading Reggie to feel even more self-loathing.

The afternoon is hot, the family – Reggie, Elizabeth, their daughter Linda (Sally-Jane Spencer), son-in-law Tom[6] (Tim Preece) and two grandchildren – trapped in the vinyl-upholstered hell of a Ford Cortina Mk III Estate. Perrin's mood declines from berating Tom to seeing if the 'wild animals' are as homogenised as much as the rest of his life. In a great comedy, one glance is worth pages of extraneous dialogue and Elizabeth regards the frightened, isolated Reggie with the look of someone who knows their partner is becoming ill. When Perrin fakes his suicide as part of a desire to return to a mythical past of 'the steam engine, the brass bedstead and the pyjama cord' in the guise of 'Martin Wellbourne', the consequences are often pain for others – and Reggie has the self-awareness to realise this.

The potential for danger in unbridled dreams is one that runs through 1970s comedy; Tom Good chooses prison over being bound over to keep the peace and Reginald Perrin momentarily contemplates actual suicide. 'Why not do it – why not prove once and for all?' With *Fawlty Towers* and *Yes Minister*, we have two double acts who are trapped within their respective statuses, one pair where the anger has turned inwards and the other whose combination of delusion and ego can have literally deadly consequences. The John Cleese/Connie Booth masterpiece ran for two series, one in 1975 and the second in 1979, by which time you can quite easily envisage Basil Fawlty watching *To The Manor Born* and ranting at the screen. Basil is even taller than De Vere, has a similar moustache and his RP accent is equally polished, so why does that cad reside in a mansion while Fawlty has to deal with the ungrateful habitués of a hotel in Torquay?

Cleese believed that 'it's the people who try desperately to put a measured surface over secret anger seething away underneath who give you the sense of most violence' (quoted in Gilliatt, 1990: 228). Anthony Aloysius Hancock may have displayed a sense of belligerence, but Basil takes the approach to the edge of desperation. If farce is tragedy plus time, then *Fawlty Towers* is a nightmare and at its core is a desperate

---

6   A further detail that fascinatingly dates the scenario; a left-wing liberal priggish estate agent would have been unthinkable in a comedy made only ten years later.

marriage. In the sublime performance of Prunella Scales, Sybil Fawlty hints at a blue-collar background while Basil has all the hallmarks of a card-carrying member of the embittered lower middle classes. His rants about 'proles!' are borne of frustration – in 'The Anniversary' we meet Roger (Ken Campbell), who is not only a vulgarian but also drives a new Wolseley 2200, the sort of car that Basil aspires to, and Graham McCann very acutely observes that Fawlty is:

> Not against the Establishment as such; he is just against an Establishment that has no place within it for him. In his own mind, one suspects, he is convinced that, if only contemporary England would change for the better then so, too, would he. (2012).

Nor does Basil ever attempt to leave Torquay; as with Tony Hancock, the local elite is his goal, in his quest for acceptance by polite local society. In this, Basil is following in the path of Captain Mainwaring and Margo Leadbetter before him, his quest exacerbated by his formidable physical presence and his alarming mood swings. One theory to explain the behaviour of the proprietor of Fawlty Towers is that he is on the autistic spectrum and has little comprehension of human codes of behaviour. Basil melts down on regular occasions, he depends on Polly (Booth) as a maternal substitute and he simply cannot understand why his guests are so illogical – 'That's not the fire bell – that's a semi-tone higher!' His fear in 'The Psychiatrist' is palpable; could it be that Fawlty has previously encountered such a professional? As with any great television programme, the backstory is palpable but only obliquely hinted at.

To negotiate such a confusing and threatening world Basil has adopted a persona with the clipped diction and the attempt at a Savile Row wardrobe on a Marks and Spencer budget – redolent not so much of 'play up and play the game' but a grammar-school boy taking careful mental notes while watching every David Niven film on release. Another picture the younger Basil may have viewed was *Room at the Top* (Jack Clayton, 1959) and while he might have dismissed Joe Lampton as a 'North Country prole' Basil would have identified with the attempted escape from a white-collar Hades. Was the vibrant younger Sybil initially taken in by Basil's carefully rehearsed 'officer and gentleman' routines? Possibly, for in Prunella Scales's performance of sheer brilliance, Mrs Fawlty is not a gorgon but a vivacious lady whose unsatisfying marriage is now sublimated in ever-more elaborate wigs and manicures. The actress reflected that 'I thought she was quite smart and quite attractive in her way', but the reaction of the public appeared to be that 'I had created a monster whom no one would go to bed with if you paid them. I'm very surprised by that' (quoted in Woddis, 1991: 40). One theory, and it is only that, is that she hailed from a prosperous family in the licensed trade, and they put up the money for the hotel venture as a wedding gift. 'My wife enjoys herself! I *worry!*' Basil is heard to wail, but this is not exactly the case.

Over a decade later, the dream has subsided not into the seediness that a lesser sitcom would have indulged in but a faded but respectable torpor. Sybil understands the routine of running a business that, if not a roaring success, at least ticks over and that her husband's social pretensions are commercially ruinous. The world of *Fawlty Towers* will be familiar to many Britons who lived through the 1970s or who read Derek Cooper's classic book *The Bad Food Guide*, with its memorable descriptions of how a lack of knowledge or budget undermined various attempts at haute cuisine. The encounter of one diner who ordered a 'house specialty' of pate only to be confronted with a suspiciously tin-shaped dish, and the response of the waitress, could have been scripted by Cleese and Booth '"I've had a word with Ernie," she said, "and he says he's never seen paté Maison come in tins any other shape"' (Cooper, 1967: 177). If the Fawltys' establishment has not quite sunk to this level of incompetence this is probably due to Sybil, for if she did not appear as a termagant the litany of complaints from the council inspector – 'lack of proper cleaning routines, dirty and greasy filters, greasy and encrusted deep fat fryer' – would have been even more extensive. To be the straight woman is a thankless task, especially when your husband's various delusions of grandeur place him above the mundanities of actually running a business.

And so, the hotel's staff and guests deal with their thwarted dreams. Polly is an artist working in the hotel by economic circumstance, Manuel (Andrew Sachs) dreams of commanding respect from Basil and the Major (Ballard Berkeley) now lives in the past. Terry the Cook (Brian Hall) has the shifty manner of one on the run from the police and a sense of anger of his lack of recognition – 'I have been to catering college you know!' At the front desk Sybil dreams of romance – Mr Johnson (Nicky Henson) in 'The Psychiatrist' the sort of flamboyant chap her husband will never be – and it is strongly inferred that Basil and sexual intimacy are terms rarely uttered in the same sentence. The leather-trousered young guest reminds Mrs Fawlty of the commercial travellers or even local Teds that she spurned in favour of a 'Brilliantined stick insect'.

As for Basil, he craved acceptance by colonels, barristers and minor members of the aristocracy, but the reality was unimpressed hotel inspectors or commercial travellers who specialise in spoons (Bernard Cribbins, never better), who carefully counted their expenses and who dare to demand service. On one occasion, a guest even has the inconsideration to die during the night, and throughout these distractions the Fawltys' relationship is not entirely dormant. 'The Anniversary' shows that Basil does care about Sybil – his preparations for the surprise party are quite elaborate – but he still does not understand the best way to communicate with his sometimes vulnerable spouse. It is nearly impossible to cite the finest moment of Prunella Scales in *Fawlty Towers,* but her distress at being seemingly forgotten is a key to the series as she does, after all these years, crave attention from this awkward, embittered man. The conclusion to 'The Anniversary' has Basil not howling in rage but wryly saying to Polly 'Now for the tricky bit' – he may have been the catalyst for utter chaos but for once he is secure about having acted correctly.

Basil Fawlty's dreams have corroded his marriage and his business, but those of Jim Hacker MP (Paul Eddington) and Sir Humphrey Appleby (Nigel Hawthorne) have the potential to destroy lives. We have come across the double act of the conniver and the comparative innocent with the Aldwych farces and, in *Yes Minister* (BBC, 1980–84) we have two idealists of different motive and social background. If Hacker was a Labour Minister of the Ernie Bevin school, the subtly of the relationship would be lost but in Anthony Jay and Jonathan Lynn's creation the MP is a middle-class eager-beaver with a Third from the LSE, and the senior civil servant with a First in Greats from 'Baillie College', is patrician and disdainful of overt emotion.

The scenario is that Hacker, after years on the back benches, has been made the Minister for Administrative Affairs, where his efforts at reform are often confounded by his Permanent Secretary – or at least that would have been the case in a lesser programme. With *Yes Minister* the reason why Hacker has only been promoted to a middling Cabinet position is made quite apparent; he is egotistical, very easily swayed and his progressive agenda can be undermined with an appeal to his vanity. Sir Humphrey, in his own fashion, is more of a visionary than his political master, believing that with more power, all would be well. Although the programme was made in the 1980s, Lynn was inspired by 'the media-obsessed politics of the Wilson/Heath/Callaghan years, not the conviction politics of Margaret Thatcher' (2011: 108).

The Hacker/Appleby relationship is at its most sharply defined in 'The Whisky Priest'. Major Saunders (John Fortune) approaches Hacker with the confidential information that terrorists in Italy are using bomb-making machinery exported from the UK to Italy. For the Minister, this is a moral issue; for Sir Humphrey, there is no difference between ends and means, to which Hacker responds that his Permanent Secretary will go to hell if those are his beliefs. For his part, Appleby indoctrinates the Principal Secretary Bernard Woolley (Derek Fowlds):

I have served eleven governments in the past thirty years. If I had believed in all their policies, I would have been passionately committed to keeping out of the Common Market, and passionately committed to going into it. I would have been utterly convinced of the rightness of nationalising steel. And of denationalising it and renationalising it. On capital punishment, I'd have been a fervent retentionist and an ardent abolitionist. I would've been a Keynesian and a Friedmanite, a grammar school preserver and destroyer, a nationalisation freak and a privatisation maniac; but above all, I would have been a stark, staring, raving schizophrenic.

On the surface, it is the smooth assurance of Screwtape writing to his nephew, but the subtext of *Yes Minister* as demonstrated by Hawthorne's subtly frenetic performance is that Sir Humphrey is slowly being driven mad by the moral compromises inherent in his position. Bernard absorbs his lesson from his senior and devises a solution: a letter couched in deliberately vague terms that is designed to arrive on the day the Prime Minister is due to leave on an overseas tour.

'The Whiskey Priest' ends with Hacker, distraught at the limitations of his moral compass and resorting to alcoholic ranting. His wife Annie (Diane Hoddinott) comforts her husband with the faint solace that while Sir Humphrey has 'lost his sense of right and wrong, you've still got yours' – except that Hacker 'doesn't use it very much'. Careerism has replaced the moral urgency that the Minster felt towards the issue; Major Saunders, who had presumably risked his position to inform Hacker, has been betrayed, the arms sales continue, and civilians will continue to be killed. The episode aired at a time when CI5's finest double act was also encountering such issues but, in *The Professionals*, Bodie and Doyle would resolve matters with a display of gunfire and driving a Ford Capri really badly. With *Yes Minister*, the episode ends with Hacker, one of the great self-deluding characters of all time, seeking a form of solace in being 'Whisky Priest' from a Graham Greene novel except, as McCann contends, 'he too knows that he is on his way to Hell' (2014).

Victoria Wood and Julie Walters: Clear-headed Nostalgia

At its best, *New Faces* (ATV, 1973–78) showcased the talents of Lenny Henry, the Chuckle Brothers, Les Dennis and Joe Pasquale; at its worst, it was the reason why alternative comedy had to happen. One contestant was a 21-year-old undergraduate whose songs at the piano were far too accomplished for an ITV talent show and largely wasted on *That's Life* (BBC, 1973–94): 'I found out a few years later there never had been a clap-o-meter, it was a vanity case with some paper round' (Wood, 1998: ix). Victoria Wood had never forgotten witnessing a Joyce Grenfell performance at the age of 6, and how talent, stagecraft and, yes, genius, could dominate an auditorium. Her ability to create and define a character with a single line – 'face to face with a Marks & Spencer's individual spotted dick' – was very much in the Grenfell tradition, and although both were solo artists they were equally at home with a partner.

In 1978 Wood wrote *Talent* for the Crucible Theatre, and Granada televised it in 1979. She played the 'best friend' character of Maureen, who exists in a fog of depression and mild self-loathing where 'the legendary giants are Des O'Connor and Russell Harty, where literature is represented by Pam Ayres and celestial music laid on by Freddie and The Dreamers – sour middle-age is defined as 'watching *Jackanory* in the afternoons' (Raban, 1979: 20). Maureen's friend Julie (Julie Walters) is sharp and with the brittleness that masks desperation: 'I was also interested in the relationship between attractive sparky girls and big fat plain ones' (Wood, 1988: ix). Julie is determined to make the break into show business, to make life happen for her, rather than acquiesce; whether the journey into the provincial abyss that is 'Bunter's' nightclub was worth the effort is a judgement for the audience to make.

Victoria Wood requested to be teamed with Julie Walters for her television revue, which was eventually titled *Wood and Walters* (Granada, 1982) and the partnership continued in the BBC's *Victoria Wood: As Seen on TV* (1985–89). The latter show was suffused with an affection for the television of Wood's youth; her version of Ena Sharples, Minnie Caldwell and Martha Longhurst could have been an out-take from *Coronation Street* in 1962. The utterly divine 'Knock Knock' musical number was a tribute to BBC light entertainment past when Billy Cotton and his band still dominated the television listings, but the programmes are not exclusively a tribute to monochrome visions of the past and tributes to the glory that was *Crossroads* (ATV/Central, 1964–88).[7] Chrissie (Woods), the would-be long distance swimmer, is determined and childlike – her secondary ambition is to meet Bonnie Tyler. She galumphs in the manner of Joyce Grenfell in *The Happiest Days of Your Life* (Frank Launder, 1950) but while Chrissie embarks on an adventure that is designed to gain her some form of recognition her parents plan to see an Andrew Lloyd Webber musical in London. Parents who were useless to the point of inertia also feature in *Wood and Walters* – 'My mother lost three children before she was 20, they weren't hers of course' – as did a sense of ambivalence towards her fanbase. One very strange sketch in which a pair of middle-aged groupies terrify their idol, a fading rep theatre actor (Alan Lake).

The elements of ruinously negligent parents and the price of ambition versus the cost of remaining a torpor-like rut were explored in Wood's 1994 feature *Pat and Margaret* (Gavin Millar). The play lies outside of our period but comedy is all about breaking the rules, as a talking head on a badly assembled clip programme is bound to utter at a certain point. Margaret Mottershead (Wood) works at a motor services café and looks permanently defeated – even her perm has declared surrender. While in the audience of the very bad TV show *Magic Moments* she is reunited with her long-estranged sister Pat (Walters), who is now Patricia Bedford, the sort of US-based soap opera actress who could give Joan Collins and Kate O'Mara a run for their money. After the show Margaret plaintively asks, 'Do you not want to know about me?' and the response comes with the sound of defences being established. If Pat entertains no fondness for her background – and little at first for her dowdy sibling – this is for reasons beyond mere careerism.

Wood perceived Margaret as embodying 'all the people who don't have a voice and don't have any way of getting themselves up the ladder', but Pat's escape was due to desperation. When she became pregnant at 15 her mother Vera (Shelia Stelfox) threw her out of the house, and when

---

7   If anyone should ever doubt the accuracy of *Acorn Antiques*, the earliest surviving edition of *Crossroads* opens with the actress playing the motel receptionist visibly awaiting her cue.

she is finally traced, her excuse is the standard one of those who should never raise children: Pat should be grateful for being made 'hard', but this is little compensation for years of emotional devastation. Worse, Vera has so damaged herself that expelling her daughter may have represented her warped form of maternal encouragement. The conclusion, of Pat buying a café for Margaret and her fiancé Jim (Duncan Preston) and taking Shelia back to the USA as a career gimmick is affectionate but not lachrymose. *Pat and Margaret* is the Wood and Walters screen partnership at its zenith, for the sisters are a double act in that they embody the disparate aspects of ambition. One is fearful of starting the assent, and the other keeps climbing out of fear.

'So, Follow Me Now into the Fatal Bathroom, Meticulously Reconstructed for this Programme': The National Theatre of Brent

The accent is one of suburban pedantry – one thinks of the clerical tones of Timothy Bateson in countless films and television programmes – and the manner brisk and formal. The National Theatre of Brent is an educational experience, even if our principal lecturer Desmond Olivier Dingle has only the slenderest grasp of his subject matter and his supporting cast consists of a bemused chap named Wallace.

This gem in Britain's theatrical firmament is the creation of actor and writer Patrick Barlow, and his hero – for he is at times – began as one Desmond Dingle. He notes that, 'he was a Max Miller style entertainer at the tail end of the Variety era, and he had the voice to match'. It was while serving as an entertainments officer on a cruise liner that was not in the *Queen Mary* category that Dingle evolved the aspiration to better himself. Surely life had more to offer than a round of deck quoits, bingo and fancy-dress parades and so an interest in the arts and history, together with a monumental degree of pretention, led to a new persona. The music-hall stage costume was dispensed with, along with his original accent. Desmond 'Olivier' Dingle may have used 'the telephone box outside of his flat in Dollis Hill' as an initial form of communication, but he was ready to embark upon a career in the arts. Desmond's creator points out, 'He probably read one page of a Peter Brook discourse on theatre, and although he did not understand it, he found the language fascinating.'

Barlow's early influences in comedy are from 'the Ealing films, Tony Hancock, Peter Sellers and Laurel and Hardy'. And Desmond needs a partner, preferably one who will be in awe of his newly acquired grandiloquence and will treat him with the deference that is now his due. The first member of 'my entire company' was Julian Hough and they staged a very special interpretation of *The Charge of the Light Brigade* at the Old Red Lion Theatre in Islington in 1980. For future productions, Hough was succeeded by 'Bernard' (Robert Austin), 'Wallace' (Jim Broadbent) and 'Raymond Box' (John Ramm). Desmond does not reward his company in monetary terms – Raymond is obliged to work at the World of Foam in Croydon – and nor does he recruit from the ranks of up-and-coming actors: 'Wallace is a gardener for the council'. Such casting decisions have the joint benefit of saving the company's funds and ensuring that Dingle's supremacy is rarely challenged. Desmond always 'ensures that he has the better costumes' but after a time he and his cast 'act like a married couple as they know each other's vulnerabilities. Desmond can be very spiteful at times' and in *Messiah* (1984) Wallace is driven to telling Dingle that 'you might as well go back to calling the bingo on Cunard!' This prompts a masterpiece of self-pity from the would-be heir to Laurence Olivier: 'I'm just a spiritual bingo caller, hacking about on the fringes of eternal truth!'

The comical lecturer and ill-trained teacher have a long pedigree in British Variety – Will Hay, Stainless Stephen, Jimmy Edwards – as is the comedy that emerges from the difference between ambition and achievement. One of the highlights of Morecambe and Wise's stage act was their ventriloquist's routine in which Eric fails to understand the art of throwing one's voice, thus driving Ernie to despair:

Wise (shouting): Don't you understand?
Morecambe: No, but does it matter at this late stage?
(Quoted in Tynan, 1989: 227).

But with the National Theatre of Brent the source material is never mocked as the double act of Desmond and his company creates two dramas – the one that they are attempting to re-enact to am-dram standards and 'the personal battle between the actor-writer-manager ... and his hapless assistant' (Billington, 1987: 26). Against the reasonable considerable odds – including Desmond's petulance and costumes of a quality usually associated with a Woolworth bargain basement sale – do come moments of truth, often from Wallace and his ilk. 'I don't understand ... I don't know what's going on ...' says a tall man wearing a towel on his head and a charity shop suit in the reconstruction of the Flight to Egypt, but Wallace's sense of fear in that moment is real. If the National Theatre of Brent has a message it is one that Keith Pratt – and especially Basil Fawlty – are unlikely to understand; that theatrical trappings cannot create truth by osmosis. Desmond cannot quite understand why or how Wallace can act in this way, but he is also capable of performances that move the audience when he forgets the 'Olivier'. Unfortunately, the Wallaces will always be on hand to innocently remind Dingle of his many limitations. *Revolution!* (1989), which boldly sets outs to tell the story of Louis XVI and Marie Antionette, contains the following masterpiece of cross-talk:

Wallace: Why are the people without bread, Demsond?
Dingle (hissing): What are you calling me that for?

With thanks to Patrick Barlow.

Bibliography

Books

Banks, Morwenna and Swift, Amanda (1988), *The Joke's on Us: Women in Comedy from Music Hall to the Present*. London: Virago Press.

Cooper, Derek (1967), *The Bad Food Guide*. London: Routledge & Kegan Paul.

Gilliatt, Penelope (1990), *To Wit: In Celebration of Comedy*. New York: Weidenfeld and Nicolson.

Kavanagh, Ted (1974), *The ITMA Years*. London: The Woburn Press.

Lewis, C.S. (2009), *The Screwtape Letters: Letters from a Senior to a Junior Devil*. London: Harper Collins.

Lynn, Jonathan (2011), *Comedy Rules: From the Cambridge Footlights to Yes, Prime Minister*. London: Faber & Faber.

McCann, Graham (2012), *Fawlty Towers*. London: Hodder & Stoughton.

McCann, Graham (2014), *A Very Courageous Decision: The Inside Story of 'Yes Minister'*. London: Aurum.

Masterman, C.F.G. and Boulton, J.T. (eds) (2012), *The Condition of England*. London: Faber and Faber.

Meades, Jonathan (1979), *This Is Their Life: An Insight into the Unseen Lives of Your Favourite T.V. Personalities*. London: Salamander Books.

Meades, Jonathan (2014), *An Encyclopaedia of Myself*. London: Fourth Estate.

Medhurst, Andy (1997), 'Negotiating the "Gnome Zone": Versions of Suburbia in Popular Culture', in Silverstone, Roger (ed.), *Exploring Visions of Suburbia*. Abingdon: Routledge.

Merriman, Eric (2007), *Hattie: The Authorised Biography of Hattie Jacques*. London: Aurum Press.

Nobbs, David (1999), *The Reginald Perrin Omnibus*. London: Arrow Books.

Nobbs, David (2009), *I Didn't Get Where I Am Today: An Autobiography*. London: Arrow Books.

Sandford, Jeremy and Law, Roger (1967), *Synthetic Fun: A Short Soft Glance*. London: Penguin Books.

Simpson, N.F. (2013), *N. F. Simpson: The Collected Plays: 'A Resounding Tinkle'; 'The Hole'; 'Gladly Otherwise'; 'One Way Pendulum'; 'The Form'; 'The Cresta Run'; 'Was He Anyone?'; 'If So, Then Yes'*. London: Faber and Faber.

Sykes, Eric (2006), *If I Don't Write It Nobody Else Will*. London: Harper Perennial.

Taylor, John Russell (2013), *Anger and After (Routledge Revivals): A Guide to the New British Drama*. Abingdon: Routledge.

Tynan, Kenneth (1989), *Profiles*. London: Nick Hern Books.

Woddis, Carole (1991), *Sheer Bloody Magic: Conversations with Actresses*. London: Virago Press.

Wood, Victoria (1998), *'Good Fun' and 'Talent': Modern Plays*. London: Bloomsbury.

Journals and Periodicals

Billington, Michael (1987), 'Joys of the Bible Belters', *The Guardian*, 15 April, pp. 26.

Cookman, Anthony (1952), Review: The Bells of St. Martin, *The Tatler*, 10 September, pp. 16.

de Jongh, Nicholas (1980), Obituary: Hattie Jacques, Mistress of Comedy, *The Guardian*, 7 October, pp. 2.

Nobbs, David (2015), Obituary: Pauline Yates, *The Guardian*, 26 January.

Raban, Jonathan (1979), Television Review: Talent, *The Observer*, 12 August, pp. 20.

'Sykes and a Following' (1964), *The Stage*, 19 March, pp. 12.

12

Double Act: Single Vision

As soon as the orchestra played *Mary from the Dairy* I usually began to cry before he came on. And when he did appear, I went on crying and laughing until the end. (John Osborne on Max Miller)

As I suggested at the start of this book, a favourite double act is inevitably a personal decision, in the same manner that various polls decree what is the greatest comedian, singer or brand of chocolate bar. By the same token, comedy teams may perform with diligence, professionalism, charm and good humour for decades, may commission or write material that is witty and polished – yet their memory is destined to fade with the era they once almost embodied. But some duos became an aspect of a nation's folklore, for reasons due to public affection, their timing – both of their routines and their rise to fame – and their combined talents.

The records of Bud Flanagan and Chesney Allen were still receiving radio airtime long after the station identities 'Home', 'Light', and 'Third' had been confined to history. The subject matter of 'Run Rabbit' now belonged to the war stories of visiting grandparents; the way in which the voices of Bud and Ches combined surpassed memories of rationing and black-out curtains. They could sometimes be glimpsed on black and white footage, and as they sang, they performed a curious set of steps that could hardly be called a dance, as Chesney Allen walked behind Bud Flanagan with a hand on his shoulder (Medhurst, 2007: 122). In the midst of economic depression and a rigid class system the moon-faced zany and his elegant and ever-supportive straight man could never be deprived of dreaming of what might have been.

Tony Hancock and Sidney James remain the definitive unofficial British double act of the twentieth century, an accolade that was not sought by the comic but remains one of his legacies. The 'Hancock Story' ended on 25 June 1968 when, in the words of John Fisher, 'he had locked himself out, and neither Sid James nor Galton and Simpson were at his side with a spare key in their illegal possession' (2013: 350). The finest achievement of *Hancock's Half Hour* is that their legacy can transcend the memories of the star's personal tragedy. With Tony Hancock and Sidney James, Galton and Simpson created their own version of Vladimir and Estragon of the outer suburb. In the front parlour of 23 Railway Cuttings they would be playing games to pass the time, one awaiting the next opportunity with belligerent optimism, the other secure in the knowledge that it will never come to pass.

And then there is Morecambe and Wise, whose work has already been the subject of insightful analysis by many writers, beginning with Kenneth Tynan in 1973. However, one challenge when considering Eric and Ernie is that they are often taken for granted precisely because of their position within the national consciousness. To many who grew up in the 1970s they truly were as much a part of the Christmas celebrations as stockings, Meltis Newberry Fruits and the queen's speech.

One reason behind their success was their ages; Wise was born in 1925, Morecambe a year later, which meant they were both of an age to have been trained in the last days when Variety was a major entertainment force, but sufficiently young, and adventurous, to venture into television in the 1950s. Their first starring venture, *Running Wild*, was an infamous disaster[1] but a guest appearance on *The Good Old Days* in 1959 shows a double act entirely at ease with the medium.

A second factor is the capricious element of luck; Gary Morecambe points out that it was by pure coincidence that Morecambe and Wise encountered each other in London after they had temporarily gone their separate ways. He also observes how they were musically trained, and although having a play-off song was a standard device for a Variety act, by no means all of them had the skills of Eric and Ernie. And their act developed. They never swapped roles (except, says Gary Morecambe, in the late 1940s when they were touring with Lord Sangster's circus) but they developed their on-stage characters. Some double acts remained much the same, barring the effects of age – Mike and Bernie were recognisably Mike and Bernie in 1977 as they were in 1958 – while Morecambe and Wise transformed into themselves. Their early influences were obviously Abbott and Costello, who defined the US quick-fire and hard-edged cross-talk act. Bert Wheeler (the innocent-looking straight man) and Robert Woolsey (the brash, cigar-smoking and bespectacled comic) were other role models, as were Laurel and Hardy: 'The first of the screen's new-type comedians. They didn't have funny clothes, red noses and big eyebrows. They didn't have to rely on things like that for their laughs although of course, there was plenty of slapstick' (Morecambe, in *Showtime*, 1965).

The first successful television series for Morecambe and Wise, *Two of a Kind* (ATV, 1962–68), displays how the riding comic/straight man combination is slightly diffused; if Eric is amiably vacant, Ernie is the harassed paternal figure rather than sharp-suited foil in a snap-brim hat. When the series was being recorded, the last of the Variety halls were closing their doors, but Morecambe and Wise were never a 'nostalgia act'; they continued the comedy traditions of previsions generations, but in tailored suits. A 1966 interview in *The Tatler* explained their philosophy:

---

1   Clifford Davis, in the *Daily Mirror* of 22 April 1954, was not a fan of Morecambe and
    Wise's crosstalk:
    Wise: I've got a fear of being locked up. It's called a complex.
    Morecambe: The magistrate calls it six months.

'I believe we shall only survive as long as we stay together … The whole essence of our act depends on mutual titillation. There has to be a masterful type and a foil. Ernie is the foil and his is the harder job because he is responsible for the continuity. We call this the "Well-mah-boy' act"', explains Ernie. 'I have to supply the cues for Eric.' (Quoted in Eldridge, 1966: 16).

The use of the term 'masterful' is key, for although the scripts of Dick Hills and Sid Green present Eric as ostensibly vague there are moments – usually when the writers are corralled into appearing in a sketch – when Morecambe delights in highlighting their deficiencies as performers. It is such moments that the 'Eric' of the 1970s is fleetingly visible. The myth that Morecambe and Wise were in dire straits by 1968 after Eric's heart attack and losing the services of Hills and Green is just that: the BBC was unlikely to have commissioned a series that was recorded in colour from such an act. Eddie Braben emphasised the Eric/Ernie relationship and their fallibility. Some of the best Morecambe and Wise routines were not the elaborate musical numbers[2] or those with the guest stars, but those where the pair were within the confines of their flat or even their bedroom, bickering in the manner of a long-term married couple.

The transfer to Thames in 1978 was, in hindsight, an error but an understandable one; the company's Euston Films division was world famous, and it did seem to present Morecambe and Wise with a real chance to make cinema features. But asides from the shows, there was the simple fact that Eric and Ernie, as with Flanagan and Allen, and so many other acts before them, were starting to look their ages. The highlight of their ITV years is, without doubt, the Andrews Sisters tribute with Leonard Rossiter. Eric Morecambe died in 1985, Ernie in 1999, and the fact that they were never 'Sir Eric' and 'Sir Ernie' is little short of a disgrace.

The greatest of the Morecambe and Wise shows were the creations of Braben, Ernest Maxim, John Ammonds and so many other professionals.

---

2 That said, Tom Jones should have employed them as permanent backing singers on the evidence of 'Exactly Like You'..

But – and there almost inevitably a 'but' in these narratives – the key to the act remains that Ernie was the greatest possible partner for Eric and vice versa. John McCabe once referred to the 'white magic' that was a part of Laurel and Hardy's comic business (2004: 149) and maybe that is the *mot juste* for the comic relationship between Morecambe and Wise.

Let us conclude with two Morecambe and Wise routines, both dating from the 1960s and neither listed among their 'classic' moments. The first has Ernie singing 'Can't Get Used To Losing You' while Eric remains ('You give me confidence' say s Wise) to perform some quite remarkable free-form dancing. 'Cause no-one else could take your place' croons Ernie to his partner, half breaking up and half utterly serious, as Eric does his utmost to throw him off track.

The second is one of a series of cinema/TV commercials that the duo made for Watney *c.* 1967 and as Morecambe and Wise dance on to the pub set, many of the extras are clearly breaking into spontaneous laughter. The closing two-shot is of Morecambe looking aggressively bemused and Wise bearing the expression 'I should be far too responsible and dignified to be enjoying this'. These vignettes contain the three elements that double acts can spend careers trying to emulate: Morecambe and Wise liked each other, they liked performing with each other, and they performed as one.

With thanks to Gary Morecambe.

Bibliography

Books

Fisher, John (2013), *Funny Way To Be A Hero*. London: Preface Publishing.

McCabe, John (2004), *The Comedy World of Stan Laurel*. London: Robson Books.

Medhurst, Andy (2007), *A National Joke: Popular Comedy and English Cultural Identities*. Abingdon: Routledge.

Osborne, John (1994), *Damn You England: Collected Prose*. London: Faber & Faber.

Journals and Periodicals

Davis, Clifford (1954), '"Running Wild" is about right', *Daily Mirror*, 22 April, pp. 4.

Eldridge, Roger (1966), 'The Magnificent Two', *The Tatler*, 24 December, pp. 16.

Morecambe, Eric and Wise, Ernie (1965), *Showtime*. May.

Index